Day By Day in Orioles History

Ted Patterson

Sports Publishing Inc.

ACKNOWLEDGMENTS

Thanks go out to the unheralded and hardworking media and public relations staffs who have served the Orioles over the last several decades, beginning with Bob Brown, continuing with Rick Vaughan and moving to the present day with John Maroon. Also to former support staff such as Mac Barrett, John Blake and current assistant PR Director Bill Stetka for their help and cooperation. Special thanks go to present day staffers Kevin Behan and Chris Skandalis for assisting in research gathering and providing facts and files. Thanks to Blair Jett and Ron Menchine for their help with Oriole memorabilia and to all-time Oriole historian Jim Bready.

Thanks also to photographer Rich Riggins, who took the many memorabilia photos that adorn the book. Appreciation also goes out to photographers Jerry Wachter, Mort Tadder, Michael Zagaris, Stu Zolotorow, Kevin Allen, Richard Lippenholz, John Cummings, Joe Giza, George Brace and Scott Hubert.

Last, but not least, I want to thank Mike Pearson of Sports Publishing, for conceiving the idea of the update and for his support and friendship on this and other projects.

Director of Production: Susan M. McKinney
Interior/photo insert layout: Michelle R. Dressen
Cover design: Terry Hayden

ISBN: 1-58261-017-7
Library of Congress Card Number: 99-63462

Printed in the United States

Sports Publishing Inc.
804 N. Neil St.
Champaign IL 61820

www.SportsPublishingInc.com

To Mark Belanger, Cal Ripken, Sr. and Jerry Hoffberger, three all-time Oriole greats who have passed away in recent months. Each in his own way—"The Blade" at shortstop, Cal, Sr. as a coach and manager, and Mr. Hoffberger as an owner—brought both prestige and distinction to the Oriole organization.

CONTENTS

INTRODUCTION

When Mike Pearson of Sagamore/Sports Publishing first phoned in 1997 and asked about updating *Day By Day in Orioles History,* I said, "Sure, 30 years are already in the book. What's another 14." Boy was I wrong. Since *Day By Day in Orioles History* was first published in 1984, baseball in Baltimore has undergone huge changes. There has been new ownerships, the move to Camden Yards, players, skyrocketing payroll, exploding fan base, and expanding media coverage, to name a few of those changes. Just about the only constants were Cal's never missing a game and the great tradition that began under Paul Richards in the 1950s and continues to the present day. From a thrifty organization that fielded great teams that drew average crowds, the Orioles have become one of baseball's elite franchises, drawing well over three million fans a year, and ranking at the top of the list in player salaries..

The Colts had barely fled to Indianapolis when the 1984 season dawned and the Orioles found themselves the only game in town. Unfortunately they weren't able to seize the momentum from their 1983 World Championship, and a slow descent to unfamiliar second division territory began.

The changes at the outset surrounded the health of owner Edward Bennett Williams and his fervent hope to bring the Orioles back to the top in rapid order, before the cancer he had so valiantly battled for years would take his life. Unfortunately the farm system took a back seat to the signing of several high priced free agents. Long range thinking gave way to the quick- fix. The strategy backfired and despite the bringing back of Earl Weaver in another desperation move by Williams, the Orioles sank to even deeper depths.

The bottom was reached in 1988 when the once proud Orioles sank to seventh place in the American League East, losing a franchise record 107 games and finishing 34 $1/_2$ games behind the first place Red Sox. Soothed considerably by the undying loyalty of the fans, the 1988 season would, nonetheless, go down as the most painful in the club's 35-year history. It was made even more painful when, on August 13, Edward Bennett Williams passed away, ending his dream of seeing the Orioles win another championship.

Williams' legacy lived on, however, as before his death, he gave the city of Baltimore renewed hope for the future in the form of a long-term committment to keep the Orioles in Baltimore. On an early May evening with over 50,000 fans at Memorial Stadium to welcome back a team that had finished off a 1-21 April, Williams and Governor William Donald Schaefer electrified the throng by announcing agreement on a 15-year lease and the building of a new ballpark in the Camden Yards area of downtown Baltimore which would be ready for occupancy hopefully by 1992. The start of the long climb back had begun.

The "Yes We Can" Orioles of 1989, managed by Frank Robinson and picked by most to finish last, astounded the baseball world by winning 87 games for a 32½ game improvement from the year before. With 13 rookies and 22 players out of the 40 man roster with less than two years major league experience, the Orioles battled Toronto down to the final weekend before losing two of three and falling two games short.

The Orioles drew a club record 2,552,753 fans in their Memorial Stadium swansong in 1991, the curtain closing on 38 seasons on 33rd street with emotional ceremonies that saw several former Orioles return for a Field of Dreams-like farewell sequence. The Orioles responded to the opening of their state-of- the-art ballpark at Camden Yards the next year by winning 89 games, a 22 game improvement from the year before, and drawing 3,567,819 in the process. Under the ownership group led by Peter Angelos, who bought the club from Eli Jacobs in 1993, Orioles success on the field and at the box office has zoomed. Under the managerial leadership of Davey Johnson the Orioles reached the playoffs in both 1996 and 1997, coming within one run of reaching the World Series in '97, losing to the Indians and drawing over 3,700,000 fans. The Orioles had made it back, falling just short of a seventh World Series appearance.

Now, once again, the Orioles find themselves in transition. Fielding a star studded but aging lineup under new manager Ray Miller in 1998, the Orioles proved a major disappointment, limping home with a sub .500, 79-83 record. Needless to say, the Orioles will embark on the last season of the century with several new faces and a new attitude. 1998 saw the return of all- time Oriole Eddie Murray, who hit his 500th homer as an Oriole in 1996. This time Eddie was back as a bench coach. Cal Ripken, the lone constant from long-ago 1984, was still adding to his incredible consecutive games streak until he ended it on the final home game of the season on September 20, playing in an incredible 2,632 games.

Day By Day In Orioles History pays tribute to one of baseball's most successful franchises, a franchise that started at rock bottom in 1954 with the transfer of the lowly St .Louis Browns. By 1957 the Orioles had reached the .500 mark and over the next 27 years they compiled more victories and the higest winning percentage of any team in baseball. Paul Richards began building the tradition as combination general manager and manager and Earl Weaver, who won over 100 games five times in his 14 full seasons as manager and led the Orioles to four World Series appearances, helped perpetuate it. Weaver has joined three of his former players, Brooks Robinson, Frank Robinson and Jim Palmer in baseball's Hall of Fame.

Proud history. Proud tradition. Hall of Fame and All-Star performers. Camden Yards. All the ingredients that spell baseball at its finest. Now let's relieve it all, *Day By Day in Orioles History.*

FOREWORD
By Boog Powell

Even though a quarter of a century has gone by since I last donned that familiar orange, black and white uniform, I still look upon myself as a Baltimore Oriole. In fact I feel privileged to be refered to in that select circle of Oriole all-time greats. The Orioles have always stood for class, on the field and in the front office, and I really didn't discover what a first-class operation the Orioles had until I was traded to Cleveland after the 1974 season. I had been in Baltimore for 13 years and it was one of the saddest days of my life to get traded away.

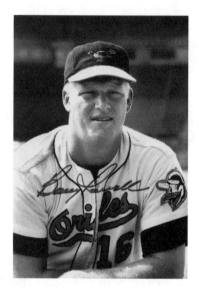

Boog Powell

Along with Brooks Robinson, Dave McNally, Davey Johnson, Steve Barber and Paul Blair, I felt I helped lay the foundation that later helped thrust the Orioles into the elite. Back in 1961 when I came up, as an outfielder I might add, the Orioles were just beginning to jell under Paul Richards. The Kiddie Korps pitching staff was starting to mature and the farm system was churning out top prospects. Still we were missing leadership and the belief that we could win, and Frank Robinson's acquisition in 1966 put us over the top. Frank keyed us to the 1966 pennant but not many gave us a chance against the favored Dodgers of Koufax, Drysdale and company. So all we did was sweep them four straight for our first World championship. Five more division titles, three American League pennants and one more World Series victory followed as the Orioles became the winningest team in baseball and continued to be long after I was gone. In 1969 we won 109 games and I'm still wondering how we lost to the Mets in the World Series. In 1970 we won 108 games and stopped Cincinnati's Big Red Machine in five games. Then in 1971 we won 101 games and lost the World Series to Pittsburgh in seven games, not so much because of what the great Roberto Clemente did, but rather the likes of Bob Robertson, Steve Blass and Nellie Briles. Being named American League MVP in 1970 remains the top individual honor of my career.

After two seasons in Cleveland, I finished my career with the Dodgers in 1977. Al Campanis, then the Dodger general manager, gave me a manual explaining how the Dodger way is the only way. Getting this guidebook from Campanis irritated me very much. I had spent 13 seasons in Baltimore in a model organization that had beaten Campanis' Dodgers in four straight games in 1966, and he wanted to tell me, after 15 seasons in the big leagues, how I should play. I learned how to act and conduct myself in 1959 at Bluefield, in 1960 at Fox Cities and 1961 at Rochester when I was first introduced to "The Oriole Way." By the time I reached Baltimore in 1961, I knew how to play sound, fundamental baseball and Paul Richards, Hank Bauer and Earl Weaver only put a exclamation point on it.

Saying goodbye to Memorial Stadium in 1991 was one of the saddest days of my life. So many memories. So much nostalgia. But being able to come back to Baltimore and be a part of the Orioles again with "Boog's Barbecue" at Camden Yards, has given me a new lease on life. Remember what I said at the beginning, "Once an Oriole, always an Oriole." And when I underwent colon cancer surgery in 1997, the outpouring of support from the city of Baltimore and Oriole fans everywhere was something I'll never forget.

My friend of long standing, Ted Patterson, never played a game for the Orioles but after 26 years in Baltimore covering the Orioles on radio and television, he's watched it all unfold, from Brooks to Cal, Frank to Eddie and Palmer to Mussina. From Memorial Stadium to Camden yards, he's chronicled it all in *Day by Day in Orioles History*. It's a book you won't want to put down because there were some mighty good days to talk about. I ought to know. I was there for many of them.

This Date in Baltimore Orioles History

JANUARY

January 3
1955— Hoot Evers begins the second of two tours of duty with the Orioles. Hoot hit only .238 before being put on waivers in July. In May, 1956, the O's sent Dave Pope to Cleveland to get Hoot back. He hit .241 in 48 games before calling it quits.

January 7
1987— Former Red Sox and Angel shortstop Rick Burleson signs a one-year contract with the Orioles.

January 8
1933— Outfielder Willie Tasby, remembered by Oriole fans as the man who played the field one rainy afternoon in his stocking feet rather than take a chance that his metal spikes might attract a lightning flash, is born in Shreveport, Louisiana.

January 10
1991— In a blockbuster deal with Houston, the Orioles obtain slugging first baseman Glenn Davis but give up three outstanding future prospects, pitchers Pete Harnisch and Curt Schilling, and out-fielder Steve Finley.

1996— Mike Devereaux, who left Baltimore after the 1994 season to file for free agency and played the '95 season with the White Sox and Braves, resigns with the Orioles, agreeing to a one-year free agent contract. Mike was named MVP of the 1995 NLCS with Atlanta.

January 11
1984— Shortstop Luis Aparicio, who spent five years in an Oriole uniform including the 1966 World Series season, is voted into Baseball's Hall of Fame along with Harmon Killebrew and Don Drysdale.

January 12
1983— Brooks Robinson is elected to the Baseball Hall of Fame, receiving 92% of the vote, the ninth highest total in history.

January 14
1963— Luis Aparicio, one of the greatest shortstops of all time, is traded to the Orioles along with Al Smith.

Going to the White Sox in this blockbuster are Hoyt Wilhelm, Ron Hansen, Pete Ward, and Dave Nicholson.

1993— Harold Baines, born and raised on Maryland's eastern shore in St. Michael's, Maryland, is acquired by the Orioles from Oakland for pitchers Bob Chouinard and Allen Plaster. The 14-year vet was originally scouted by Bill Veeck of the White Sox, who remembered Baines as a school boy star while living on Peach Blossom Creek outside Easton.

1994— Chris Sabo, who led the Reds in seven offensive categories in 1993 and connected for three grand-slam home runs among his 21 total, signs a free-agent contract with the Orioles after six seasons in Cincinnati.

Chris Sabo

January 15
1949— Bobby Grich is born in Muskegon, Michigan.

1999— In keeping with a recent trend, the Orioles activate their pipeline with the Seattle Mariners by signing 32-year-old reliever Heathcliff Slocumb to a one-year contract. Slocumb will be used to set up closer Mike Timlin, who also pitched in Seattle. Slocumb, who averaged 30 saves a season from 1995 through 1997, had only three in 1998 to go with a 2-5 record and a 5.32 ERA.

January 16
1999— After arriving the previous night, Oriole owner Peter Angelos and a contingent of officials from Major League Baseball and Catholic Relief Services begin negotiating with Cuban officials for a humanitarian home and home series with a team of Cuban all-stars. The U.S. State Department approved the series, as long as proceeds go to charity and not to the Castro government.

January 17
1925— Jehosie Heard, who pitched in two games in 1954 and was the Orioles' first black player, is born in Atlanta, Georgia.

January 18
1954— Just months before the Orioles returned to the major leagues, Scott McGregor is born in Inglewood, California.

January 22
1925— Bobby Young, a Baltimore-area native who played on the old International League Orioles and was the starting second baseman in 1954, is born in Granite, Maryland.

January 23
1928— Shortstop Chico Carrasquel, who played the 1959 season with the Orioles and in one game was hit in the head with the bases loaded, forcing in the game winner, is born in Caracas, Venezuela.

January 26
1958— Dave Nicholson, the strongboy from St. Louis who never overcame his propensity for striking out, signs for the biggest bonus in club history.

January 27
1947— John Lowenstein is born in Wolf Point, Nevada.

January 29
1994— Baseball's all-time saves leader Lee Smith signs a free agent contract with the Orioles. Smith has amassed a record 401 total saves over 13 seasons, 36 more than runner-up Jeff Reardon.

Memorial Stadium.

FEBRUARY

February 1
1944— Paul Blair is born in Cushing, Oklahoma.

1982— The Orioles trade third baseman Doug DeCinces to California for Dan Ford.

February 2
1937— Don Buford is born in Linden, Texas.

February 6
1895— Babe Ruth is born on Emory Street in Baltimore, Maryland.

February 8
1977— Billy Smith, a switch-hitting second baseman who played out his option with the Angels, signs a two-year contract with the Orioles. Smith was the lone free-agent acquisition from the reentry draft that saw the Orioles lose Reggie Jackson, Bobby Grich, and Wayne Garland.

February 10
1933— Billy O'Dell, the first bonus baby signed by the Orioles, is born in Whitmere, South Carolina.

February 11
1987— Veteran National League infielder Ray Knight signs a one-year contract with the Orioles.

Billy Smith

February 12
1939— Jerry Walker is born in Byng, Oklahoma.

1942— Pat Dobson is born in Depew, New York.

February 15
1938— Chuck Estrada, a member of the early 1960s Kiddie Korps and who won 33 games his first two years before developing arm troubles, is born in San Luis Obispo, California.

February 16
1947— Terry Crowley, known as "The King of Swing" while playing with the O's as primarily a pinch hitter, is born on Staten Island.

February 18
1954— In an ill-fated trade made just before the Orioles' first spring training, Roy Sievers is sent to Washington for Gil Coan. Whereas Sievers emerged an authentic power-hitting threat of long standing

with Washington, Coan had two lackluster seasons in Baltimore before being sold to the White Sox in 1956 for the waiver price.

February 22
1954— The former St. Louis Browns, now known as the Baltimore Orioles, hold their first spring workout at Yuma, Arizona.

February 24
1956— Eddie Murray is born in Los Angeles.

February 25
1975— Long-time favorite Boog Powell, who slipped to only 12 home runs and 45 RBIs in 1974, is traded to Cleveland for catcher Dave Duncan.

February 27
1993— Popular Dodger lefthander Fernando Valenzuela, who won 141 games and pitched in five All-Star games in 11 seasons in Los Angeles before being released and joining the Mexican League, signs a minor league contract with the Orioles.

Boog Powell

MARCH

March 16

1954— Oriole general manager Art Ehlers purchases long-time Phillie first baseman Eddie Waitkus. Unbeknownst to Ehlers, O's first baseman Dick Kryhoski fractured his left wrist in spring training on the same day. After hitting .238 in 1954, Waitkus was released in 1955.

March 18

1999— Former Oriole first base great Eddie Murray and former General Manager Frank Cashen, who oversaw the club when it reached the post-season six times in a 10-year span, are announced as the newest inductees to the Orioles Hall of Fame. Murray, currently an Orioles bench coach, spent 12½ of his 21 big league seasons with the Orioles, batting .294 with 343 homers. He returned via trade in 1996 after a six-year absence and hit his 500th career homer to join Hank Aaron and Willie Mays as the only players with 500 homers and 3,000 hits.

March 21

1939— Tommy Davis, the Orioles' first full-time designated hitter, is born in Brooklyn, New York.

March 23

1943— The "Big Bopper," Lee May, is born in Birmingham, Alabama.

March 24

1925— Original Oriole Dick Kryhoski is born in Leonia, New Jersey.

March 25

1999— Cal Ripken, Sr., who spent 36 years in the Orioles organization as a player, manager, scout and coach, dies of lung cancer at the age of 63. Ripken, who became the only manager in big league history to manage two sons simultaneously in 1987, preached fundamentals, hard work and attention to detail, all assets exhibited by son Cal Jr., who didn't miss a game for over 16 years. Ripken, Sr., who left the Oriole organization in 1993, was diagnosed with cancer in October, 1998.

*Gene Woodling with
author Ted Patterson*

March 26

1982— The Orioles acquire catcher Joe Nolan from Cincinnati for two minor leaguers, Dallas Williams and Brooks Carey.

March 28

1999— In the first game played on Cuban shores involving a major league team since 1959, the Orioles eke out a 3-2 win over the Cuban Nationals before over 50,000 fans in Havana. With Fidel Castro looking on, the Orioles get a two-run second-inning homer from Charles Johnson and an RBI single in the 11th from Harold Baines. In between Cuban reliever Jose Contreras pitched two-hit ball over eight innings, striking out 10. The Orioles will host the Cubans at Camden Yards on May 3.

March 31

1958— Just two weeks before opening day, Gene Woodling and Dick Williams come back to Baltimore for their second tour of duty, along with pitcher Bud Daley, as Larry Doby and Don Ferrarese are sent to Cleveland.

Cal Ripken Jr.'s 1982 Orioles cap.

APRIL

April 1

1998— The Orioles bounce back from a rocky opening-day performance the day before by routing Kansas City 10-1 and reaching several milestones in the process. Cal Ripken hits his eighth career grand slam, Scott Erickson notches his 100th career victory and Lenny Webster enjoys his first two-homer game in the majors. It is also Ray Miller's first win as Oriole manager and first managerial win since 1986 when he managed the Twins.

April 2

1976— In Hank Peter's first major deal as general manager, the Orioles trade Don Baylor, Mike Torrez, and Paul Mitchell to Oakland for Reggie Jackson, Ken Holtzman, and Bill Van Bommel. Reggie did not report for a month—a full three weeks into the season—which helped account for a 6-9 April.

1984— President Ronald Reagan becomes the 13th president to throw out an opening day first ball (the third outside of Washington) when the Orioles open with the White Sox in Baltimore. The president spent the first inning sitting in the Orioles dugout with Commissioner Bowie Kuhn and owner Edward Bennett Williams before returning to Washington. The Orioles win, 5-2, before over 51,000 fans.

1986— An opening day crowd of 52,292, the largest regular season crowd in Oriole history, goes home disappointed as Cleveland's Ken Schrom beats Mike Flanagan, 6-4.

1997— Jimmy Key, replacing the injured Mike Mussina as Opening Day starter, the first lefty to start an opener since Jeff Ballard in 1989, beats Keven Appier and the Royals, 4-2, to improve his Opening Day career record to 7-0.

Owner Edward Bennett Williams, President Reagan and Commissioner Peter Ueberroth at the 1986 Opening Day game.

Camden Yards

1998— Jeffrey Hammonds' two-run single in the bottom of the ninth caps a four-run rally and carries the Orioles over the Royals, 4-3. Harold Baines, with the only two Oriole hits entering the ninth, homers to lead off the inning. Royal reliever Jeff Montgomery hits one batter, and walks another with the bases loaded before Hammonds' big hit.

April 3

1960— The Orioles trade second baseman Billy Gardner to Washington for Clint Courtney. Courtney, nicknamed "Scrap Iron" and still holder of the club mark for the fewest strikeouts in a season (seven in 437 at bats in 1954), begins his second of three tours of duty in Baltimore, hitting only .227 in 83 games for the 1960 Orioles.

1989— The new season dawns with heavy rains and the opener with Boston is in doubt, but at 11:30 A.M. the clouds disappear, the sun comes out, and it becomes one of Baltimore's best weather openers ever, the first of many miracles for the improbable '89 Orioles. After President George Bush tosses out the ceremonial first pitch, the Orioles proceed to nip the Red Sox, 5-4, in 11 innings. Cal Ripken Jr. hits a three-run homer off Roger Clemens and rookie Craig Worthington singles in the game winner in the 11th in front of 52,161 fans. There would be no 0-21 start this year. The win snaps a four-game Presidential losing streak, three with Ronald Reagan and one with Jimmy Carter.

April 4

1983— A sellout crowd of 51,885 is on hand to usher in the Orioles' 30th season, but the Royals spoil the occasion with a 7-4 win, breaking a string of five straight home opening wins.

1994— Rafael Palmeiro, the most celebrated of the Orioles off-season acquisitions, hits a seventh-inning homer to help Mike Mussina beat Keven Appier and the Royals on Opening Day, 6-3. The 29-year-old Palmeiro had homered in his first intrasquad game, his first exhibition game, his first game as an Oriole at Camden Yards in an exhibition game against the Phillies, and now on Opening Day.

April 5

1982— The Orioles hit four home runs, including a grand slam by Eddie Murray and three-run shots by Cal Ripken, Jr. and newcomer Dan Ford, to beat Kansas City, 13-5, before a record crowd of 51,958.

1989— The crowd of 22,041, the second biggest second day house in club history, watches the Orioles beat Boston, 6-4, and suddenly the O's are two games over .500 for the first time since June, 1987. Jose Bautista uses only 94 pitches and retires 16 straight at one point to get the win.

1999— The Orioles open their season in the American League by outlasting the Tampa Bay Devil Rays before over 46,000 fans at Camden Yards. Before the game a moment of silence was observed for departed Orioles Mark Belanger and Cal Ripken, Sr., with the number "7" emblazoned on the third base coaching box where Cal Sr. coached for over a decade. Newcomer Albert Belle electrified the fans with a three-run homer and Mike Mussina won his fifth opening day start.

April 6

1979— Earl Weaver becomes the 32nd manager in baseball history to win 1,000 games in the majors on opening day when Jim Palmer defeats the White Sox, 5-3, in Baltimore.

1987— Larry Sheets' 10th-inning sacrifice fly lifts the Orioles to a 2-1 opening day win over Texas. Don Aase gets the win in relief of Mike Boddicker. It would be Aase's only win of the season and one of just seven appearances because of a sore shoulder that required surgery.

1992— In the historic first game at Oriole Park at Camden Yards, Rick Sutcliffe, making his Orioles debut as the oldest opening-day starter in club history and pitching his eighth opener overall, blanks Cleveland, 2-0, on five hits. The O's hadn't had an Opening Day shutout since 1976 when they beat Boston, 1-0. The Orioles become the first team to christen a new park with a shutout since the San Francisco Giants blanked Los Angeles, 8-0, on April 15, 1958, in the Giants' first game at Candlestick Park. The Orioles were also the first team since Toronto in 1977 to win their first game in a new home. Since then, the Blue Jays at Skydome, Chicago at the new Comiskey, Minnesota at the Metrodome and Montreal at Olympic Stadium, all lost their new stadium openers. A crowd of 44,568 watched President George Bush throw out the first pitch. The Orioles scored both runs off loser Charlie Nagy in the fifth inning when Chris Hoiles doubled home Sam Horn and Bill Ripken squeezed home Leo Gomez. Cleveland's Paul Sorrento had the distinction of collecting the first hit in the new ballpark with a second-inning single. Sorrento also hit the new park's first home run, a three-run shot off Bob Milacki in the Indians 4-0 win on April 8 in game two. Glenn Davis had the Orioles' first hit, a second-inning single to center off Nagy, who also went the distance.

April 7

1970— Dave McNally fans a career-high 13 batters and the Orioles break loose for seven runs in the last three innings, including a Frank Robinson home run, in an 8-2 opening-day win in Cleveland.

1979— Lerrin LaGrow of the White Sox hits Gary Roenicke in the face with a pitch, inflicting a 25-stitch cut that put him out for a week. When he returned a week later, Roenicke wore a batting helmet, designed by Earl Weaver and Colts equipment head Marty Daly, that was equipped with a football-type facemask.

1993— Reliever Gregg Olson allows a home run to Doug Strange, the first batter he faces in '93, in a 3-1 loss to Texas at home, but doesn't allow another homer the rest of the season in 49 games and 44.1 innings pitched.

April 8

1963— The Orioles win the Presidential Opener in Washington, 3-1, scoring all their runs in the second inning off Don Rudolph on a solo homer by Jim Gentile and Boog Powell's two-run belt.

April 9

1959— Vice President Nixon throws out the first ball at Griffith Stadium. The Orioles lose the Presidential Opener, 9-2, to the Senators.

1970— Tom Phoebus wins his first of the year and the Birds take their third straight with a 13-1 bombing of Cleveland. Don Buford hits two of the Orioles' four homers, one from each side of the plate.

1976— A record opening-day crowd of 46,425 at Memorial Stadium watches the Orioles blank Boston, 1-0, with Jim Palmer and Dyar Miller combining on the shutout.

1983— Cleveland wins its home opener, 8-4, as Tippy Martinez, who would enjoy his best season in the majors, gives up his first career grand slam, to George Vukovich. Julio Franco follows with a solo shot as Tippy gives up two homers in one game for the first time.

1990— Sam Horn, signed to a minor league contract after being released by Boston in February, enjoys the greatest Opening Day and Orioles debut in club history. Horn belts a pair of three-run homers to help the Orioles defeat the Kansas City Royals in come-from-behind fashion, 7-6, in 11 innings at KC. His first homer comes off Cy Young winner Bret Saberhagen. It was the most RBI by a major league player on Opening Day since Jim Presley had six for Seattle in 1986. Brant Alyea had seven for the Twins against Chicago on April 7, 1970.

Sam Horn

1992— Ben McDonald tosses a two-hitter and beats the Indians, 2-0. It's the third shutout in as many games to inaugurate Camden Yards. It's just the second time in major league history shutouts are thrown in the first three games of a new ballpark. The other time it happened was way back in 1913 when Ebbets Field opened. The O's two complete-game shutouts after three games matches their total from the entire '91 season. Mike Devereaux hits the Birds' first homer in their new park off Jack Armstrong.

1998— Joe Carter drives home the go-ahead run in the eighth inning and the Orioles tie a club record with five double plays in winning their seventh straight, 2-1, over the Royals in Kansas City. The 7-1 start equals the best start in club history.

1999— Jerold C. Hoffberger, former President of the National Brewing Co. and principle owner of

Four Oriole immortals—Jim Palmer, Earl Weaver, Brooks Robinson, and Frank Robinson.

the Orioles from 1965 until 1979, dies suddenly just two days after celebrating his 80th birthday. Under Hoffberger's leadership, the Orioles won five American League pennants, two World Championships in 1966 and 1970 and six divisional crowns. Hoffberger sold the Orioles to Edward Bennet Williams after the 1979 season for when the Williams family sold to Eli Jacobs. Hoffberger, a great philanthropist, was called one of the most generous men in America by Town and Country magazine. He gave over $10 million to various charities.

April 10

1968— Brooks Robinson hits his third straight opening-day home run in a 3-1 win over Oakland.

1970— Brooks Robinson's hit scores the winning run in the last of the 10th as the Birds beat Detroit, 3-2, in the O's home opener.

1975— Lee May smashes a three-run homer in his first at bat in the American League, connecting off Joe Coleman. Jim Palmer pitches a 10-0 shutout in Detroit on opening day.

1983— Eddie Murray has four hits, scores four runs, and drives in four as the Orioles pound Cleveland, 13-2.

1987— The Orioles edge Cleveland, 12-11, in 10 innings in the Indians home opener. The crowd is 64,540, the most people to ever watch the Orioles in a regular season game.

April 11

1963— Milt Pappas pitches a five-hitter as the Birds beat Whitey Ford and the Yankees, 4-1, in the first meeting between the two teams. Boog Powell hits two home runs.

1970— A four-run outburst in the eighth lifts the O's to their fifth straight win, 5-3, over Detroit. The win sets a club record for most victories at the start of the season.

1973— The Orioles help the Tigers open their home season before more than 46,000 fans in Detroit. But the Birds spoil the occasion with a 3-1 win in 12 innings. Jim Palmer, Grant Jackson, and Eddie Watt hold the Tigers hitless over the last eight innings.

1974— The Orioles spoil Boston's home opener by coming back to win, 7-6, in 11 innings. The game had been postponed twice because of four inches of snow that fell in Boston.

1988— Frank Robinson replaces Cal Ripken Sr. as manager of the Orioles after the Orioles' 0-6 start. They proceed to lose 15 more in a row under Frank before finally winning at Chicago. The Birds were 54-101 under Robinson. On October 4, two days after the season, Robinson appoints Ripken as the O's third base coach for 1989.

1997— Rafael Palmeiro becomes the first player ever to hit two home runs in one game onto the Eutaw St. promenade, the walkway in front of the warehouse at Oriole Park. "Raffy" connects twice in a 9-3 win over Texas.

1998— Mike Mussina allows only two hits through eight innings, striking out nine and notching his 1000th career strikeout as the Orioles blank the Tigers, 2-0, at Tiger Stadium. Mussina required just two outfield putouts in winning his second game of the season.

April 12

1966— The Orioles beat Boston, 5-4. Jim Lonborg balks home the winning run with the bases loaded and two outs in the 13th inning.

1974— Two straight wild pitches by Jim Slaton with the bases loaded in the fourth inning give the O's a 5-3 win over Milwaukee.

1989— The Orioles break a 15-game losing streak to the Royals with a 5-4 win in 15 innings in Kansas City in the longest game in Royals history, 5:07. Leading, 4-1, in the ninth, KC ties the game, but Mark Williamson comes to the rescue and retires all 14 Royals he faces. Mike Devereaux' sac fly off Steve Farr scores the game winner.

1993 cap

April 13

1954— The Orioles play their first game since returning to the major leagues in Detroit before 46,994, and lose to the Tigers, 3-0, as Steve Gromek beats Don Larsen.

1966— Jim Palmer pitches his first career complete game and hits a two-run homer to help his cause as the Orioles beat Boston, 8-1, at Fenway Park. Frank and Brooks hit back-to-back homers in the first inning.

1968— Elrod Hendricks, in his first major league at bat, singles home the first run of the game in the seventh as the Orioles and Jim Hardin beat California, 3-0.

1969— Comebacking Jim Palmer, making his first appearance since September 19, 1967, strikes out eight Senators, including Frank Howard four times, blanking Washington, 2-0. Frank Robinson's two-run homer in the third accounts for the Oriole scoring. In the second game of the twin-bill, Tom Phoebus wins his first of the season and extends the O's scoreless-inning streak to 30.

1975— Mike Torrez, making his first start in the American League, benefits from 15 hits as the Birds bomb Boston, 11-3.

1991— Cal Ripken bangs out four hits, including a triple and two home runs while driving in seven in an 11-4 rout of the Rangers in Arlington.

1997— Jimmy Key blanks the Rangers, 9-0, at Camden Yards. It's his first complete game since May 6, 1994 and his first shutout since May 28, 1993.

April 14

1954— Duane Pillette has the distinction of winning the first-ever game for the modern day Orioles, going the distance in a 3-2 victory in Detroit.

1983— The longest nine-inning game in Orioles history is played amid 27 mph winds at Comiskey Park. The White Sox lead, 9-2, after five innings before the Birds rally to tie. The White Sox win, 12-11, as rookie Ron Kittle drives in six runs.

1991— Nolan Ryan wins his first game against the Orioles in nearly 15 years, 15-3, in Texas. Ryan had lost nine straight decisions to the Orioles since last winning in 1976 with the Angels.

April 15

1954— In the first game ever played in Baltimore's new Memorial Stadium, 46,354 watch the Orioles defeat Chicago, 3-1, behind Bob Turley's seven hit, nine strikeout performance. Both Clint Courtney and Vern Stephens hit home runs off loser Virgil Trucks.

1987— Milwaukee's Juan Nieves becomes the only opposing pitcher to no-hit the Orioles at Memorial Stadium. Centerfielder Robin Yount makes a great catch of an Eddie Murray drive to right center to end the game. Milwaukee wins, 7-0.

1989— A seven-run ninth inning, featuring three-run homers by Brady Anderson and Larry Sheets off Mike Smithson, propels the Orioles to a 12-4 win over the Red Sox at Fenway Park.

1991— Glenn Davis and the Orioles spoil Milwaukee's home opener with a 7-2 win as Davis hits his first American League homer off Chris Bosio. Sam Horn hits a three-run homer for the Orioles.

April 16

1959— George Bamberger goes 6⅓ innings in his first and only major league start, but Billy O'Dell gets the win in a 7-4 victory over the Yankees at Memorial Stadium.

1972— After nine games have been cancelled due to the players' strike, the Orioles open the season with a 3-1 win over the Yankees before only 13,153 fans at Memorial Stadium.

1994— The Orioles begin a 16-6 stretch by coming back from a 3-0, seventh inning deficit to beat the Rangers, 6-4, in the new ballpark at Arlington. Rafael Palmeiro homers against the club who let him go and Harold Baines delivers a pinch- hit, three-run triple to break the game open in the eighth.

April 17

1958— Brooks Robinson hits his first home run at Memorial Stadium off Washington's Russ Kemmerer. It is Brooks' fourth career homer, all hit off Senator pitching.

1966— The biggest walk-up gate sale in club history (21,140) watch the O's come from behind with two runs in the eighth to defeat New York, 5-4. The crowd total is 27,802.

1968— The Orioles help unveil major league baseball in Oakland but spoil the occasion as Dave McNally pitches a two-hitter to beat Lew Krausse, 4-1. Boog Powell hits the first home run in the Coliseum. Mark Belanger and Brooks Robinson also homer before a crowd of 47,233.

1973— Earl Williams hits his first home run as an Oriole, a three-run shot in the eighth, to provide Dave McNally with all the runs he needs in a 4-2 win over the Yankees. Williams nails a 0-2 pitch from Sparky Lyle into the left-field seats to provide Mac with his third straight win.

1977— After Rich Dauer goes 0-for-16 in the first five games of the season, Billy Smith takes over in a Sunday double-header in Texas and goes 6-for-8, hitting his first major league home run, a shot off Bert Blyleven. With his parents from San Antonio in the stands at Arlington, Billy goes 10-for-19 in five games with the Rangers.

Brooks Robinson

1992— Randy Milligan becomes the first player to have a multi-homer game at Oriole Park when he hits two against Detroit, driving in six runs in an 8-0 win over the Tigers. Milligan hit his second career grand slam off Les Lancaster. Rick Sutcliffe pitches his second straight shutout at the new park.

1993— The Orioles spot the Angels a 5-0 lead, roar back to tie, then blow it with a classic base-running blunder in the eighth when Jeff Tackett, Brady Anderson and Chito Martinez all end up in the vicinity of third base at the same time. Two were tagged out to end the inning, and the Angels prevail, 7-5.

1996— The Orioles edge Boston, 6-5, for their 11th win in 13 games to open the season, their second best beginning in club history after 1966's 12-1 start.

April 18
1975— Lee May hits two home runs and drives in seven in his first-ever game at Fenway Park. The O's came back to beat the Red Sox, 9-7.

April 19
1977— Brooks Robinson hits his 268th and last home run in dramatic fashion. The Orioles trail Cleveland, 5-2, in the bottom of the 10th. With one out and runners on first and second, Lee May singles in a run. Then Brooks comes up as a pinch hitter for Larry Harlow. He runs the count to 3-2 and fouls off several pitches before homering into the left-field seats off of lefty Dave LaRoche to produce a 6-5 win.

1980— Harold Baines, the St. Michaels, Maryland, resident (and Easton, Maryland, native), is 1-for-25 at the start of his rookie year when he hits his first big league homer, a solo shot off Jim Palmer in Baltimore. He also makes a game saving catch in the 12th as the White Sox win, 5-4.

1983— With the chill factor hovering around five degrees and snow falling, John Lowenstein hits a towering home run into the flurries for a 4-2 win over the Texas Rangers at Memorial Stadium.

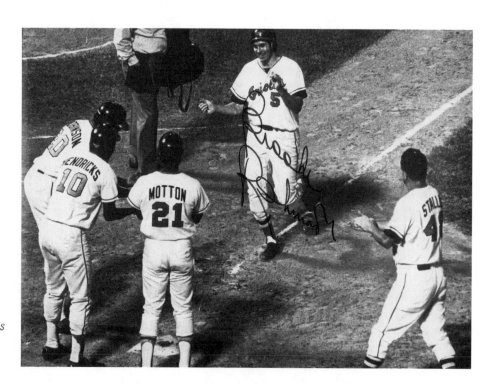

Brooks Robinson crosses home plate.

April 19

1985— Rookie Fritz Connally, whose first two major league home runs were grand slams, hits his first off Doyle Alexander in Toronto on the 14th pitch thrown to him in that plate appearance. Connally fouls off nine pitches before connecting to give the Orioles a 4-1 lead in the fifth in a game they eventually lose, 6-5.

1990— The Orioles' home opener draws 49,288 who watch the Tigers issue eight walks in the first four innings and commit four errors as the Birds win, 4-2, behind hometown boy Dave Johnson, who becomes the first Baltimore native to start a home opener.

1996— No it isn't a football result. The Orioles are clobbered in Texas, 26-7. Infielder Manny Alexander makes his pro pitching debut as he allows five earned runs and four walks in ⅔ of an inning in the rout.

April 20

1962— The Orioles beat the Senators in the first night game ever at D.C. Stadium (now RFK) by a 5-4 score.

1968— Baltimore clubs California 10-1 behind Boog Powell's three-run homer. Frank Robinson goes 3-for-4, but leaves the game with a stiff neck. The Angel team doctor diagnoses Frank's ailment as mumps and the entire team is given shots.

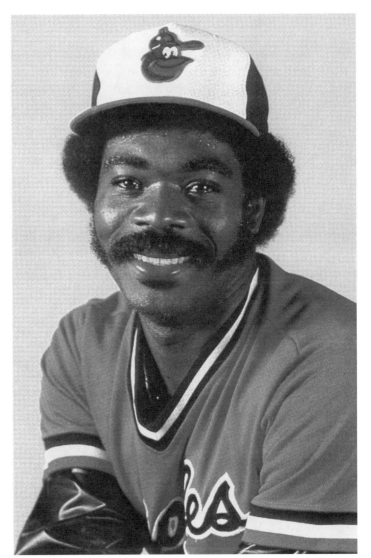

Eddie Murray

1972— The Orioles get only two hits off Tom Timmerman and Chuck Seelbach, but one is a homer by Paul Blair. The Birds win, 1-0, and Pat Dobson wins his second without a loss.

1984— Trailing the Twins, 2-1, at home in the seventh inning, Eddie Murray hits a game-tying two-out single off Ron Davis, then hits a two-run 10th-inning homer off Davis to win the game, 4-2, and launch the Orioles on a 29-12 stretch.

1985— John Lowenstein, playing the next-to-last game of his 16-year career, drives in the game winner with a sac fly off Tom Waddell in the eighth as the Orioles rally from a 7-1 deficit to beat the Indians, 8-7.

1989— Jeff Ballard beats Bret Saberhagen and the Royals, 2-0, at Memorial Stadium in the shortest game of the year at 2:03. Saberhagen has already pitched two complete games versus the Orioles, allowing only one earned run and yet he's only 1-1.

1992— After the Tigers hit three consecutive homers (Alan Trammell, Cecil Fielder, Mickey Tettleton) in a span of seven pitches off Ben McDonald in the fourth inning to take a 4-0 lead, the Orioles bounce back with five runs in their half of the fourth and seven more in the seventh to beat Detroit, 12-4. Tettleton's homer bounces off the Warehouse, landing 406 feet from home plate. Sam Horn becomes the first player to hit a ball into the centerfield bleachers, a 420-foot shot off Eric King.

April 21

1954— More than 43,000 fans are on hand for the first night game ever at Memorial Stadium. Bob Turley leads the Cleveland Indians, 1-0, and has a no-hitter going with one out in the ninth when Al Rosen singles and Larry Doby follows with a two-run homer that gives the pennant-bound Indians a 2-1 win. Turley loses on a two-hitter, striking out a club-record 14.

1986— Floyd Rayford sets a club record for most errors in a game when he makes four in a 7-0 loss at Cleveland. He also ties an American League record for most errors in a game by a third baseman.

1996— Brady Anderson sets a record with a leadoff homer in the 9-6 loss at Texas. It's Brady's fourth straight game with a leadoff homer, setting a major league record. The previous mark was two straight games, done 33 times.

1998— Lefty reliever Jesse Orosco celebrates his 41st birthday, becoming the third oldest Oriole ever behind Rick Dempsey (43) and Dizzy Trout (42).

April 22

1914— Nineteen-year-old Babe Ruth makes his pitching debut in organized baseball for his hometown Orioles of the International League and defeats Buffalo, 6-0, on six hits. He collects two hits in four times at bat against George McConnell, a right-hander.

1965— The Orioles lead Washington, 8-0, after two innings, and then bomb the Senators, 18-4, to set a club record for the largest winning margin, 14 runs.

1989— A crowd of 34,698, swelled by a walk-up of more than 11,000, cheers the Orioles into first place with a 4-1 win over the Twins. Rookie outfielder Steve Finley collects his first two big league hits, including the game winner. It's the first time since May 11, 1985 that the Orioles have first place to themselves.

Bob Milacki

1990— The Orioles nip the Tigers, 3-2, in 12 innings as Joe Orsulak goes four-for-four. With three hits the next night against Kansas City, Orsulak has a total of seven consecutive hits and a walk in eight plate appearances.

April 23

1954— The Orioles win the first extra-inning game in their history as Ray Murray doubles home two runs in the 10th at Chicago to beat the White Sox, 3-1.

1969— In an early duel between the two pitchers who would tie for the Cy Young Award balloting, Mike Cuellar tops Denny McLain, 3-2, in 10 innings. McLain retires 21 straight before Ellie Hendricks leads off the 10th with a double, while Cuellar sits down 20 in a row. Mark Belanger drives in Hendricks with a single to right to win it.

1983— Scott McGregor out-duels Tommy John at Anaheim Stadium, 3-1. A crowd of 63,073, the largest crowd ever to watch the Orioles play, watch Scotty win his 13th in his last 14 decisions against the Angels.

1989— Bob Milacki goes the route, tossing a three-hit shutout and blanking Minnesota, 3-0. Milacki uses only 100 pitches and becomes only the third Oriole ever to face the minimum 27 batters (Jim Palmer in '67 and Mike Flanagan in '82). It's only the third complete-game shutout in the Orioles' last 252 games, and Milacki has pitched two of them.

1992— The Orioles win their seventh straight, 8-1, in Kansas City as Mike Mussina tosses the Birds fifth complete game. It took them until September 4 to notch five complete games in '91.

1997— Eric Davis hits his ninth career grand slam and matches his career-high with six RBI in a 11-9 loss to the White Sox at Camden Yards.

April 24

1966— Steve Barber goes the distance to beat the Yankees, 2-1, on a four hitter as Brooks Robby drives in both runs on doubles. It is the 11th straight win for the Orioles at Yankee Stadium and 16 of the last 18.

1973— In his first appearance against the Orioles since being traded from the Dodgers to the Angels, Frank Robinson hits a three-run homer to key a six-run explosion and 6-5 Angel win in Anaheim. Frank's blast travels 435 feet over the left field wall.

1982— The Orioles snap a nine-game losing streak, the longest in six years, beating the White Sox, 7-4.

1994— Seattle's Ken Griffey Jr., facing rookie Brad Pennington, blasts the fourth-ever homer onto the Eutaw Street corridor, 438 feet from home plate and 25 feet short of the warehouse as the Mariners came back to win, 7-6.

April 25

1954— The Orioles' first doubleheader ends in defeat, 4-3 and 3-2, to Chicago.

1978— Jim Spencer, a Baltimore native, hits his 100th career home run in the ninth inning of a 4-3 Yankee victory over Baltimore at Memorial Stadium.

1985— Rookie pitcher Ken Dixon wins his first major league start, going the distance in a 7-1 win over Cleveland at home. Dixon takes a one-hit shutout into the ninth and finishes with a three-hitter.

1989— The Orioles, with President George Bush looking on at the Big-A in Anaheim, hit into five double plays but get home runs by Mickey Tettleton, Jim Traber, Bill Ripken and rookie Steve Finley to beat Mike Witt and the Angels, 8-1. Finley's three-run shot is his first in the major leagues. Jeff Ballard ups his record to 4-0.

1998— Cal Ripken Jr. plays in his 2,500th consecutive game, driving in three runs in an 8-2 win over the Oakland

Cal Ripken, Jr.

Athletics. The crowd of over 47,000 Camden Yards fans gives Ripken a huge ovation when the game becomes official in the fifth inning. Less than a year earlier, Ripken gave thought to ending the streak when a herniated disk in his back was pressing against a nerve that runs down his left leg. Doctors prescribed six to eight weeks of rest. Ripken rejected the advice, although he almost removed himself from the lineup on August 2 in Oakland. He stuck it out although he ached so much he couldn't sit in the dugout. He spurned off-season surgery and instead worked to strengthen his back. And the streak, now in its 17th season, just keeps going on.

April 26

1901— In the first American League game in Baltimore, league president Ban Johnson throws out the first ball. The Orioles beat Boston, 10-6. This Orioles club moved to New York in 1903 and became known as the Highlanders and eventually the Yankees.

1959— The Orioles sweep the Yankees in three straight for the first time ever at Yankee Stadium. Lenny Green's inside-the-park homer accounts for two runs.

1970— Frank Robinson becomes the only Orioles player ejected all season when Jim Odom thumbs him for arguing called strikes. The Birds beat Kansas City, 10-9, as Don Buford hits a three-run homer in the eighth.

1974— Andy Etchebarren hits a sacrifice fly to drive in Don Baylor with the winning run in the 15th inning. The Birds edge Oakland, 6-5.

1989— Oakland's Bob Welch leads, 1-0, on a two-hit shutout through seven innings but the Birds tie it on a bases loaded walk in the eighth, followed by a run-producing single by Steve Finley. Gregg Olson preserves the 2-1 win by retiring six in a row to save it, striking out Dave Parker, Dave Henderson and Mark McGwire in the ninth.

1994— On a gorgeous Tuesday afternoon, the Birds wallop Oakland, 10-4, before the largest regular season crowd ever to that point at Oriole Park, 47,565. Brady Anderson delivers a pair of homers and a pair of doubles to account for 12 total bases, one shy of the club record.

1995— The strike is finally over. It began in August of 1994 and cut out 40 regular season games as well as the playoffs and World Series and knocked out the first 18 games of the 1995 season. The Orioles lose to Kansas City, 5-1, before only 24,170 fans.

1997— Roberto Alomar homers three times in one game and collects a career-high six RBI in a 14-5 win over the Red Sox at Oriole Park. It is Robbie's first ever three-homer game and the 16th time it's been done in Oriole history, first at Camden Yards.

April 27

1942— A crowd of over 13,000 at old Oriole Park watches future Hall of Famer Bob Lemon hit four home runs, a triple, and a single as the Orioles split a doubleheader with Montreal in the old International League. Lemon, who converted to pitcher after joining the Cleveland Indians, played third for Baltimore. He hit three home runs, plus a triple and single in the 10-5 first-game win, driving in five runs and scoring five.

1961— Dick Hall has a one-hitter until Joe Hicks' two-out ninth-inning single, walking only one in a masterful, 5-0, win over Washington.

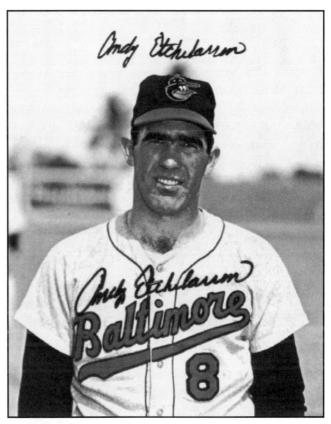

Andy Etchebarren

Tom Phoebus

1968— Tom Phoebus, a Baltimore native, tosses a no-hitter against Boston, 6-0, striking out nine and walking three. The game was delayed an hour and 23 minutes at the start because of rain. Brooks Robinson saves the no-hitter by making a spectacular catch of Rico Petrocelli's eighth-inning line drive. Curt Blefary, normally an outfielder/first baseman, is the catcher.

1969— In a doubleheader at Memorial Stadium, Frank Robinson has six hits, including two home runs and eight RBI to pace a sweep of the Yankees, 6-0 and 10-5.

1979— The Orioles win their ninth straight as Mike Flanagan beats Matt Keough, 7-1, at Oakland. Third baseman Doug DeCinces hurts his back in pregame practice and misses the next 33 games.

1988— Just one day after being recalled from Rochester, third baseman Craig Worthington homers off Minnesota's Bert Blyleven for his first major league hit in a 7-6 defeat at the Metrodome.

1994— The Orioles blast the Angels, 13-1, in Anaheim to give Ben McDonald a perfect 5-0 record for April. It's the fastest an Oriole pitcher has won five games (club's 20th game). McDonald would go on to win his first seven starts.

April 28

1960— Steve Barber, who won 95 games in an Oriole uniform, wins his first major league game, going the route over Boston, 6-1.

1981— Ken Singleton sets a club record with his 10th consecutive hit, a home run off Chicago's Richard Dotson. Ken hit .472 in April and was voted American League Player of the Month.

1987— Mike Boddicker pitches the second one-hitter of his career, beating the Royals, 3-0, while allowing only a single to Willie Wilson in the sixth inning.

1988— Mike Boddicker drops to 0-5 to start the season as the Orioles lose at Minnesota, 4-2, to give them 21 straight defeats to start the season, eight games worse than any other start in major league history and the second longest losing streak in history, topped only by the '61 Phillies who lost 23 straight.

1991— Dwight Evans, signed as a free agent on December 6, 1990, after 19 seasons in Boston, homers off Erik Hanson of Seattle becoming the 17th player in Major League history to hit a homer in 20 consecutive seasons. The Orioles edge Milwaukee, 5-4, at Memorial Stadium.

April 29

1970— Paul Blair becomes the third Oriole in club history, joining Boog Powell and Curt Blefary, to smash three home runs in a game, in an 18-2 trouncing of the White Sox at Comiskey Park.

1972— Don Baylor's first major league home run, a three-run blast off Andy Messersmith, helps lead the Orioles to a 6-1 win over the Angels.

1980— Rick Dempsey enjoys his first two-home-run day as the Orioles lose to New York, 4-3. Dempsey connects off Luis Tiant and Rudy May.

1988— After losing their first 21 games, the Orioles blank the White Sox, 9-0, in Chicago. Mark Williamson, making just his third big league start, is the winner, his only win in 10 starts.

1990— Rene Gonzales belts a "sudden death" game-winning home run in the bottom of the ninth inning off Mike Jackson to beat Seattle, 5-4, at Memorial Stadium.

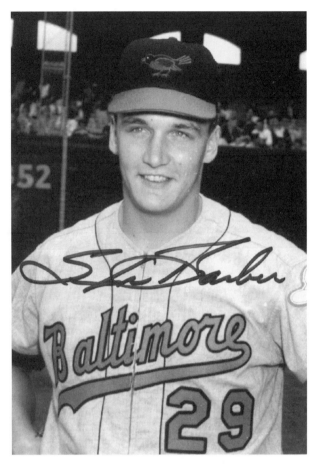

Steve Barber

1998— Twenty-one-year-old rookie Sidney Ponson makes his starting debut, giving up six runs and six hits in four innings in a 16-7 loss at Chicago. Ponson is the third native of Aruba to play in the majors. Orioles prospect Eugene Kingsale played in three games for the O's in 1996, and former Orioles farmhand Calvin Maduro made his big league debut with the Phillies in September, 1996. On June 7, 1998, Sidney's cousin, lefthander Radhames Dykhoff made his debut with the Orioles. All four Arubans were signed by Orioles scout Jesus Halabi.

April 30

1961— Consecutive home runs by Jim Gentile, Gus Triandos and Ron Hansen key a four-run seventh inning off Paul Foytack as the Birds beat Detroit, 4-2.

1967— Steve Barber and Stu Miller combine to no-hit Detroit at Memorial Stadium, but lose, 2-1. The Tigers get both their runs in the top of the ninth, one scoring on a wild pitch by loser Barber and the other on an error by Mark Belanger, who dropped the ball on a potential game-ending double play.

1989— Unbeaten Jeff Ballard becomes the first Oriole ever to win five games in April, beating the Mariners, 4-3, in Seattle. Mickey Tettleton's two-run eighth inning homer puts the O's up for good.

1990— Steve Finley's over-the-wall catch of a Lance Parrish fly ball in the eighth inning, saves a tie score and allows the O's to post a 2-1, 12-inning victory over the Angels at Memorial Stadium. If not for Finley's catch, Parrish's drive would have resulted in a three-run homer and given California a 4-1 lead.

1993— Rightfielder Mark McLemore walks twice in one inning in a 12-5 win over the Royals, tying a club record set by Merv Rettenmund in June, 1970.

1994— Mike Mussina runs his record to 5-1, beating Randy Johnson and the Mariners, 6-4, in Seattle. The win proves costly, however, as rookie Jeffrey Hammonds, trying to score on a sacrifice fly, crashes into the mask of catcher Bill Haselman, cutting his face, receiving a concussion, and later injuring his knee during his recovery which forces off-season surgery. Reserve Jack Voigt stepped in and went 3-for-5 that day with a homer off the dangerous Johnson. The win concluded a 15-8 April, third best in club history.

Merv Rettenmund

MAY

May 1

1960— The Orioles score six runs in the fourth inning to overcome a 5-2 Yankee lead as Chuck Estrada goes on to win his first major league start, 9-5.

1964— Jim Palmer makes his professional debut at Aberdeen, South Dakota.

1966— The Orioles knock off Detroit, 4-1, to set a club record of 10 straight wins.

1970— Terry Crowley's first major league homer, a three-run shot in the fourth inning, is the key blow in a 9-3 win over the Twins.

1977— Pat Kelly begins a long-ball streak of five homers in six games by hitting two homers against the Angels, the second a 10th-inning game winner off Paul Hartzell, and a 3-2 victory. The two homers begin a 19-game hitting streak, longest in the American League in 1977.

1984— Mike Boddicker pitches a six-hit, 3-0 shutout over Bert Blyleven and the Indians, which includes a season-high nine strikeouts. It's the first of 20 wins for Boddicker.

Chuck Estrada

1992— The Orioles belt five homers and take advantage of 13 Seattle walks to blast the Mariners, 15-1, at Camden Yards. Tall Randy Johnson is charged with 10 walks, four of them in the six-run fifth, which is capped by Mike Devereaux' grand slam, the first of his two homers on the night. Chris Hoiles, Leo Gomez and Bill Ripken also homer.

May 2

1962— In Minnesota, Boog Powell hits his first major league home runs, one to right field off Jim Kaat, and the other to left off Ted Sadowski. Just three of Boog's 15 homers in '62 were hit on the road and two came in one game.

1968— In his first start since tossing a no-hitter, Tom Phoebus strikes out 11 Yankees in a 6-3 win.

1972— Dave McNally, making up for lost time due to the players' strike, hurls his third shutout in four starts, blanking Chicago, 3-0.

1984— Brook Jacoby's sacrifice fly in the 16th inning scores the game winner in a 9-7 Cleveland win in the Orioles' longest game of the year. The loss goes to Jim Palmer, the last decision of his illustrious career.

1988— Fantastic Fans Night. A crowd of 50,402 turns out at Memorial Stadium to greet the 1-23 Orioles coming off a 12-game road trip which finishes off a 1-22 April. In a pre-game ceremony that night, Maryland Governor William Donald Schaefer and Orioles owner Edward Bennett Williams announce the agreement of a 15-year lease on the newly proposed downtown ballpark. The Orioles beat Texas, 9-4, their first home win of the season. It would be the last time Williams, battling cancer, would see the Orioles in person. Earlier that day the Orioles released classy lefthander Scott McGregor, who held an emotional farewell press conference before the game.

1993— The Orioles edge Kansas City, 4-3, as Harold Baines completes a stretch of reaching base 13 consecutive times. His eight hits and five walks match Jim Dwyer's effort in 1982 to tie the club record. Baines had eight consecutive hits, second behind Ken Singleton's 10 straight hits in 1981. Harold's eighth hit drove in the game winner in the "sudden death" win over KC.

May 3

1959— Tenth-inning home runs by Billy Gardner and Chico Carrasquel give the O's a win in Chicago. It is the Birds' eight come-from-behind victory of the season and 11th win in their last 16 starts.

1980— Ferguson Jenkins becomes the fourth pitcher in history to win 100 or more games in each league. The Texas right-hander beats the Orioles, 3-2, at Arlington Stadium. The other pitchers to achieve this milestone are: Cy Young, Jim Bunning and Gaylord Perry.

1982— Despite allowing three hits and a walk, Mike Flanagan faces the minimum number of batters in a 6-0 blanking of the Mariners. "Flanny" had two runners erased on double plays, one picked off, and another thrown out while attempting to stretch a double.

1963— Pitcher Buster Narum becomes the only Oriole to homer in his first major league plate appearance, connecting off lefthander Don Mossi in the fourth inning with John Orsino aboard in a win at Detroit. It was to be Narum's only at bat in an Oriole uniform.

1992— The Orioles sweep Seattle for the first time at home in 12 years with a 8-6 victory. It's the Bird's fifth straight win and gives them a 9-1 record at home. Gregg Olson becomes the youngest pitcher to record 100 saves (25 years, 204 days), surpassing Bruce Sutter by more than a year.

1996— B.J. Surhoff and Brady Anderson both homer twice in an 8-2 win over the Brewers at Camden Yards. It's the first time the Orioles have two players homer twice in a game since Mike Devereaux and Randy Milligan in 1992.

1998— Mike Mussina, on the disabled list since April 17 after a wart on the index finger of his pitching hand cracked open, allows only two hits over 7⅔ innings in blanking the Twins, 2-0, at Camden Yards. Solo homers by Rafael Palmeiro and Eric Davis account for the Oriole runs. Mussina combines with Arthur Rhodes for a three-hit shutout as the O's win their first series since April 12 in Detroit.

May 4

1961— Trailing the Angels, 6-3, in the ninth, the Orioles rally to tie as Ron Hansen hits a two-run homer in the comeback. Hansen drives in two more runs in the 13th and the Birds win, 5-4. The Orioles hit nine homers in three games, winning two. Both wins are credited to Hoyt Wilhelm.

1973— Frank Robinson, making his first appearance at Memorial Stadium since being traded after the 1971 season, is presented with his retired Oriole jersey, number 20. Frank made the night a memorable one by scoring the only run in the Angels' 1-0 win. Fittingly, the other Robinson, Brooks, singled to set a major league record for hits by a third baseman (2,417), breaking Pie Traynor's record.

1975— The Orioles snap a six-game losing streak by beating Cleveland. Doug DeCinces hits his first big league homer off Tom Buskey.

1983— The Orioles absorb their worst pasting of the season, 16-8, at the hands of the California Angels. In a separate development, Hank Peters announces that Mike Boddicker has been recalled from Rochester to replace the ailing Jim Palmer.

1990— The Orioles outlast Seattle, 9-8, at the Kingdome as Gregg Olson's consecutive scoreless innings streak is snapped at 41. The streak began on August 4, 1989 and matches the 13th longest streak in major league history and longest ever by a reliever. It is also the longest streak in the American League since 1968, when Luis Tiant also had a streak of 41 with Cleveland.

1992— Chris Hoiles' grand slam caps a seventh-inning rally as the Orioles beat Texas, 8-5, for their sixth straight win. The win moves the O's to 10-1 at home, the best mark any team has ever had opening a new ballpark. Mike Devereaux steals home in the first inning, the O's first steal of home since Lee Lacy did it in 1986 at Oakland.

1994— Chris Sabo homers off star reliever Dennis Eckersley with two outs in the ninth in Oakland to give the O's a 3-2 lead. Lee Smith, 12 for 12 in save situations, blows his first save but gets the win, 4-3, in 10 innings.

1996— Brady Anderson, on his way to an incredible 50-homer season, hits his 15th home run in the Orioles' 10-5 win over Milwaukee. It's the earliest date anyone has hit 15 in club history. Brady ties the major league record with 11 home runs in April, breaking the club record of 10 set by Frank Robinson in 1969.

May 5

1962— The Angels' Bo Belinsky, a former Orioles farmhand, pitches a no-hitter against the Orioles at Dodger Stadium, Los Angeles, winning, 2-0. The losing pitcher is Belinsky's former minor league roommate,

Steve Barber. Between the publicity of dating movie queens like Mamie Van Doren and his escapades with teammate Dean Chance, Belinsky compiled a major league record of 28 and 51.

1964— In his first start of the year and his second big league game, 19-year-old Wally Bunker throws a one-hitter, beating Washington, 2-1. Bunker, who also one-hit Kansas City in '64, was named Rookie Pitcher of the Year with a 19-5 record.

1968— The Orioles blank Washington, 8-0, for their seventh straight win as Gene Brabender goes the route. In winning eight of nine, Oriole pitchers combine for a 1.56 ERA, posting two shutouts, a no-hitter, and holding the opposition to six hits or less in each game.

1979— Lee May hits the 10th grand-slam homer of his major league career to propel the O's to a 9-1 win over the Angels at Memorial Stadium. It is the fourth straight win for the O's and their 14th in 15 games. Jim Palmer brings his career record to 21-8 vs. the Angels.

Wally Bunker

1985— The day after he breaks Brooks Robinson's club record for consecutive games played, Cal Ripken goes 5-for-6 with four RBI in a 10-5 win over the Twins at the Metrodome.

1987— Lefthander Eric Bell becomes the ninth Oriole pitcher to lose a no-hitter in the ninth inning when Tom Nieto singles with none out in Minnesota. The Twins scored four runs in that inning, but Bell eventually wins the game, 5-4.

1993— Mike Mussina becomes the first Oriole to throw consecutive complete game shutouts since Jim Palmer in 1982 when he blanks the Twins, 3-0, at Minnesota. Mike shut out the Twins in his previous start April 29, 11-0 at Camden Yards. It's the first time the Twins have been blanked in back-to-back games since Sandy Koufax turned the trick in the 1965 World Series.

May 6

1934— After losing the first game of a doubleheader at Buffalo for their eighth loss in a row, the Orioles storm back to swamp the Bisons, 23-0, in the seven-inning nightcap. It remains the largest shutout victory in Baltimore history, major or minor league.

1966— The Orioles score twice in the 15th to overcome a 2-1 Cleveland lead and win, 3-2. Dave Johnson homers and Boog Powell singles in the winner off Oriole killer Lee Stange in the bottom of the 15th.

1968— Dave Leonhard pitches a one-hitter, the O's sixth straight complete game win and eighth victory in succession, shutting out Detroit, 4-0.

1979— Dennis Martinez shuts out California, 6-0. Since a 3-8 start, the O's have won 15 out of 16.

1984— Cal Ripken hits for the cycle in a 6-1 win at Texas, homering off Dave Tobik in the ninth inning to complete the job. Brooks Robinson had been the only Oriole to hit for the cycle back in 1960.

1987— Scott McGregor snaps a personal five-game losing streak by tossing a three-hit shutout over Bert Blyleven and the Twins, winning, 6-0.

1993— After going 0-for-3 in his major league debut at Minnesota on May 4, Damon Buford, son of former Oriole leadoff hitter Don Buford, collects his first big league hit off Willie Banks on May 5 and then, on May 6, gets two hits including his first major league home run at Toronto off Scott Brow in a 10-8 Blue Jay win.

Cal Ripken Jr.

1994— Former Oriole greats Eddie Murray and Dennis Martinez return to Baltimore as members of the Cleveland Indians and both have a hand in defeating the Orioles, 4-2. Eddie hits a two-run blast off the right field foul pole while Martinez pitches all 10 innings, allowing only three hits and strikes out nine to gain his first American League win since 1985.

1997— Eric Davis goes 4-for-4 and ups his league-leading batting average to .388 in an 8-4 win over the Anaheim Angels.

May 7

1968— The Orioles set a club record with their seventh straight complete game, but the Birds' eight-game winning streak is snapped, 2-1, by Detroit. Tom Phoebus is the hard-luck loser as Mickey Lolich records his ninth straight win over the Orioles. The Birds' last win over Lolich was May 26, 1964.

1970— It looked like the Orioles' 16-game winning streak against Kansas City would end, but Frank Robinson kept it going with a three-run homer with two down in the ninth off Moe Drabowsky, and a 7-6 win.

1974— The Orioles tie a club record and an American League record with a 21-hit outburst while downing Oakland, 9-3. It is the fourth time in club history the O's had 21 hits in a game and all nine regular hitters had at least two hits, which ties a league mark.

1990— Gregg Olson allows his first run of the season at California in his ninth game, breaking a streak of 41 consecutive scoreless innings in 29 appearances. Olson hadn't allowed a run since July 31, 1989. Olson breaks the club record of 36 straight scoreless innings set by Hal Brown in 1961. Olson went another 12 appearances before yielding another run.

1991— Maryland native Harold Baines enjoys the biggest game of his career at the Orioles' expense, hitting three home runs, driving in seven runs and setting an Oakland club record with 14 total bases (he doubled and walked the other two times up) in an 11-3 romp.

1992— In the most thrilling game at young Oriole Park, the Orioles enter the ninth trailing the Twins, 4-1, but parlay four hits, two mistakes by Minnesota outfielders and a game-ending wild pitch by Rick Aguilera into a 5-4, sudden-death victory. Cal Ripken Jr. is walked intentionally to load the bases just ahead of Aguilera's wild pitch that scores Joe Orsulak.

Harold Baines

May 8

1966— Frank Robinson becomes the first player to ever hit a ball completely out of Memorial Stadium when he homers off Luis Tiant of Cleveland in the second game of a doubleheader. The ball clears the left field seats, landing in the parking lot 451 feet from home plate, rolling to a stop 540 feet away.

1977— Pat Kelly caps a five-home-runs-in-six-games explosion with a grand slam off Dick Pole and the Seattle Mariners at Memorial Stadium. Jim Palmer is the winner, 6-4.

1979— Consecutive home runs by Eddie Murray, Lee May, and Gary Roenicke in the sixth inning power the Orioles over Oakland, 8-5. Murray's blast extends his hitting streak to 19 games.

1991— Mark McGwire hits two three-run home runs, one off Mike Flanagan and the other off Mark Williamson in a 9-3 Athletics win in Oakland.

1994— Ben McDonald becomes the majors' first seven-game winner (he has yet to lose) with an 8-6 win over the Indians. After a home run and bases-loaded triple, outfielder Mike Devereaux is struck on the cheek by a pitch from rookie Chad Ogea. Remarkably, there was no fracture and he played the next day wearing a protective flap on his helmet.

1997— Mike Mussina beats Randy Johnson and the Mariners, 13-3, at Camden Yards. The Oriole win snaps Johnson's 16-game winning streak, one shy of the American League record of 17 straight wins set by Cleveland's Johnny Allen in 1936-37 and the Orioles' Dave McNally in 1968-69.

1998— In the first meeting ever between the two teams, the Orioles score five runs in the seventh and two in the eighth to beat the expansion Tampa Bay Devil Rays at Tropicana Park in St. Petersburg. Eric Davis' solo homer off Baltimore area native Tony Saunders ties the game, and Harold Baines' pinch-hit two-run single puts the Orioles up for good.

May 9

1961— In Minnesota, Jim Gentile becomes the first player in big league history to hit grand-slam home runs in successive turns at bat in the same game. Diamond Jim hit his first off Pedro Ramos in the first inning and followed in the second with another off Paul Giel. Later in the game, he drove in his ninth run of the game, a club record, on a sacrifice fly. The Birds clobber the Twins, 13-5.

1962— Brooks Robinson hits his only two grand slams of the season in consecutive games, on May 6 in Los Angeles off Ken McBride, and May 9 at home against Ed Rakow of Kansas City.

1965— Four pitchers combine to set a club record by fanning 15 Tigers in a 5-4, 12-inning win. Jim Palmer, making his first big league start, strikes out six in seven innings.

1970— The Orioles nip Chicago, 4-3, for their fifth straight win as Brooks Robinson hits his 200th career home run off Tommy John, a two-run shot at Comiskey Park.

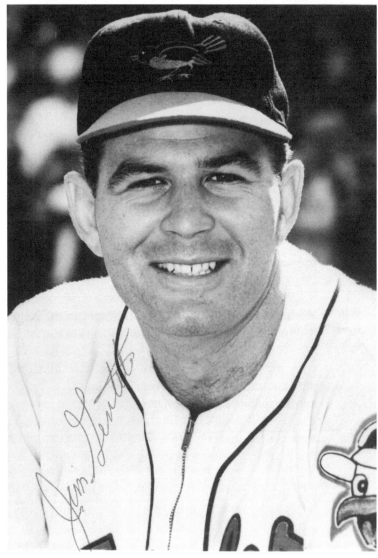

Jim Gentile

1971— A bat-day crowd of 43,300 watches Vida Blue out-duel Jim Palmer, 2-1. Blue fans nine in winning his eighth straight. Palmer, losing his first against five wins, retires 18 straight A's at one point, striking out 11 in seven innings of work.

1973— Look-alike rookies, Al Bumbry and Rich Coggins, hit their first major league homers back-to-back off Oakland's Jim "Catfish" Hunter.

1987— Eddie Murray becomes the first player in baseball history to hit a home run from both sides of the plate in consecutive games when he does it at Chicago, May 8-9. Eddie connects off Jose DeLeon and Ray Searage the first day and Joel McKeon and Bob James the second.

1987— Larry Sheets, who led the Orioles in homers with 31, clears the right-field roof at Chicago's Comiskey Park, connecting off Bob James. It is the 42nd roof shot in Comiskey history and second by an Oriole. Boog Powell did it on July 18, 1966 off Juan Pizarro.

1993— Damon Buford, recalled six days earlier when Mike Devereaux went on the disabled list, homers off Juan Guzman in the third, and then in the ninth singles with two out off Duane Ward to drive in the go-ahead run as the Orioles rally from a 3-2 deficit to beat the Blue Jays at the Skydome, 4-3.

1994— Sid Fernandez, signed by the Orioles as a free agent, wins his 100th game in the majors, 4-1, over Toronto at Camden Yards.

1998— The one-two punch of Mike Mussina and Cal Ripken Jr. leads the Orioles over Tampa Bay, 7-0. Mussina struck out 10 and didn't allow a walk in twirling a five-hit shutout. He capped his masterpiece by striking out the side on 10 pitches in the ninth. Ripken's three-run homer off knuckleballer Dennis Springer was his first home run since April 9 and his first extra-base hit since April 22.

May 10

1960— Oriole catcher Joe Ginsberg ties the modern American League record with three passed balls in the second inning and four in the game while trying to handle Hoyt Wilhelm's knuckler. Kansas City wins, 10-0.

1969— Pitcher Jim Hardin hits a one-out homer in the bottom of the ninth to key the Orioles over Kansas City, 6-5. It is Hardin's first relief appearance after 54 straight starts.

1972— Dave McNally wins his fourth of the year (all shutouts), 1-0, over Texas. Texas owner Bob Short, who had moved the team from Washington to Texas that winter, is doused with a cup of beer by an irate female fan of the Senators.

1978— A two-run homer by Eddie Murray in the bottom of the ninth lifts the O's to a 3-2 victory, ending the Red Sox winning streak at seven games.

1998— B.J. Surhoff clubs his 100th career home run in a 4-3 loss at Tampa. B.J. has now hit 56 homers in two-plus years with the Orioles after hitting 57 homers in nine years in Milwaukee.

May 10-11

1985— Fred Lynn sends the fans home happy two nights in a row with game-winning "sudden death" homers in the bottom of the ninth off Minnesota's Ron Davis and Curt Wardle. The scores were 6-5 and 4-2. His three-run homer off Wardle in the 11th was before a crowd of 49,094. Lynn homered in the ninth inning the following afternoon off Frank Viola, but the Birds lost, 7-3.

Jim Palmer

May 11

1973— Last-minute sub Ellie Hendricks hits a two-run homer to help the O's and Jim Palmer shut out New York, 3-0. Starting catcher Earl Williams, who had numerous clashes with Earl Weaver in his two seasons in Baltimore, was late arriving due to a traffic jam.

1974— The Orioles set an all-time club record for hits with 22 while trouncing Cleveland, 12-1. Mark Belanger ties a club record with five straight hits.

1983— Mike Flanagan hurls his 15th career shutout and outduels the ancient Mariner, Gaylord Perry, who went the route in a losing cause. The Birds beat Seattle, 1-0, the only run scoring on a fifth inning double by Cal Ripken. Flanagan is now, 6-0.

1989— Dave Stewart, who came to Baltimore last May at 8-0 and lost, is 6-0 this time and loses again. The Orioles send Stewart to his fifth straight loss in Baltimore, 6-2, behind Mickey Tettleton's homer and three RBI. Only 1,201 show up, the third smallest home crowd ever, because it's a hastily scheduled make-up game on a Thursday afternoon following a Wednesday night rainout, the fifth rainout already in the season.

1998— Scott Erickson breaks a string of five straight winless starts by blanking his former team, the Twins, 4-0, at the Metrodome. It's the Orioles' third shutout in the last seven games. Erickson coaxes 15 groundball outs in winning for the first time since April 12. Rafael Palmeiro and Roberto Alomar homer.

May 12

1956— Left-hander Don Ferrarese pitches a brilliant two-hit shutout over the Yankees, 1-0, for his first major league win. He loses the no hitter in the ninth when Andy Carey and Hank Bauer single to open the inning.

1964— The Orioles set a club record by stealing five bases at Washington. Luis Aparicio stole three, Willie Kirkland, two.

1967— Jim Palmer faces the minimum 27 batters as the Orioles thump the Yankees, 14-0. Palmer retires the first 18 Yankees in succession before Horace Clarke's leadoff single in the seventh. Clarke was erased on a double play and Palmer settled for a one-hitter.

1971— Jerry May's third-inning single is all Kansas City can muster as Mike Cuellar shuts out the Royals, 6-0.

1976— Reggie Jackson hits his first home run as an Oriole at County Stadium in Milwaukee, a grand slam off Jerry Augustine that helped produce an 8-6 win. It is the first of three grand slams that Reggie hit during the season, all off left-handers. He hit only one in his eight-year career with the A's.

1984— Jim Palmer appears in his 558th and last game against the A's in relief. Oakland wins, 12-2, in Baltimore. Palmer does not figure in the decision.

1987— Larry Sheets' pinch-hit "sudden-death" three-run homer off Jeff Reardon beats the Twins, 10-7, at Memorial Stadium.

1993— Boston's Roger Clemens sets a Camden Yards strikeout record by fanning 13 Orioles in a 4-0 win.

1995— The Orioles reach the 10 million mark in attendance at Oriole Park at Camden Yards in a 3-2 loss to Cleveland. It comes in the 221st date at Oriole Park, making it the second quickest ballpark to reach the 10 million mark in attendance. Toronto's Skydome did it in 206 dates.

May 13

1965— Milt Pappas, in his final year with the Orioles, wins his 100th game, 3-2, over Luis Tiant and the Indians as Boog Powell homers.

1975— The Birds snap Jim Kaat's 12-game win streak with a 3-2 win over the White Sox as Ross Grimsley wins his first game of the year.

1988— Oakland pitcher Dave Stewart, whose 8-0 start is one win shy of Paul Lindblad's club record set in 1975, loses to Jay Tibbs and the Orioles, 4-1, in Baltimore. Eddie Murray's and Fred Lynn's back-to-back homers end Stewart's homerless skein at 57.1 innings.

1993— The Orioles are shutout in back-to-back games for the first time since May 21-22, 1983, as Danny Darwin, Greg Harris and Jeff Russell combine on a two-hitter, blanking the Orioles, 2-0.

Boog Powell

1995— Mike Mussina beats Mark Clark and the Indians, 6-1, at Oriole Park with a complete-game three-hitter. It's the first complete game of the year in the American League.

May 14

1967— Mark Belanger hits his first big league home run off New York's Mel Stottlemyre at Yankee Stadium. Belanger hit only 20 home runs in 5,784 at-bats in the major leagues.

1968— In one of the biggest turnarounds in their history, the Orioles drop their seventh straight, 4-0, to the Tigers, after winning eight straight. It is the O's longest losing streak in 10 years.

1983— The Orioles outlast the Rangers in Arlington, 14-11, in 11 innings. The two clubs combine for 41 hits (most ever in an Orioles game), and the Rangers had 22 of them. Lenn Sakata drove in two runs in the four-run 14th, as did Rick Dempsey.

1987— The Orioles hand Kansas City's Bret Saberhagen his first loss of the year after a 6-0 start. Cal Ripken hits a two-run homer in the first, but it's Terry Kennedy's solo home run leading off the eighth that breaks a 3-3 tie and gives the O's a 4-3 win.

1998— Oriole ace Mike Mussina is struck in the face by a line drive off the bat of Cleveland's Sandy Alomar. The sixth-inning smash breaks Mussina's nose and leaves him with a gash above his right eye that requires several stitches. Mussina never loses consciousness, but there is a great deal of swelling that requires Mussina to go on the disabled list for the second time. The game, which becomes secondary to the blow to Mussina's head and numbs both benches and the fans who witness it, is won by Cleveland, 5-4, at Camden Yards.

May 15

1962— Boog Powell hits his first two Memorial Stadium homers in the same game to power the O's to a 7-1 win over the Angels. Boog's second blast travels 425 feet to right center.

1968— The Orioles get three-run homers from Boog Powell and Curt Motton, and solo shots from Dave Johnson and Ellie Hendricks to beat Denny McLain and the Tigers, 10-8. McLain's win streak is snapped at five and the O's losing streak ends at seven.

1969— Dave McNally pitches 8⅓ hitless innings before Cesar Tovar spoils the no-hit bid with a ninth-inning single. Mac settles for a one- hit, 5-0 win over the Twins.

1971— The Orioles set a club record by leaving 18 on base, but still score enough runs to beat Boston, 7-4.

1983— Texas edges the Orioles, 2-1. But umpire Ken Kaiser was the dominant figure. First he ejected Eddie Murray for "mimicking" him. Then Kaiser called Pete O'Brien safe at the plate in a controversial call that set off a wild argument. It resulted in Joe Altobelli's first ejection as Orioles manager.

1991— The Orioles host Queen Elizabeth II and Prince Philip, along with President and Mrs. Bush, but lose to Oakland, 6-3, despite Randy Milligan's two homers off Bob Welch. The Queen and the other dignitaries meet the players from both teams in the Oriole dugout before the game.

1992— The Orioles move into first place by blanking the White Sox, 2-0, as Mike Mussina comes within an out of a complete-game shutout. Gregg Olson comes in to save the game.

May 16

1954— The largest crowd to attend a day doubleheader, and the largest crowd in the first 10 years of the franchise, 46,796, sees the Birds lose the opener, 2-0, to the Yankees, and then bounce back to take the second game, 6-2, behind Don Larsen.

1965— Jim Palmer picks up his first big league win in relief of Dave McNally as the Orioles beat the Yankees, 7-5, in Baltimore. The O's trailed, 4-2, when Palmer came in and he hits his first major league homer in the fourth to tie it.

1975— Bobby Grich's homer provides the only run of the game as Jim Palmer beats the Angels, 1-0. Grich had homered to provide Palmer with a 1-0 win against Milwaukee on April 22.

Bobby Grich

1987— Scott McGregor notches his 138th and last major league win, 4-2, over Mike Witt and the Angels, his 20th career victory over California.

1992— The Orioles hand Jack McDowell his first loss of the season against seven wins with a 7-2 win at Comiskey Park. Frank Thomas hits a 466' homer to left that is the longest in the new Comiskey's 13-month history.

1993— Mike Mussina ties a club record by striking out 14 Tigers at Detroit in a 3-2 Oriole win. Mussina ups his record to 5-1. The last 14-strikeout effort was more than 35 years ago when Connie Johnson did it in September 1957 against the Yankees. Bob Turley in 1954 and Mike Boddicker in the 1983 ALCS also share the record.

May 17

1967— Baltimore sets a club record as seven Orioles homer at Boston in a 12-8 win. Four of the homers are in one inning (Etchebarren, Bowens, Powell and Dave Johnson). Paul Blair, Brooks and Frank Robinson also homer as the O's score nine runs in the seventh inning.

1975— A regular-season record crowd of 48,042 watches the Orioles lose to California, 6-3. In the fifth inning, third base umpire Ron Luciano calls Tommy Harper's drive down the left-field line a three-run homer. After Earl Weaver and the Orioles complained, the umpires huddled and the call was changed to a foul ball. Dick Williams of the Angels then was ejected for arguing when the call was reversed. Luciano admitted afterwards he never saw the ball but felt he had to make a call. "I had a 50-50 chance of being right," he said.

1983— The O's sweep the White Sox, 7-2 and 5-0, but pay a stiff price. Mike Flanagan tears a ligament in his left knee while fielding a Tony Bernazard ground ball. The hottest pitcher in baseball missed the next 11½ weeks. Mike Boddicker, making his first start, pitches a five-hitter in the nightcap to record his first big league shutout.

1984— Jim Palmer, whose 268 wins, eight 20-win seasons and three Cy Young awards make him unquestionably the greatest pitcher in Oriole history, is granted an unconditional release after starting 0-3 with a 9.17 ERA in 17.2 innings.

1994— A duel between respective aces Mike Mussina and Boston's Roger Clemens lives up to its hype as Cal Ripken breaks a 2-2 tie in the eighth with a sacrifice fly, and Lee Smith preserves the 3-2 win with his 16th save in 17 opportunities. Mike is now 7-1, while Clemens drops to 4-2.

1996— Chris Hoiles hits a dramatic two-out ninth inning grand slam to stun the Mariners, 14-13. It is only the 12th, two-out sudden-death grand slam to win a game by one run in major league history. Rafael Palmeiro enjoys the fifth five-hit game of his career and first since July 1992 while with Texas.

1997— Jimmy Key and the Orioles edge Seattle, 4-3, at the Kingdome. It's Key's eighth straight win to start the season, making him the fourth pitcher in Oriole history to get off to an 8-0 start. Key joins Dave McNally (15-0) in 1969, Hoyt Wilhelm (9-0) in 1959, and Arthur Rhodes (9-0) in 1996.

May 18

1957— The White Sox were leading, 4-3, in the ninth inning at Baltimore just seconds before a 10:20 p.m. curfew, prearranged to enable Chicago to catch a train, would have ended the game. Paul LaPalme was pitching for Chicago and Dick Williams was the Oriole hitter. With none on, all LaPalme had to do was hold on to the ball or throw it against the backstop to assure a win. Instead, he threw a strike and Williams hit a homer to tie at 4-4. The game had to be played in its entirety at a later date and the Orioles won the rematch.

1979— Don Stanhouse squeezes out a 7-6 win in Toronto on Lee May's 11th-inning hit. The Birds move back into first place, a position the O's would occupy for all but one day (June 5) the rest of the way.

1983— Richard Dotson takes a no-hitter into the bottom of the eighth at Memorial Stadium, but the White Sox right-hander loses his bid for no-hit fame and the game when Dan Ford hits a solo home run with one out in the eighth inning. It is the only run in the game and the only hit for the Orioles. Storm Davis and Tippy Martinez combine on a four hitter.

1993— Fernando Valenzuela hurls the eighth two-hitter of his career, an eight-inning rain-shortened 7-0 win over the Indians at Camden Yards. It's Fernando's first win in the majors since September 14, 1990, when he pitched the Dodgers over the Reds. It had been 975 days in between wins. It is his first complete-game shutout since his no-hitter against St. Louis on June 29, 1990.

May 19

1956— The Orioles even their record at 15-15, but never see the .500 mark again the rest of the year.

1959— Billy O'Dell wins his own ball game when he hits a 120 foot home run off Billy Pierce. Chicago was winning, 1-0, when O'Dell looped a ball over first base that hit the right-field foul line, which was made of wood. The ball bounced over the head of onrushing right fielder Al Smith, and by the time the ball was retrieved, O'Dell had made it home on the heels of the base runner for a 2-1 win.

Fernando Valenzuela

1963— Robin Roberts becomes the 15th pitcher in major league history to strike out 2,000 batters in a win over Chicago.

1968— Curt Blefary foils Sonny Siebert's bid for a no-hitter with a seventh-inning double. Siebert and the Indians win, 2-0, on a one-hitter for the veteran Cleveland right-hander.

1972— The Orioles lose for the first time since June of 1970 at County Stadium in Milwaukee. The Birds had won 10 straight in Milwaukee.

1974— The Orioles set a club record with six errors in one game in a loss to Boston. Frank Baker had two errors, and Boog Powell, Bobby Grich, Brooks Robinson, and Dave McNally had one each.

1976— All-time home run king Henry Aaron hits the only home run of his career at Memorial Stadium, but the Orioles prevail over the Brewers, 5-3.

1980— Gary Roenicke hits into a double play and steals home in the same inning as the Orioles down Cleveland, 4-1.

1983— The Orioles nip Toronto, 2-1, at Exhibition Stadium as Dan Ford hits another eighth-inning home run, this one with a runner aboard, and picks up his third straight game-winning RBI.

1987— The Orioles rout Seattle at the Kingdome, 15-4, behind a season-high 19 hits, including nine for extra bases, which was one shy of the club record. The beneficiary is lefthander Jeff Ballard who picks up his first big league win.

1993— Rookie Sherman Obando's first major league homer off Mark Clark helps the Orioles to a 6-3 win over Cleveland. Combined with the 7-0 win over the Tribe the day before, Obando went 6-for-7 with five RBI and the home run.

1998— Relief pitcher Armando Benitez, frustrated over surrendering a three-run homer to Bernie Williams in the eighth, drills Tino Martinez, the next batter, in the shoulder blade, sparking a wild bench-clearing brawl that spills dangerously into the visitors dugout at Yankee Stadium. The brawl lasts 10 minutes and is highlighted by Yankee relief pitcher Graeme Lloyd's flailing at Benitez, Darryl Strawberry's sucker punch at Benitez, and Alan Mills, retaliatory haymaker to the jaw of Strawberry. Various suspensions are handed out, the longest (eight games) to Benitez. The Yankees win the game, 9-5, as the Orioles sink to their deepest depths of the still-young season.

May 20

1963— Popular favorite Gus Triandos, traded to Detroit in the off season, returns for the first time in a Tiger uniform, striking out in a pinchhitting role. Gus said he was the first player to have a press conference for striking out.

1981— The Orioles win their eighth straight, 5-3, over the Angels behind the pitching of Dennis Martinez. It is the longest win streak of the season and it puts the Birds in the eastern lead by 1½ games.

1983— The Orioles lose 7-5 in Toronto, and lose the next two games, 6-0 and 5-0, to plunge into the depths of a seven-game losing streak.

1988— The Orioles drop a 3-2 decision to Seattle and fall to 6-34, the worst 40-game record in major league history. The Orioles lead, 2-0, after six innings, but Seattle ties it in the seventh on a Ken Phelps homer and win it on an eighth-inning unearned run.

1989— Jeff Ballard ups his record to 7-1 with a 5-1 win over Cleveland. Ballard gets help from Gregg Olson, who has fanned 19 in his last 14.1 innings. Craig Worthington is now 5-for-5 with the bases loaded.

May 21

1956— The Orioles acquire George Kell, Mike Fornieles, Bob Nieman, and Connie Johnson from the White Sox in a trade for Dave Philley and Jim Wilson.

1962— Robin Roberts, released by the Yankees two weeks before, is signed by the Orioles. Robin, who was 1-10 the year before, won 10 games in '62 with a sparkling 2.78 ERA.

Tommy Davis

1985— Mike Boddicker's win streak is snapped at five as he walks in the game winner with the bases loaded and two outs in the 10th inning at Oakland, the first of five straight losses for the Oriole ace.

May 22

1973— Tommy Davis' 18-game hit streak begins. The streak is snapped on June 16 by the Texas Rangers. Davis, the Orioles' first regular designated hitter, also had hitting streaks of 11 and 13 games in 1973.

1976— After Doug DeCinces belted a grand-slam homer to beat the Tigers the day before, Ken Singleton hits one out with the bases loaded in the ninth inning to give the O's an 8-4 victory at Memorial Stadium.

1980— Retiring the last 17 batters, Scott McGregor pitches a two-hitter. The Orioles defeat the Tigers, 5-1, in Baltimore.

1992— It was a rough ride for the Angels, losing, 5-3, at Camden Yards, but not as rough as the bus ride they experienced on their trip from New York on the New Jersey Turnpike. The lead bus in the two-bus caravan went off the road and turned over, inflicting serious injuries to manager Bob Rogers and lesser ones to Alvin Davis and Bobby Rose. Fast reaction by players in the second bus prevented more injuries, and a tree the bus hit prevented the vehicle from rolling down a hill. This was the last game the Orioles didn't sell out all season. They hung the SRO sign in each of their last 59 home games. Another footnote: Randy Milligan becomes the first player to hit a ball off the rightfield scoreboard at Oriole Park. He was the 1,530th player to come to the plate.

1993— In the longest game by time at Oriole Park, (5:34), the Orioles edge the Brewers, 5-4, in 14 innings. Harold Reynolds drives in the game winner with a sac fly. It's the second longest game by time in Orioles history, exceeded only by the 5:46 game played against the Yankees at Memorial Stadium in 1988.

1994— After losing back-to-back games to the Yankees, the Orioles salvage an exhausting 10-inning tussle, 6-5, as Rafael Palmeiro establishes a personal- and club-record 24-game-hitting streak, the longest in the majors in 1994.

May 23

1954— Bob Feller beats the Orioles, 4-3, for his 250th major league win.

1963— Robin Roberts pitches his 36th lifetime shutout, his first in the American League, a two-hitter against the Washington Senators.

1970— The Orioles score seven runs in the fourth inning, a season high, en route to a 12-3 win over Boston before 40,267 fans.

1978— Mike Flanagan tosses a two-hit shutout over Detroit, handing the Tigers their first whitewash of the season, 2-0.

1979— Pat Kelly's three-run, sudden-death homer in the 10th beats Boston's Bob Stanley.

1983— The Twins, making their 51st trip to Baltimore since the franchise moved from Washington in 1961, win, 12-4, to key their first sweep ever in Memorial Stadium. Minnesota wins the next two nights, 6-1 and 7-4.

1989— The Orioles bash four homers, by Mickey Tettleton, Mike Devereaux, Billy Ripken and Larry Sheets, and move into a first-place tie with Boston with a 9-3 win over the White Sox in Chicago. It's the latest the Birds have been on top since 1983. The Orioles are 20-21 and yet tied for first, as all seven A.L. East clubs are below .500.

Robin Roberts

1990— Jeffrey Hammonds cracks a grand-slam home run and scores three times in support of Doug Drabek's four-hit pitching as the Orioles drub Oakland, 9-1, snapping a nine-game losing streak, their longest since the 0-21 start in 1988.

1991— Coach Johnny Oates replaces Frank Robinson as Orioles skipper, guiding the club to 54 wins and 71 losses. Oates signed a two-year contract to return as manager the day after the season ended.

May 24

1962— The Orioles accuse Detroit pitcher Jim Bunning of cutting baseballs after several balls used in the game were discovered with inch-long gashes. The umpires refused to check Bunning's belt buckle, which was where Oriole manager Billy Hitchcock thought the balls were being doctored. There were at least 16 people involved in the melee on the mound with Hitchcock, Bunning, Detroit manager Bob Scheffing, and umpire Charlie Berry. After the game, at least 11 balls were returned to Hitchcock from fans who had caught them in the stands and all were cut in the same manner.

Reports were submitted to the league office but, as Berry said, "We have to catch them in the act, before we can accuse them of something." The Tigers win the game, 5-4, in 11 innings.

1964— Harmon Killebrew hits the longest home run ever measured at Memorial Stadium, 471 feet, on the fly off Milt Pappas over the hedge in left center field. It beat Boog Powell's 1962 blast by two feet. Killebrew hit 67 homers against the Orioles, more than any other player.

1970— Brooks Robinson, beaned by Boston's Mike Nagy In the fourth, leads off the 10th with a solo home run to give the Orioles a 2-1 win.

1991— Johnny Oates' first game as Oriole manager is a forgettable 7-1 loss to the Yankees. The Orioles commit three errors.

1994— Cal Ripken hits his 300th career home run in a 13-5 win over the Brewers in Milwaukee.

1997— Eric Davis leaves the game in Cleveland with severe stomach cramps, the first outward indication of a potentially serious problem with his health. Three days later he leaves the team in New York to be examined in Baltimore.

May 25

1962— All 10 players in the Oriole lineup hit safely as the O's beat Boston, 9-5, at Fenway with a 16-hit attack. Jim Gentile hits his sixth homer in the last seven games, driving in four. Gentile had 12 RBI in that same seven-game span.

1963— All-time Oriole relief pitcher Stu Miller collects his first American League win in relief of Milt Pappas.

1969— A record 28,960 tickets are sold at the gate as a Bat Day crowd of 39,860 turns out to see the O's beat the A's, 5-3.

1974— With a national television audience watching, Mike Cuellar makes it look easy, pitching a two-hitter and beating New York, 5-1, for his fifth straight complete-game victory.

1981— Mark Belanger hits his first home run in four years, off Ron Guidry at Memorial Stadium, as the Orioles top the Yankees, 10-1.

1993— In his first game back off the disabled list after a partial shoulder separation diving for a double on May 2, Mike Devereaux delivers a game-winning RBI single in the 10th to lift the Birds to a 4-3 win over the Yankees in New York.

Stu Miller

May 26

1958— Kansas City A's pitcher Murray Dickson, 41 years old, homers in the 10th to give himself a 5-4 win over the Orioles in Kansas City.

1963— Reliever Wes Stock becomes the only Oriole pitcher ever to win both ends of a doubleheader as the Orioles sweep Cleveland.

1979— In a 5:17 struggle at Detroit, the Orioles win their 26th in 32 games, beating the Tigers, 7-5, in 16 innings. Both teams use five pitchers, the Oriole hurlers striking out 16, the Tiger pitchers fanning 14. Lee May's two-run single in the 16th wins it.

1989— The Orioles begin a 98-day stay in first place with a 5-2 win in Cleveland as Jeff Ballard ups his record to 8-1 as he reaches the eight-victory level in fewer starts than any previous Oriole pitcher.

May 27

1955— Center fielder Chuck Diering makes a spectacular catch of a long Mickey Mantle drive in the hedge some 440 feet from home plate and only 10 feet shy of the old scoreboard at Memorial Stadium. Before the fences were moved in, center field was a distant 450 feet away.

1960— The Orioles unveil "the big mitt," an oversized catcher's glove designed by manager Paul Richards to help the Bird catchers handle the dancing knuckleballs of Hoyt Wilhelm. Later outlawed by the rules committee, the glove worked. Clint Courtney doesn't allow one pitch to get by and the Orioles edge the Yankees, 3-2, as Wilhelm goes the route.

1962— Jim Gentile hits his eighth homer in the past nine games and Wes Stock wins his seventh straight in a streak going back to 1960 as the Birds beat Boston. At this point, the Orioles have hit 48 homers in 40 games. Brooks Robinson hits his seventh, the same number he hit in all of 1961.

1972— A crowd of 39,714 on "Ball Night" sees Terry Crowley's eighth-inning homer give the O's a 4-2 win over Cleveland. Earl Weaver is ejected for piling dirt on second base following an argument with umpire John Flaherty.

1981— Terry Crowley beats the Yankees with a sudden-death, 10th-inning single off Goose Gossage.

1983— The Orioles snap their seven-game losing streak by beating Kansas City, 7-4, at Royals Stadium. Eddie Murray, who had gone a career-high 31 straight games without a home run, hits a two-run shot off loser Larry Gura.

1989— Mickey Tettleton's two-run eighth inning homer, his sixth in his last 12 games, breaks open a close game and propells the Orioles to a 5-1 win in Cleveland. The Orioles are 5-0 on the road swing, outscoring their opponents, 32-7. Dave Schmidt and Mark Huismann combine on a four-hitter.

1990— Jeff Ballard, the ace of the pitching staff the year before, wins his only start of the season at Texas, beating Bobby Witt, 9-2. Ballard finishes the season 2-11, 1-10 as a starter with a 5.09 ERA. In his defense, the O's scored three runs or less in 10 of his 17 starts, and he was shut out twice.

May 28

1954— Chicago beats the Orioles, 11-6, as Baltimore sets an American League record by using eight pinch hitters. Collectively they went 1-for-7, plus a walk. The Orioles left 16 on base. Cass Michaels of the White Sox hit the first grand slam in Memorial Stadium.

Earl Weaver

1969— Earl Weaver catches Seattle manager Joe Schultz with his lineup cards mixed up in a game at Sicks Stadium. Schultz made out a second lineup after Weaver decided to pitch Dave McNally instead of Jim Palmer. However, at the home-plate meeting, Schultz handed Weaver the first card. Mike Cuellar noticed the error because he couldn't spell Gerry McNertney's name as the lineup was given on the PA system. Cuellar, charting pitches for McNally, asked Weaver for the Seattle card and noticed the difference. The Orioles led, 9-2, in the fifth when Weaver sprang his surprise. Tommy Davis had just doubled home two runs for the Pilots when Weaver notified the umpires that Davis had batted out of turn. The umps agreed, ruled Davis out, and nullified the runs. The Orioles won, 9-5.

1978— At Memorial Stadium, Jim Palmer becomes the Orioles' first 200-game winner, pitching the Birds to a 3-0 win over Cleveland in the second game of a doubleheader. Gaylord Perry is the loser.

1983— Scott McGregor pitches a two-hit shutout and wins, 1-0, on the strength of Eddie Murray's seventh-inning homer. The Royals lost Dennis Leonard for the season when his knee gives out in the third inning.

1987— In a 12-inning, 8-7 win over California, the Orioles hit a Memorial Stadium club-record six home runs and the two teams combine for eight homers, another mark. Mike Young hits two for the Orioles, one in the 10th and another in the 12th, a two-run game winner, tying the major league record for most extra-inning home runs in one game. Young becomes the fifth player in major league history to hit two extra-inning homers in the same game. Larry Sheets also hits two and Cal Ripken and Rick Burleson hit one apiece.

1991— After four straight losses, Johnny Oates gains his first win as Oriole manager. Randy Milligan's three-run homer off Charles Nagy is the key blow in the 5-2 win.

1996— Bill and Cal Ripken Jr. homer in the ninth inning at Seattle, marking the sixth time in major league history that brothers have homered in the same inning. The Ripkens were also the last duo to do it, September 15, 1990, at Toronto. Other brothers to do it were Paul and Lloyd Waner, Hank and Tommie Aaron and Wes and Rick Farrell. The Orioles beat the Mariners, 12-8, as Cal enjoys his first three-homer game, driving in eight runs in the 12-8 Oriole win.

May 29

1967— The Orioles acquire Pete Richert from the Nats for Mike Esptein and Frank Bertaina.

1970— Mike Cuellar ties a major league record by striking out four batters in one inning against California.

1971— The Birds blow a big, 7-0, lead, but come back to get a win for Baltimore native Dave Boswell in his first Oriole appearance, 11-8, over the Twins.

1974— The Orioles bomb Kansas City, 10-3, as Mike Cuellar notches his sixth straight complete game. That gives Mike 100 complete games in 200 starts for the Orioles in five-plus seasons.

1979— After losing the night before on George Brett's 16th-inning homer (he had two homers, a triple, double, and single), the O's beat the Royals, 8-1, at KC. It had been nearly two years since their last victory at Royals Stadium, having lost 10 in a row on the Royals' carpet.

1981— The Orioles cap their winningest May ever (21-8) by edging the Tigers, 6-5. Dennis Martinez, who tied for the league lead in wins (14), is the winner. The Orioles lead the eastern division by three games over the Brewers.

1989— The Orioles beat Nolan Ryan and the Texas Rangers, 6-1, at Memorial Stadium, hitting three home runs off the Ryan Express, the most the fireballing righthander has allowed in one game since 1982. Mickey Tettleton, Cal Ripken and Larry Sheets connect off Ryan, who strikes out 10 but sees his lifetime record against Baltimore drop to 5-14. He hasn't beaten the Birds in 13 years.

1996— Cal Ripken hits his 334th career homer in Seattle, moving past Eddie Murray for first place on the Orioles' all-time list.

May 30

1954— It was a struggle in '54. The Orioles break a 10-game losing streak with a 5-2 win over the White Sox, which snaps Chicago's eight game winning streak.

1955— Brooks Robinson, two weeks past his 18th birthday, signs his first professional contract with the Orioles in his hometown of Little Rock, Arkansas. Assistant General Manager Art Ehlers offers $4,000 and a major league contract.

1962— Minnesota's Pedro Ramos shuts out the Orioles, 7-0, in Baltimore and hits two home runs, one a grand slam.

1966— Dave Johnson's string of seven straight hits is snapped in the ninth when he flies out. The Orioles beat the Twins, 5-1, as Johnson goes 4-for-5.

1982— The streak begins. Cal Ripken's amazing consecutive games streak begins when Earl Weaver starts Cal at third base in a 6-0 loss to Toronto at Memorial Stadium.

1991— In a poignant and memorable moment, the Orioles beat Boston, 9-3, in Dwight Evans' return to Fenway Park. Evans, who patrolled rightfield for 19 seasons in a Red Sox uniform, receives three standing ovations in the game while another ex-Red Sox, Sam Horn, hits a three-run homer off Jeff Gray in the eighth inning to cinch the victory.

1992— Gregg Olson's two-inning effort sets the club record for career saves at 106 as "the Otter" passes Tippy Martinez by striking out Jose Canseco with the potential tying run on base. The Orioles beat Oakland, 7-6, on the 10th anniversary of the start of Cal Ripken Jr.'s consecutive games streak.

1997— Mike Mussina comes within two outs of a perfect game, retiring 25 straight Cleveland batters at Camden Yards before Sandy Alomar lines a 1-1 pitch to left for a clean hit, ending "Moose's" bid for perfection and a no-hitter. Mussina retires the next two batters, settling for his second career one-hitter in a 3-0 win. It's the 10th time an Oriole pitcher has lost a no-hit bid in the ninth and the first since Eric Bell in 1987.

May 31

1966— Sparked by a season-high 19 hits, the O's score six runs off Camilo Pascual in the first inning, the big blow a Dave Johnson three-run triple. Of the 12 players in the line up, 11 got at least one hit, and Boog lumbers in from second on a wild pitch. The Birds cream the Twins, 14-5.

1970— Paul Blair suffers a multi-fractured nose, damage to his left eye, and other facial injuries when struck by a Ken Tatum pitch in California. Blair underwent surgery in Orange, California, and remained hospitalized eight days.

1971— After hitting two home runs in Chicago, Don Buford is struck in the back by a Bart Johnson pitch. Buford charges the mound, but no blows are struck. After being pelted with garbage, paper, and part of seats in left field, Buford is attacked by a fan while waiting in the on-deck circle in the ninth. The entire Oriole ball club came to Buford's aid. The Birds score five in the ninth to win, and begin a nine-game winning streak.

Mike Mussina

1975— Mike Cuellar stops the Angels on one hit, a fourth-inning single by Bruce Bochte, in winning, 1-0, at Anaheim. Brooks Robinson provides the game's only run with an eighth-inning homer off Bill Singer.

1980— Ken Landreaux's 31 game hitting streak is stopped by Scott McGregor as the Birds clobber Minnesota, 11-1. Landreaux's streak is the longest in the American League since Dom DiMaggio hit in 34 straight games in 1949.

1989— Mickey Tettleton cracks a three-run homer off Texas' Cecilio Guante, giving the O's switch-hitting backstop 13 roundtrippers, the most by any American League catcher entering the month of June in history. The Orioles withstand a five-run Ranger rally in the sixth as Tettleton connects for the eighth time in his last 16 games in the bottom of the sixth. Mark Williamson wins in relief, giving him wins on two consecutive nights. He's now retired 43 of the last 49 batters he's faced.

Mickey Tettleton

JUNE

June 1

1975— Nolan Ryan pitches the second no-hitter of his career, beating the Orioles, 1-0, in Anaheim. It is Ryan's 100th career victory.

1978— Firing his third straight shutout, and the 49th of his career, Jim Palmer pitches the Orioles to a 1-0 triumph over the Yankees in New York.

1998— The Orioles, trailing, 4-0, before the game's first out and trailing, 8-4 and 9-6, at other junctures, come back to out-slug the Seattle Mariners, 10-9, at Camden Yards. The two clubs combine for eight home runs. In the eighth inning Brady Anderson hits a two-run homer and Eric Davis also homers to set in motion the Orioles most inspirational comeback of the season. Rafael Palmeiro ends the homer barrage with a deep drive to right center off loser Tony Fossas to cap the four-run eighth.

June 2

1959— In pursuit of his eighth straight win, Hoyt Wilhelm is attacked by a swarm of gnats while on the mound at Comiskey Park, Chicago. The pesky insects refuse to leave under the counterattacks of the groundskeepers and the umpires' "flit" guns. The gnats are finally driven away by a fireworks barrage, brought in from center field where they had been set up for a postgame display. Hoyt won the game, 3-2.

1960— The Birds complete a three-game sweep of the Yankees to take a three-game lead in the standings. Jerry Walker beats Whitey Ford, 3-2; Hal Brown pitches a one-hitter in game two; and Gene Woodling provides the margin of victory with an eighth-inning homer and a 6-5 victory.

Steve Stone

1974— Wayne Garland relieves Mike Cuellar in the fifth and pitches two-hit shutout baseball for the last six innings to notch his first big league victory.

1980— Lenn Sakata homers in his first big league pinch hit appearance to beat his old team, the Brewers, in the 11th inning in sudden-death fashion, 9-8.

1982— Steve Stone, bothered by tendinitis in his right elbow ever since his Cy Young season of 1980, tearfully announces his retirement. Stone, who won 25 games in 1980, fell to 4-and-7 in 1981, spending three months on the disabled list with elbow and shoulder miseries. The 34-year-old right-hander, signed as a free agent after the 1978 season, won 40 games and lost only 21 as an Oriole.

1989— The Orioles beat the Tigers, 4-1, at Tiger Stadium for the 3,000th win in the franchise's history. Only four other major league franchises won 3,000 in fewer games: New York Yankees, Chicago Cubs, Pittsburgh Pirates and New York Giants. Bob Milacki's two-hitter gives the O's their 15th win in their last 20 games and a 3½-game lead in the A.L. East.

1994— The Orioles emerge from a five-losses-in-six-games slump by hammering Detroit, 11-5. The win goes to rookie Scott Klingenbeck, who joined the club the night before to fill in for the injured Ben McDonald. McDonald had made 80 consecutive starts before aggravating a pulled groin on May 28. The 23-year-old Klingenbeck, who had been drafted but failed to sign with the Tigers five years earlier, pitches seven strong innings and is helped by Cal Ripken's three-run homer. Scott returns to Double-A Bowie one week later, winning his only major league appearance of the season.

1995— Rookie outfielder Curtis Goodwin arrives from AAA Rochester and singles off Oakland's Steve Ontiveros in his first major league at bat in a 2-1 win over the Athletics. Curtis keeps it going, with at least two hits in 10 of his first 11 games in the big leagues. Goodwin reaches every hit plateau from six to 49 faster than any Orioles rookie ever.

1998— For the second straight game, Rafael Palmeiro hits a game-winning homer as the Orioles come back to nip Seattle, 9-8, in 10 innings. Ken Griffey had given the Mariners an 8-7 lead in the top of the 10th off Norm Charlton with his second homer of the game. After Harold Baines' single in the bottom of the 10th, Palmeiro blasts a Bobby Ayala pitch over the fence in right center to win it. Brady Anderson, B.J. Surhoff and Cal Ripken homer for the Birds. The teams combine for 15 homers in two games. It is the seventh sudden-death win in the six-year history of Camden Yards and second by Palmeiro.

June 3

1968— Dave McNally strikes out 12 Angels and pitches a two-hitter as Boog Powell supplies both runs of the game with a two-run homer.

1977— The Orioles execute a game-ending triple play to beat the Royals in Kansas City, 7-6. It happens in bizarre fashion. John Wathan hits a sacrifice fly to Pat Kelly in right. Fred Patek is caught off first and is out, Kelly to Mark Belanger to Billy Smith back to Belanger. Belanger then noticed Dave Nelson standing off third base. He ran at him and tagged him out, completing the game-ending triple play. The scoring went 9-6-4-6. This game also marked the 2,842nd and last major league hit by Brooks Robinson, who delivered a seventh-inning single.

1985— Lee Lacy's first American League homer, a two-run shot in the bottom of the ninth off Angel reliever Donnie Moore climaxes a four-run rally that sees the Orioles win, 7-5, after entering the inning down, 5-3.

1989— Kevin Hickey picks up his first win in nearly seven seasons as the Orioles beat Detroit, 4-2.

1998— Doug Johns, a mystery-man journeyman lefthander who had spent time on the disabled list for insomnia, comes to the rescue of the Orioles' beleaguered

Dave McNally

starting staff, tossing 7⅓ scoreless innings in a 3-0 win over the Red Sox at Fenway Park. Johns doesn't allow a hit until Damon Buford's leadoff single in the bottom of the sixth. It's the first shutout suffered by the Red Sox this season. Johns, who has pitched for the Athletics and the Parma Italian team, has allowed only four earned runs in 24⅔ innings.

June 4

1957— Third baseman George Kell, playing his final season in the big leagues, records his 2,000th career hit in a 9-7 Kansas City win.

1967— Andy Etchebarren's two-run homer off Bob Priddy in the 19th inning gives the Orioles a 7-5 win over Washington in their longest game ever. A club record 21 strikeouts was set by five Oriole pitchers—Barber, Bunker, Watt, Eddie Fisher and Stu Miller.

1969— Don Buford hits the first pitch of the game for a home run and Boog Powell follows with another a few minutes later. The Birds beat Oakland, 6-1. Tom Phoebus ups his record to 6-1.

1972— The O's are shut out by Oakland in a doubleheader for the first time since June 15, 1958. Both scores are 2-0. Jim "Catfish" Hunter wins his 100th in the first game.

1983— The Orioles jump on eight-game-winner Dave Stieb for three homers in three innings (Murray, Bumbry, Lowenstein) and a 6-4 win over the Blue Jays in Baltimore.

George Kell

1988— The Orioles and Yankees play 14 innings in five hours and 46 minutes, the longest game by time in club history. It finishes at 1:22 a.m., the latest a game has ever finished on 33rd street. The Orioles come from behind twice in extra innings to win it, scoring once in the bottom of the 10th on Rene Gonzales' double to tie it at 4-4. And in the bottom of the 14th, with the bases loaded and two out and the Orioles trailing, 6-4, Cal Ripken Jr.'s grounder to third is thrown wildly to first by Mike Pagliarulo, allowing Rick Schu, Gonzales and Bill Ripken all to score to win it, 7-6, for the Birds.

1989— On the same day the Red Sox blow a 10-0 lead and lose, 13-11, to Toronto, the Orioles ride Randy Milligan's three-run homer to a 7-4 win in Detroit, completing a four-game sweep. Thanks to 12 wins in the last 13 games, the Orioles lead in the east grows to four games.

1993— Jack Voigt hits his first major league homer off Seattle's Randy Johnson and goes 3-for-5 with three RBI, singling in the 10th in a 6-5 "sudden death" win over the Mariners at Camden Yards.

June 5

1966— It takes just 18 minutes to complete a suspended game from the night before against the A's. With the score tied 5-5 in the 12th, Stu Miller retires the A's one-two-three while Russ Snyder drives in the game winner in the bottom of the 12th to complete the second suspended game in Oriole history.

1971— The guns begin firing late in a 12-4 win over the Brewers. Trailing, 2-1, in the sixth, the Birds score six runs on Paul Blair's first career grand slam and Merv Rettenmund's two-run shot. Frank Robinson ties a club record by scoring four runs.

1985— Dennis Martinez pitches the first one-hitter of his career for his 100th major league win as he blanks California, 4-0, at Memorial Stadium. Jerry Narron's single in the third is the only hit Martinez allows, retiring the last 16 batters in order.

1989— For the first time in history, the Orioles have the first overall selection in the free agent draft, and for the first time since the draft was initiated in 1965, the Orioles become the only team to be in first place on the day they drafted the first player in the draft. The Orioles select two-time All-America pitcher Ben McDonald out of LSU. That night, the Birds, despite being out hit 13 to 9, pound New York, 16-3, for their eighth straight win as Jeff Ballard ups his record to 9-1. The big blow is supplied by Steve Finley, a third-inning grand slam off Chuck Cary. Only four of the O's 16 runs are earned as the Yankees commit six errors.

1992— The Orioles move into first place by percentage points over Toronto behind the masterful pitching of Rick Sutcliffe, who pitches eight scoreless innings and wins, 1-0, on an eighth-inning RBI single by Cal Ripken Jr.. Gregg Olson is superb in gaining the save by pitching the ninth. David Segui snatches a two-run homer from Candy Maldonado in right field in the fifth inning and Mike Devereaux makes a sensational leaping grab on Joe Carter's bid for a three-run homer in the sixth. It is just the O's second 1-0 win in 932 games, since Mike Flanagan beat the Twins in July, 1986. The other came in Kansas City in '91. The Orioles go over the million mark in attendance on their 24th date. Just two franchises have reached it quicker, Toronto in 21 dates in 1992 and 22 dates in '91, and the Dodgers in 22 dates in '81 and on their 24th date four times.

1994— The White Sox are leading, 5-1, in the fifth, but red-hot Rafael Palmeiro, who had reached base safely nine straight times, homers. The next batter, Harold Baines, does the same and with the help of reliever Mark Eichhorn, who pitches his 15th and 16th straight scoreless innings of a streak that would reach 22, the Orioles come back to beat Chicago 8-5 at Camden Yards.

1998— Scott Erickson coaxes 19 ground ball outs and beats the Atlanta Braves, 3-2, in the shortest game ever at Camden Yards, 3-2, before over 48,000 fans. The time of one-hour and 53 minutes makes it the shortest game in the majors this season and the Orioles' shortest game since they played Toronto in 1:48 in 1983. All the runs are solo homers, with Eric Davis, Lenny Webster and Joe Carter connecting off local product Denny Neagle.

June 6

1967— The Orioles sweep a pair from the Angels at Anaheim Stadium by scores of 16-4 and 11-1. California uses 12 pitchers as the Birds rap out 23 hits in the two games. In the opener, Curt Blefary drives in seven runs with three homers (one a grand slam) while Paul Blair drives in four.

Scott Erickson

1977— Lee May's seventh home run in eight games gives the Orioles a 5-2 win over the Brewers at Milwaukee.

1979— The Orioles move into first place to stay behind Dennis Martinez, who shuts out Kansas City, 3-0.

1993— In game 1,790 of his streak, Cal Ripken Jr. suffers a twisted right knee when his spikes catch in the infield grass during the Orioles-Mariners melee that sees Seattle skipper Lou Piniella ejected along with seven players. Although Cal doesn't come out of the game, his knee is swollen and painful the next day. Still, he doesn't even miss infield practice. Cal says later, "It was the closest I've ever come to not playing." The Orioles and Mike Mussina beat the Mariners, 5-2. The fight begins when Mussina hits catcher Bill Haselman with a pitch and Haselman charges the mound, emptying both benches.

June 7

1959— Hoyt Wilhelm shuts out Kansas City, 3-0, to win his ninth of the season without a loss and eighth complete game. In notching his third shutout, Hoyt lowers his ERA to 0.996. Hoyt's streak brought more national attention on the Birds than any previous individual accomplishment in the club's history.

1961— The Orioles pick up Marvelous Marv Throneberry from the A's for Gene Stephens.

1968— John "Blue Moon" Odom has a no-hitter for 8⅔ innings against the Orioles at Memorial Stadium. Dave Johnson ruins his bid with a single to right. Odom walks eight, but wins, 6-1.

1998— Eddie Murray, who left Baltimore under a cloud after the 1988 season in which he requested a trade, has his number 33 officially retired in an emotional pregame ceremony. Murray didn't show much emotion as a player, but is choked up and teary-eyed as he thanks fans, teammates and family. One of just three players in history to amass both 3,000 hits and 500 homers, the Hall of Fame bound Murray, now an Oriole coach, is honored by the four other Orioles to have their numbers retired—Brooks and Frank Robinson, Jim Palmer and his first manager, Earl Weaver. Atlanta pitcher Greg Maddux then hands the Orioles their first shutout in 129 games, pitching a four-hitter and winning 9-0. Maddux needs only 100 pitches, coaxing 20 ground ball outs and only one fly ball out in running his record to 9-2. The four-time Cy Young winner is now 73-2 when backed with five runs or more.

Eddie Murray

June 8

1975— A fourth-inning single by Hal McRae is the only hit given up by Jim Palmer, who beats the Royals and Steve Busby, 1-0. It is Palmer's third career one-hitter, fifth shutout of the year and third by a 1-0 score.

1983— Alan Ramirez, just up from Rochester, pitches seven strong innings in his major league debut, leaving with a 2-2 tie. The Orioles score five runs in the eighth to beat

Milwaukee, 7-3. Cal Ripken and John Lowenstein each hit two-run homers off Tom Tellmann after Ken Singleton had hit a game-tying two-run homer off Don Sutton in the seventh.

1986— Lee Lacy hits three home runs at Yankee Stadium in an 18-9 thumping of the Yanks. Lacy becomes the first righthanded hitter since Ben Chapman in 1932 to accomplish the feat. The game was the longest by time in American League history, four hours and 16 minutes, which didn't include a 40-minute rain delay.

1990— Phil Bradley connects for an inside-the-park home run at Memorial Stadium off New York's Greg Cadaret. It's the 18th inside-the-park home run in club history and the first since Al Bumbry at Chicago on August 21, 1976. The O's had gone 2,148 games in between. It is the first inside-the-parker at Memorial Stadium since Bumbry did it against the Yankees on April 19, 1974. Bradley's heroics help the O's to a 5-4, 10-inning win. Billy Ripken also homers against Cadaret, his first ever at Memorial Stadium after 584 at bats.

1998— Shutout the previous day by Greg Maddux, the Orioles unleash a season-high 18 hits and score their season high in runs by pounding the Phillies, 14-8, at Veterans Stadium. The Orioles were trailing, 7-6, when they pulled ahead in the sixth on an RBI double by Roberto Alomar. Rafael Palmeiro followed with a two-run homer, and Joe Carter hit a solo shot. Carter, who beat the Phillies in the 1993 World Series with a clutch ninth-inning home run in game seven while playing with Toronto, adds an RBI double in the eighth. Carter is booed vociferously throughout the game as the Orioles play in Philadelphia for the first time since winning the 1983 World Series. The only player remaining from that World Series win is Cal Ripken Jr. Pitcher Doug Johns goes 2-for-2, becoming the first Oriole pitcher to get two hits in a game since Dave McNally on August 9, 1972.

June 9

1943— The Orioles and Rochester battle to an 0-0, 18-inning tie at old Orioles Park. Steve Gromek for the Birds and Ira Hutchinson for the Red Wings went all the way. Gromek gave up 15 hits and Hutchinson 13 safeties.

1959— In an historic bench mark, the Orioles move into a first-place tie with the White Sox. It is the first time ever that the O's are in first place after the second day of the season. The Birds beat Cleveland, 7-3, as 46,601 watch on Interfaith Night.

1962— Yogi Berra, playing in his 2,000th game with the Yankees, hits a pinch homer as New York scores five runs in the seventh to overcome a 2-0 Oriole lead. Bobby Richardson also homers for the Yankees. After this Yankee victory, the Orioles took 10 of the last 12 with New York.

1972— In their first ever game in Texas, the Orioles beat the Rangers, 7-2, thanks to four Texas errors.

1982 — Mike Flanagan, joining Jim Palmer and Scott McGregor before him, goes the route as the Orioles beat the Brewers for the third straight time in Milwaukee. The Orioles move from fifth place to third in the process.

1983 — Despite scoring seven runs in the bottom of the first, the Orioles, who committed a club-record-tying six errors, need a strong relief effort from Tippy Martinez to hold off the Brewers, 10-7.

1985 — The Orioles become the 26th and last team in the majors to be shut out, losing to Oil Can Boyd and the Red Sox, 12-0. It is the first time the Orioles have been blanked since September 21, 1984. Boyd was the perpetrator on that day as well.

1989 — Mickey Tettleton homers twice, both off Bryan Clutterbuck, to up his league lead to 16 in a 7-1 win over Milwaukee. Mark Williamson wins in relief. He's 4-0 with two saves and a 1.13 ERA.

1990 — Pete Harnisch strikes out 10 Yankees in a 10-1 thumping of New York at Memorial Stadium. It's the first time in 327 games an Oriole pitcher reaches double-figure strikeouts in one game. Randy Milligan ties a club record by belting three home runs, joining Bobby Grich and Juan Beniquez as the only Orioles to hit three homers at Memorial Stadium. Bob Melvin doubles in the game, his first Memorial Stadium hit after going 0-for-33.

1993 — Mark McLemore, producing some of the best numbers ever for a non-roster player (a .284 average with 165 hits and 72 RBI), ties a club record for most hits in a game with a career-high five in a 7-4 win over Oakland. Mark scores the go-ahead run in the seventh and drives in two insurance runs in the eighth.

1994 — Making his major league debut as an outfielder at Fenway Park, Chris Sabo tosses out Scott Cooper by a mile in the seventh to maintain a 6-6 tie, then hits a two-run homer in the eighth off Kevin Ryan to put the Orioles ahead to stay. The Orioles win, 10-7, as Sabo also doubles and is hit by a pitch.

1996 — Roberto Alomar's batting average peaks at .410 in a 12-9 loss to Chicago. Alomar becomes the fifth player this decade to be hitting .400 or better after June 1. Alomar finishes with a .328 average, one percentage point behind Ken Singleton for highest ever by an Oriole.

1997 — The Orioles announce that outfielder Eric Davis will undergo surgery involving an obstruction in his colon to be performed on June 13 by Dr. Keith Lillemoe, Professor of Surgery at Johns Hopkins Hospital.

June 10

1898 — Wilbert Robinson, Orioles catcher, makes seven hits in seven trips and bats in 11 runs as Baltimore beats St. Louis, 25-7.

1959 — Cleveland's Rocky Colavito becomes only the eighth batter in major league history to hit four

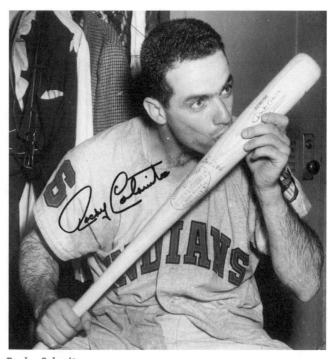

Rocky Colavito

home runs in one game. He joins Lou Gehrig as the only American League players ever to hit four consecutive homers in one game as the Indians outslug the Orioles, 11-8. Billy Martin and Minnie Minoso also homer for the Indians.

1971— Sparked by Frank Robinson's three hits and five RBI, the O's grab a 9-0 lead after three innings and coast from there for a 12-0 win over the Twins behind Jim Palmer's shutout pitching.

1979— Starting in left field for the first time as an Oriole, Benny Ayala blasts solo homers off Texas' Jon Matlack in the fourth and sixth innings. It is Ayala's first two-homer game in the majors and his first American League homers. The Orioles win, 5-4, on Terry Crowley's pinch single in the ninth, and Dennis Martinez wins his 10th straight game.

Benny Ayala

1983— Storm Davis wins, 3-0, pitching a route-going, three-hit shutout at Fenway Park in 1:59. The Orioles are in first place by three games.

1985— Lee Lacy leads off the game at Tiger Stadium with a broken bat opposite field homer and homers in the 11th to give the Orioles a one-run lead, but Detroit scores two in the bottom of the 11th to win it, 8-7. With two-down in the ninth, Floyd Rayford homers off Willie Hernandez to tie the game in one of the most exciting games of the season.

1993— Jamie Moyer, 0-11 in his previous 16 major league starts, beats Frank Viola and the Red Sox, 2-1, at Fenway Park.

1995— Jeff Manto, who spent the year before at AAA Norfolk and Rochester, becomes the 24th player in major league history to homer in four consecutive at bats when he homers against the Angels in a 6-2 win. Manto clubbed two homers on June 8 in a win over Seattle, two home runs against the Angels on the ninth and another on the 10th. Manto made an out between homers on the eighth, homered twice and walked twice on the ninth and homered in his first at bat on the 10th. He had four career homers entering the '95 season. Jeff tied the major league record for consecutive homers over three games, matching the record set by Johnny Blanchard of the '61 Yankees. He becomes the first Oriole to homer in back-to-back games since Larry Sheets in 1987.

June 11

1962— Robin Roberts makes his first Oriole win, and first in the majors in over a year, one to remember. Bud Daley beaned Boog Powell in the top of the fourth with the O's up, 3-0. Boog left on a stretcher and was taken to a hospital for observation. When Robin threw over Roger Maris' head in token retaliation, Maris charged the mound and a free-for-all ensued. Clinging to a 5-3 lead in the ninth and with two runners on, Hoyt Wilhelm strode in and struck Clete Boyer out on three pitches to preserve the victory for Roberts.

1965— Jerry Hoffberger is elected chairman of the Oriole board of directors, replacing Joseph Iglehart.

1980— The Orioles lose, 8-2, in Seattle, their 9th loss in 12 games. The loss topples them out of first place and costs a playoff berth. Baseball went on an 8½ week sabbatical that night due to the players' strike; when the game returned in August, a split season concept was devised that awarded playoff berths to the teams leading their divisions when the strike began.

1983— The Orioles win their sixth in a row, 10-6, in Boston, and lead the division by four games, the O's biggest lead until September.

June 12

1972— A crowd of 50,182 at Oakland watches Pat Dobson out-duel Vida Blue, 1-0. Don Buford drives in the only run in the eighth before the largest crowd to ever watch a game in the Bay Area.

1986— Juan Beniquez becomes the ninth Oriole to hit three homers in a game when he does it at Memorial Stadium against the Yankees in a 7-5 loss. Beniquez did it just four days after Lee Lacy did it against New York.

1990— Cal Ripken plays in his 1,308th consecutive game in a 4-3, 10-inning, win over Milwaukee and moves into second place on the all-time list ahead of Ev Scott (Yankees-Red Sox, 1918-1925) who played all 1,307 games of his streak at shortstop.

1992— Leo Gomez' first major league grand slam off Scott Eldred helps propel the Orioles and Mike Mussina to a 6-0 win at Detroit. Chris Hoiles accounts for the other runs with two solo homers. Hoiles would finish the season with the fewest RBI (40) in major league history for a player with 20 or more homers. Seventeen of his 20 homers were solo shots.

1993— Rookie first baseman Paul Carey, born and raised in Boston, has three hits and drives in the game-tying RBI in the seventh and game-winning RBI double in the ninth in a 5-1 Oriole win at Fenway Park. The double would be Carey's only extra-base hit of the season in 47 at bats.

1995— Brady Anderson sets the American League record with his 34th consecutive stolen base in a 4-3 loss in Cleveland.

Brady Anderson

June 13

1972— The Orioles win their sixth in a row to move into a first-place tie with the Tigers. Mike Cuellar goes the distance for a 5-1 win over Oakland, giving the O's six straight complete-game wins.

1983— Cal Ripken's three-run homer off Don Sutton provides all the Orioles' offense in a 3-2 win over the

Brewers at County Stadium. Tippy ends it when he induces Ted Simmons to ground into a game-ending double play with the tying and winning runs on base.

1985— Manager Joe Altobelli is fired after the Orioles return home from Detroit, losing, 6-2, the night before for their fifth straight loss. The Orioles were 29-26 at the time, in fourth place, eight games behind Toronto in the standings. Third base coach Cal Ripken, Sr. managed for one game on June 13, an 8-3 win over Milwaukee, before Earl Weaver took over on the 14th for his second tour as manager as the Birds came back to dump Milwaukee, 7-5. The Orioles went 53-52 under Weaver the rest of the season.

1988— Catcher Mickey Tettleton becomes the 36th player in major league history to homer from both sides of the plate in one game as he does it in Detroit in a 6-4 Orioles win. Only three others have done it in Orioles history, Eddie Murray, Don Buford and Mike Young.

1992— Mike Flanagan experiences an inning he'll never forget, facing 13 batters in the eighth inning in Detroit, three shy of tying the American League record for most batters faced in an inning. Flanny gave up six hits including a home run, eight earned runs, walked three and hit two batters. The Tigers pounded the Orioles, 15-1.

1997— Brady Anderson collects the Orioles first-ever interleague RBI with a single off Braves ace Greg Maddux in a 4-3 Oriole win in Atlanta. Jimmy Key ups his record to a sparkling 11-1.

Mike Flanagan

June 14
1970— Dave May celebrates Ball Day by hitting his only home run of the season, a two-run shot in the 10th to give the Orioles and Jim Palmer a 4-2 win over Oakland.

1972— The Orioles win their seventh straight game and third straight over the A's as Bobby Grich's 10th-inning homer gives Dave McNally a 2-1 win over Catfish Hunter.

1973— Trailing, 3-1, in the eighth against Kansas City, the Orioles erupt for seven runs to win, 8-3. Grant Jackson gets the win in relief. Jackson wins three and saves two in the five-game home stand.

1977— Pat Kelly's three-run homer in the 11th climaxes a four-run outburst as the Birds come from behind to defeat the Brewers, 8-5, at Memorial Stadium.

1978— Jim Palmer pitches the Orioles to a 5-2 win over California, the Birds' 13th consecutive victory— tops in the majors that year. The streak, which ended the following night, fell one short of the club record set in 1973 between August 12 and August 27.

1985— Earl Weaver returns to manage the Orioles after a 2½ years hiatus and the Birds respond with a 7-5 win over Milwaukee.

1986— Two Oriole greats, 268-game winner Jim Palmer and three-time Oriole MVP Ken Singleton, are inducted into the Orioles Hall of Fame in ceremonies before the Orioles game with the Yankees.

1987— Dave Schmidt beats the Blue Jays, 8-5, snapping Toronto's six-game win streak against the Orioles and 11-game overall win streak in the American League, a club record. The win snaps the Orioles' 10-game losing streak, longest since 1958.

1994— The Orioles acquire outfielder Dwight Smith from the Angels. He becomes the fourth Smith to grace the Oriole roster in '94, a league record for Smiths on a ballclub in the same season. Lonnie, Lee and Mark are the other Smiths.

1996— Cal Ripken Jr. sets the world record for consecutive games played by passing Sachio Kinugasa's Japanese record of 2,215 consecutive games played. The Orioles beat the Royals, 6-1, in Kansas City and Kinugasa was in KC to help honor Cal. Cal finished the year with 2,316 consecutive games played, all starts.

1997— Mike Mussina singles off John Smoltz in Atlanta, making him the first Oriole pitcher to get a hit in a regular season game since Roric Harrison homered at Cleveland on October 3, 1972 on the final day of the season in the last year before the designated hitter rule was instituted. Tim Stoddard singled in game four of the 1979 World Series.

June 15

1921— After Lefty Groves (he was called Groves during his entire career with the Orioles) beats Buffalo, 4-2, on five hits in the opener for Baltimore's 27th victory in a row, the Bisons jump all over the Birds in the second game for an overwhelming 19-8 triumph. Tommy Thomas, who started the long winning streak for the Orioles on May 20, was the losing pitcher. Walter Tragesser, the usually lighthitting Buffalo catcher, was a terror at bat with six hits in six times

1958— On a day that the Orioles should have stayed home, the White Sox shut the Birds out twice in Baltimore—3-0 on a Jim Wilson two-hitter and 4-0 on a Dick Donovan seven-hitter.

1976— In a trade that would help shape the Oriole future, Hank Peters trades Ken Holtzman, Doyle Alexander, Grant Jackson and Elrod Hendricks to the Yankees for Rick Dempsey, Rudy May, Tippy Martinez, Dave Pagan and Scott McGregor. On the day of the big trade, the Orioles put the brakes on a nine-game losing streak—their longest in 18 years—when they beat the White Sox, 4-0, in Chicago behind the shutout pitching of Jim Palmer.

1983— Down by 7-0 after six innings, the Orioles battle back to tie the Brewers in the eighth with five runs, three on a Cal Ripken homer, then win it with a four run 10th, featuring Ripken's two-run double and RBI by John Shelby and Eddie Murray. The 11-7 win kept the Birds on top of the east by 3½ games.

1989— The Orioles execute the only triple play in the American League all season and their first in 10 years. With the Yankees' Don Mattingly on first and Steve Sax on second, Steve Balboni lines out to Cal Ripken Jr. who flips the ball to brother Bill at second base to double up Sax. Bill then throws to Randy Milligan at first to get Mattingly. It is the ninth triple play in club history and undoubtedly the first in major league history involving brothers. The Orioles are 3-2 winners in 10 innings.

1991— Catcher Bob Melvin ties a club record with five hits in an 8-4 win at Toronto. Included is his only home run of the season, off Juan Guzman. Mike Devereaux hits a three-run homer for the Orioles.

1997— Catcher Lenny Webster smacks a two-run 10th-inning home run off Mark Wohlers to give the Orioles a 5-3 win and a sweep of the Braves in Atlanta.

1998— The Orioles stop David Wells' eight-game win streak with a 7-4 victory over the first-place Yankees at Camden Yards. Wells (8-2) was unbeaten in 11 starts since April 2 and was 5-0 in his last five appearances. Rafael Palmeiro and Joe Carter both homer and have three hits for the Orioles. The game features the ejection of Yankee reliever Mike Stanton, who hit Eric Davis with a pitch after serving up Palmeiro's homer. Stanton was later suspended five games by league president Gene Budig.

June 16

1959— Milt Pappas hurls his first major league shut out as he blanks Detroit, 4-0, on a two-hitter.

1962— Robin Roberts wins his second game in six days after going over a year between victories, beating Washington at D.C. Stadium.

1966— An Oriole relievers' string of retiring 37 consecutive batters over five games ends when Eddie Fisher, making his Oriole debut, allows a single in the eighth. The Senators beat the Orioles, 2-1. The streak included Eddie Watt retiring 12 straight Yankees and Moe Drabowsky 10 straight Senators.

1973— Although claiming he doesn't feel well, Jim Palmer retires the first 25 men in order before the Rangers' Ken Suarez singles to center with one out in the ninth, ruining Palmer's try for a perfect game. Palmer yielded one more hit and wins, 9-1.

1978— Dennis Martinez posts his first major league shut-out and Eddie Murray drives in four runs, as the Orioles blank Oakland 6-0 at Memorial Stadium.

1983— Scott McGregor has a 1-0 lead with two down and none on in the bottom of the ninth at Milwaukee. Then Cecil Cooper doubles and Ted Simmons singles in the tie run. In the 11th, Rick Manning's homer off Tim Stoddard wins it for the Brewers, 2-1, one of only two losses to the Brewers in 1983.

1987— Cal Ripken Jr. singles off Rich Bordi in New York for his 1,000th career hit, becoming the youngest Oriole ever to do so.

1988— The Orioles beat Boston, 8-4, despite a solo steal of home by Red Sox second baseman Marty Barrett. He was the first Red Sox to do it (not as part of a double-steal) since Tommy Harper in 1970. No Oriole had done it since Ron Hansen in 1960.

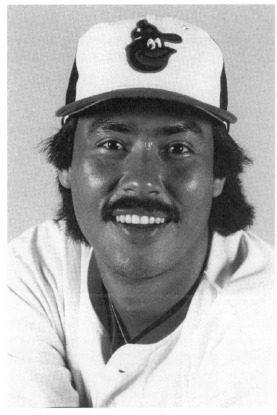

Dennis Martinez

1991— The Orioles outslug Toronto, 13-8, at the Skydome, hitting four home runs, including a pinch grand slam by Joe Orsulak off Duane Ward, his first in the big leagues.

1998— Rookie Sidney Ponson helps end New York's major league record streak of non-losing series at 24 as the Orioles blank the Yankees, 2-0. By winning the first two games of the three-game series, the Orioles assured the Yankees of not splitting or winning a series for the first time since opening the year with two straight losses at Anaheim. New York had been tied with the 1912 Red Sox and 1970 Reds for most consecutive series wins in a season. Ponson, making his first ever start at Camden Yards, allows just two hits in 6⅔ innings. The right-hander retired 20 of the first 21 hitters he faced.

June 17

1973— It takes 16 innings, but the Orioles manage to beat Texas, 5-4 at Memorial Stadium. The game took 4:07 to play. Bob Reynolds got the win and Don Stanhouse was the loser.

1974— Mike Cuellar goes the route to win his ninth straight, 1-0, over Minnesota, in the shortest game of the season, 1:43.

1984— Gary Roenicke's grand slam breaks a 2-2 eighth inning tie and propels the Orioles to a 6-2 victory at Yankee Stadium. The slam off Dennis Rasmussen also wins a million dollars for College Park, Maryland housewife Anne Sommers, whose name was drawn at random in a TV Homerun Sweepstakes Inning.

1991— The Orioles snap Minnesota's 15-game win streak as they beat the Twins, 6-5, on Randy Milligan's dramatic two-out, two-run double off Rick Aguilera in the bottom of the ninth inning.

1997— The Orioles hold a news conference during which Johns Hopkins surgeon Dr. Keith Lillemoe announces that Eric Davis had a malignant mass and ⅓ of his cancerous colon removed. The prognosis for full recovery is good. On July 11, Davis announced that he would begin chemotherapy treatments at the UCLA Medical Center on July 16.

June 18

1966— The Orioles blast five home runs, all with at least one on, to crush the Red Sox, 16-6, at Fenway Park. Frank Robinson and Boog Powell hit two-run homers in the first. Brooks Robinson adds a three-run blast, as does Dave Johnson. Curt Blefary caps the barrage with a two-run shot.

1974— Bobby Grich becomes the first Oriole ever to hit three home runs in a game at Memorial Stadium as the Birds pound Minnesota, 10-1. The first two were off Joe Decker and the third was off Tom Burgmeier.

1977— Jim Palmer becomes the winningest pitcher in Oriole history by defeating the Toronto Blue Jays, 4-2, at Toronto. It is his 182nd victory, one more than former teammate, Dave McNally.

1979— Umpire Larry Barnett ejects Earl Weaver following a disagreement on what constitutes interference between catcher and batter. Earl returned, brandishing a rule book, which he promptly tore into shreds when Barnett ignored his pleading. The Orioles won at Cleveland, 8-7.

1989— The Orioles conclude the second best attended homestand in club history (358,084 in 11 games) with a 4-2 win over Oakland. Mickey Weston, called up from Rochester that day, retires eight of nine batters to save the win for Dave Schmidt.

1990— After losing three straight to Boston the Orioles salvage a 7-2 win in the finale as Dave Johnson goes the distance to beat Roger Clemens before a crowd of 31,582. The total for the four-date series, 167,456, sets a club record. Johnson is one of just four pitchers to beat Clemens all season. The others are Dave Stewart, Kevin Appier and Kevin Tapani.

1998— Darryl Strawberry's mammoth 465-foot homer with two aboard in the first inning, the longest in the history of Oriole Park, gives the Yankees a 5-3 win and averts an Oriole sweep of the three-game series. Strawberry connects off Mike Mussina before the largest crowd in Camden Yards history, 48,269. The ball caroms off the ivy-covered wall beyond the center-field fence, beating the previous record of 463 feet by Oakland's Pedro Munoz, who hit a 463-foot homer off former Orioles starter David Wells in 1996.

June 19

1960— Hoyt Wilhelm and Milt Pappas shut out the Tigers twice, 2-0 and 1-0, on two and three hits, respectively. Jim Gentile's long belt to the third deck of Briggs Stadium wins the first one, while Brooks Robinson's ninth-inning sacrifice fly provides the winning margin in the nightcap.

1962— Chuck Estrada wins his first in over three weeks, 3-1 over the Yankees, as the Birds snap a scoreless skein of 32½ innings. Hobie Landrith's bad hop single over short drove in the first run.

1969— Dave McNally fires a two-hitter vs. the Senators at RFK Stadium. President Nixon showed up for the last few innings. It is McNally's 12th straight win.

Milt Pappas   *Hoyt Wilhelm*

1970— Despite two home runs and eight RBI by Senator first baseman Mike Epstein, the Orioles outlast Washington, 12-10, in the first of two. Merv Rettenmund's single up the middle scores Dave Johnson with the winning run in the 13th inning of the nightcap, 3-2.

1980— John Lowenstein's pinch single in the eighth scores the tying run against the A's and sends Al Bumbry to third. First baseman Jeff Newman cuts off the throw-in and nails Lowenstein in the back of the neck as he dashes for second. As John goes down, the ball caroms into the outfield and Bumbry scores the winning run. Lowenstein, lying motionless, is carried off on a stretcher. He appeared seriously hurt. But just as the stretcher disappears into the dugout, Lowenstein sits bolt upright and gives out a double-fisted salute.

1983— Jim Palmer wins his second game of the season, 6-3, over the Red Sox, as Eddie Murray hits two homers.

1984— After striking out his first three times up in Boston, Eddie Murray hits a grand slam in the eighth inning to trim the Red Sox lead to 7-5. Eddie comes up in the ninth, again with the bases loaded and Boston up 7-6 and drills a two-run single off Steve Crawford to give the Orioles an 8-7 lead. The O's eventually win, 9-7. The grand slam was Eddie's eighth, one more than Boog Powell for tops in Oriole history.

1985— The Yankees complete a three-game sweep of the Orioles in Baltimore with a 10-0 win. New York outscores the Orioles 26-4 in the three games. The Yankees out-hit the Orioles .389 to .158, 44 hits to 15.

1988— Boston bangs out 23 hits, the most ever by a visiting team at Memorial Stadium, in crushing the Orioles, 15-7. The combined total of 37 hits is a season high in the American League.

1991— On "Turn Back the Clock Day", commemorating the 1966 World Champion Orioles, the Twins, down 4-3, score five runs in the ninth off Gregg Olson (three wild pitches and a throwing error) as 44,742 look on in disbelief at an 8-4 loss. Olson tore off his throwback jersey and stuffed it in the trash barrel after the game. It was the first and only time Olson lost at Memorial Stadium.

1992— Outfielder Gene Woodling, one of the greatest clutch hitters to ever don an Oriole uniform, becomes the 23rd member of the Orioles Hall of Fame.

1992— Mike Devereaux's grand slam in the second and Randy Milligan's solo shot in the sixth, help propel the Orioles over the Yankees, 10-7, as the Birds take their last look at first place, by three percentage points over Toronto.

Dave McNally shirt—1966

June 20

1953— Frank Robinson makes his organized baseball debut with Ogden of the Pioneer League. Frank played third base and had a triple in three at bats in a 5-4 loss to Magic Valley.

1970— Brooks Robinson makes his 2,000th major league hit a big one—a three-run homer off Joe Coleman, Jr. It is the margin of victory in a 5-4 Oriole win.

1975— The Orioles and the Red Sox tie a league record by using seven pitchers in the ninth inning. The Birds use four, but it only staves off defeat. The Red Sox win, 4-3, in the 12th.

1977— The Boston Red Sox tie a major league record for most homers in six consecutive games (22) when Butch Hobson homers in the eighth to give Boston a 4-0 victory over the Orioles at Baltimore.

1982— Joe Nolan's two-run pinch homer off Rich Gossage in the 11th gives the Orioles a 5-3 win at Yankee Stadium.

1986— Mike Boddicker beats Boston, 14-3, to up his record to a glittering 10-1. A torn finger ligament led to a 4-11 record the rest of the season.

Brooks Robinson

1989— Despite spotting the Mariners a 5-0 lead, the Orioles come back to win, 8-6, at the Kingdome. Mickey Weston, in relief of Jeff Ballard, picks up his first major league win with four shutout innings.

1998— Just one out away from having the game suspended because of curfew, Rafael Palmeiro hits a two-out, three-run homer off Toronto reliever Bill Risley in the bottom of the 15th inning to give the Orioles a 7-4 win over the Blue Jays in a game that didn't end until 1:25 a.m. At 5:49, it's the longest game in club history, beating the 1988 game against the Yankees by three minutes. Altogether, 13 pitchers throw 495 pitches. The much-maligned Oriole bullpen throws 10 shutout innings. The Orioles were 1-17 with runners in scoring position until Palmeiro sent what was left of the crowd of over 47,000 home happy.

June 21

1956— Connie Johnson and George Zuverink combine to one-hit the White Sox, but Chicago pitcher Jack Harshman also tosses a one hitter and wins the game, 1-0.

1966— In the first of a twi-night doubleheader at Yankee Stadium, the Birds lead, 7-5, with two out and two on in the bottom of the ninth. Roy White hits a drive off Stu Miller that is headed for the right-field stands, but Frank Robinson leaps high in the air and catches it while tumbling backward into the seats. Instead of a Yankee win, it is a game-ending catch for Frank. New York manager Ralph Houk went crazy when Frank disappeared into the stands for 15 seconds. But Hank Soar said the catch counted and the Orioles had won their 12th straight at Yankee Stadium.

1970— Dave McNally beats the Washington Senators, 4-2, in Baltimore for his 100th career win.

1975— Jim Palmer shuts out Boston, 3-0, for his 12th win of the season and fifth in a row. Palmer's sixth shutout matches his career high. He had six in 1969 and again in 1973.

1976— Wayne Garland pitches his first major-league-career complete game and shutout when he stops the Red Sox, 2-0, at Memorial Stadium. Garland has a no-hitter for 7.2 innings before giving up a single to Rico Petrocelli.

1983— The O's beat the Yankees for the 10th straight time in Baltimore, 5-2, thanks to a pair of two-run homers by Gary Roenicke off Shane Rawley.

1985— Ray Miller resigns as Oriole pitching coach to become manager of the Minnesota Twins. In his 7½ seasons as pitching coach, Miller produced two Cy Young winners and five different 20-game winners.

1987— The Orioles need two days to snap a nine-game losing streak to the Tigers. The Orioles lead, 9-4, when the game is suspended at 1:02 am. Two lengthy rain delays are the reason, with the game still in the bottom of the first at 10:23 pm. It takes only eight minutes on the 21st to complete the Oriole win. The regular game on the 21st saw Detroit win, 9-3, in record-setting fashion. The Bengals 12 extra base hits, seven doubles and five homers, are the most ever by an Orioles opponent.

1988— Pitcher Oswald Peraza earns his first big league win, 4-2, at Toronto, over Mike Flanagan, whom the Orioles traded to the Blue Jays the year before to get Peraza and Jose Mesa.

1989— The Orioles jump out to an 8-0 lead but survive a late-inning comeback to beat Seattle, 8-6. Gregg Olson douses a Mariner threat with his 10th save, most for an O's rookie since Bob Reynold's nine in 1973. In sweeping three in Seattle, the Orioles lead in the east jumps to seven games.

1992— Catcher Chris Hoiles is struck by a pitch thrown by Tim Leary of the Yankees, fracturing his right wrist. Hoiles spent the next two months on the disabled list. The Orioles protested the game, claiming Leary was doctoring the ball, and also the fact it was an illegal pitch. Hoiles retaliated with six home runs against the Yankees in 1993, the most by an Oriole against New York since Curt Blefary hit six in 1965.

June 22

1962— Boog Powell becomes the first player to hit a ball over the hedge in center field at Memorial Stadium with a 469-foot drive off of Boston's Don Schwall. Boog's blast rolls to a stop 508 feet away. Hobie Landrith wins the game with a two- run homer off Dick Radatz in the ninth. The final is 3-2.

1969— Dave Leonhard, on weekend leave from the Maryland Air National Guard summer camp, makes his first start of the season and pitches a three-hit, 6-0 shutout over Cleveland.

1979— Doug DeCinces hits a dramatic two-run homer off Dave Tobik in the ninth to rally the Orioles to a 6-5 win over Detroit and a three game lead in the eastern standings. The win, coupled with a doubleheader sweep of the Tigers the following day and highlighted by Eddie Murray's three-run, ninth-inning game winner in the opener, symbolized "Oriole Magic" in 1979.

1989— The Orioles win their seventh straight, 6-5, in Anaheim, with Jim Traber's pinch homer in the eighth off Willie Fraser winning it.

1990— The Orioles are within one out of tying the club record for most consecutive errorless games, but left fielder Joe Orsulak commits an error with two out in the ninth inning, ending the string at nine error-free games. Boston wins the game, 4-3, at Fenway Park.

1991— Bob Milacki works eight shutout innings and Gregg Olson gets the save as the Orioles nip Tom Gordon and the Royals, 1-0, for their first 1-0 win in nearly five years. Cal Ripken walked, stole second, went to third on a wild pitch and scored on David Segui's single for the only run.

1993— Chris Hoiles connects for two home runs, including his third career grand slam and a career-high six RBI, in a 12-9 thumping of the Tigers at Oriole Park. The Orioles, down, 7-1, in the fourth inning, score eight runs in the sixth with two out.

1995— Harold Baines plays in his 1,000th game as a designated hitter in a 4-1 loss to Boston. Baines is the only player to play 1,000 games as a DH and another position (1,060 games in the outfield).

1998— Mike Mussina fires a two-hitter and retires the last 22 batters he faces as the Orioles stop the Mets, 7-2, in an inter-league game. It's Mussina's best effort since coming back from the line drive that forced him out of action with a broken nose and other lacerations. The only Mets hits are consecutive homers by Brian McRae and Butch Huskey in the second. They are the only New York batters to reach base. Rafael Palmeiro, Cal Ripken and Chris Hoiles homer for the Orioles.

June 23

1954— The Red Sox and Orioles combine to use 42 players in a 17-inning marathon at Memorial Stadium. The Birds prevail, 8-7, with Sam Mele of the Orioles hitting into a short-to-second-to-first-to-catcher triple play.

1963— Bob "Rocky" Johnson ties Brooks Robinson's then club record by beginning a string of eight consecutive hits.

1964— In one of the most memorable games ever played in Baltimore, the Orioles trail the Yankees, 7-2, with two down in the bottom of the eighth when they erupt to score seven runs and hang on to win, 9-8. The crowd of over 31,000 gives the Birds a standing ovation when they take the field in the ninth, and a song, "That Yankee Game," was written commemorating the comeback.

1977— Butch Hobson's homer boosts Boston's home-run record streak to nine consecutive games (30 homers) as the Red Sox beat the Orioles, 7-3.

1979— In the first game of a Saturday night doubleheader, the O's trail Detroit, 6-5, in the ninth when Eddie Murray hits a three-run, one out homer off Tigers veteran John Hiller to win in sudden death. In the second game, pinch hitter Terry Crowley's two-out eighth inning single breaks a 5-5 tie to give the O's their second nine-game winning streak of the year.

1990— The Orioles lead the Red Sox at Fenway in the 10th inning, thanks to a Mickey Tettleton homer, but Dwight Evans, signed by the Orioles after the season, hits a "sudden-death" two-run homer off

Gregg Olson to win it for Boston, 4-3. It is the first home run off Olson since Evans connected, also at Fenway, on April 15, 1989, a string of 114.2 homerless innings, second longest in club history behind Tippy Martinez' 123.2 from 1978-80.

1991— The Orioles sweep a pair at Kansas City, both in extra innings, as the two teams combine for 65 hits and 36 runs. The O's score four in the top of the ninth on Chris Hoiles' first major league grand slam in the first game to tie it before winning 11-8 in 10 innings. Tim Hulett and Brady Anderson homer in the 10th. In game two, the Royals score five in the ninth to send it into overtime before the Orioles win, 9-8, in 12 innings, thanks to Joe Orsulak's 12th-inning homer.

1992— Cal Ripken homers twice and drives in four runs in a 7-1 win over Milwaukee at County Stadium. Cal's three-run smash in the seventh puts the game out of reach. Cal would go 73 games until

Rick Sutcliffe

September 14 before hitting another homer. The homers were career numbers 268 and 269, which puts Cal one ahead of Brooks Robinson for the club's most homers by a righthanded hitter.

1993— Rick Sutcliffe becomes the first pitcher this year to throw a complete game against Detroit, beating the Tigers, 6-2, for his sixth straight win making him 8-2. But the rest of the season is a struggle, as Sutcliffe musters a 2-8 record with a 7.57 ERA, the result of a knee injury that required surgery.

June 24

1979— On "Silver Sunday," Ellie Hendricks hits a home run off Milt Pappas to win the 25th anniversary "old-timers" game. The teams, determined by fan vote, feature Jim Gentile, Gene Woodling, Gus Triandos, Frank Robinson, Milt Pappas and Boog Powell, plus several other stars from the O's first 25 years.

1988— Roger Clemens, who had pitched a shutout against the Orioles in Baltimore six days earlier, lasts just 2½ innings at Fenway Park, giving up six runs and seven hits in a 6-2 Oriole win. The big blow is a bases loaded two-run double by Jim Traber, his fifth-straight bases loaded safety.

June 25

1961— The Orioles edge the Angels, 9-8, in 14 innings, with Ron Hansen's homer in the 14th being the game winner. A major-league-record 16 pitchers are used in the game, eight by each side. Little Albie Pearson was up eight times in the game with two hits and five walks.

1963— Robin Roberts wins his 250th game and pitches his 37th shutout in the process as the O's break open a scoreless tie with one run in the fifth, two in the sixth, four in the seventh, two in the eighth and one in the ninth to win, 10-0, at Los Angeles. Jim Gentile drives in six runs with two doubles and a homer.

1966— Sam Bowen's solo homer off George Brunet in the top of the ninth gives Wally Bunker a 1-0 win over the Angels.

1970— In a 14-inning game at Boston, the Orioles spot the Red Sox a 7-0 lead before banging out 21 hits and winning, 13-8.

1973— Al Bumbry ties a club record with five hits in a 4-3 win over Milwaukee. Paul Blair, the only unanimous choice on *The Sporting News* American League All-Star fielding team makes a sensational catch in deep center field to take a home run away from George Scott in the fifth inning.

1974— Mike Cuellar's nine-game winning streak ends as Mickey Lolich and the Tigers blank the Birds, 2-0. The normally low-key Cuellar was ejected in the third by plate umpire Russ Goetz for disputing ball and strike calls.

1984— Ken Singleton becomes the 150th player in baseball history to record 2,000 career hits, against Boston in a 7-4 defeat.

Al Bumbry

1993— Highly touted rookie Jeffrey Hammonds makes his major league debut with a pinch hit single in the sixth off Jim Abbott. He then adds another single and an intentional walk as he helps the Orioles rally from a 6-0 deficit to beat the Yankees, 7-6, in 10 innings at Camden Yards. Chris Hoiles walks with the bases loaded and two out in the bottom of the 10th to score the game winner. Hammonds becomes the first player from the '92 June amateur draft to make the majors.

1997— Mike Mussina has a no-hitter through seven innings at Milwaukee before Jose Valentin opens the bottom of the eighth with a single. Mussina runs his record to 9-2 in the 9-1 win.

June 26

1970— Frank Robinson becomes only the seventh player in history to hit two grand slams in a game at RFK Stadium in Washington as he unloads on successive plate appearances off Joe Coleman, Jr. in the fifth and Joe Grzenda in the sixth in a 12-2 win.

1978— The Orioles absorb their worst pasting in history, losing at Toronto, 24-10. Rather than deplete his pitching staff, Earl Weaver brought in outfielder Larry Harlow and catcher Elrod Hendricks to pitch. Harlow worked ⅔ of an inning, giving up five runs, including a John Mayberry three-run homer. Harlow walked four and threw a wild pitch. Hendricks fared better, holding the Blue Jays scoreless for 2⅓ innings.

1993— In his first major league start, Jeffrey Hammonds doubles and hits a two-run homer off Neal Heaton to help the Orioles rally from a 5-2 deficit to a 12-10 win over the Yankees. Chris Hoiles becomes

Frank Robinson

the first Oriole to hit six homers in a week since Larry Sheets accomplished the feat in 1987. The Orioles won all six games. Bob Wickman, who brought an 8-0 record into the game, led 5-2 in the fifth, but the Orioles rallied behind 10 extra base hits, tying the club record.

1994— The Orioles complete their first-ever sweep at the Skydome and their first in Toronto since 1982, 7-1, as Mike Mussina ups his record to 11-4. Mark Eichhorn had earned two relief wins in the two previous games against his old mates.

1995— Jamie Moyer has a no-hitter through 5.2 innings at Milwaukee before it's broken up by a Jeff Cirillo single. The Orioles and Moyer win the game 2-0 as Jamie allows just two hits over seven innings.

June 27

1956— The Orioles lead the Indians, 9-1, after 3½ innings at Cleveland but lose, 12-11, in 11 innings. The loser is Hal Brown on Chico Carrasquel's 11th-inning single as the Orioles blow the largest lead in their history.

1961— Marvelous Marv Throneberry, who spent parts of the 1961 and 1962 seasons in Baltimore, hits two solo homers to lift the Birds to a 5-3 win over Kansas City.

1964— For the second time in his career, Boog Powell hits three home runs in a single game, the second time in as many years against the Senators at D.C. Stadium. His three homers account for all the Oriole runs in a 3-1 win.

1967— Frank Robinson slides hard into second base, trying to break up a double play and collides with Al Weis of the White Sox. Frank spent two days in the hospital with a concussion and double vision. After missing 28 days, Frank returned, but hit only .282 the rest of the season compared to .337 before the injury. Weis tore ligaments in his left knee and was out for the season.

1969— Dave McNally sets an Oriole pitching record with his 13th consecutive win, and 11th of the season, in a 4-1 win over Detroit.

1973— Dave McNally sets a club record with his 27th career shutout, scattering 10 Yankee hits in a 4-0 win.

1983— Ken Singleton hits his first homerun right-handed since August 24, 1981, off Shane Rawley, and the Birds lead the Yankees, 3-2, in the bottom of the ninth. But Steve Kemp ties it with a single off Tippy and Butch Wynegar wins it with an 11th-inning single off Tim Stoddard. The O's are out of first place for the first time since June 5.

1987— Lee Lacy's two-out, two-run double off Tiger reliever Willie Hernandez lifts the Orioles from a 2-1 deficit to a 4-2 win at Tiger Stadium.

1989— The Orioles match their top run output of the year by crushing Toronto, 16-6, at Memorial Stadium. The O's take advantage of a club-record tying 15 walks and Randy Milligan's best day in the majors. The "Moose" homered, doubled twice, singled and walked, driving in four runs and scoring four. Jay Tibbs pitches the Orioles first complete game since April, beating former Oriole Cy Young winner, Mike Flanagan. It's his first complete game in 40 starts.

1990— Chris Hoiles hits his first major league homer against the Indians, a game-winning three-run shot in the 10th inning off Sergio Valdez to give the Orioles a 6-3 win.

1993— Rookie John O'Donoghue suffers a 9-5 setback in his debut against the Yankees and is optioned to Rochester the next day. He and his father, John Sr., become the third set of father's and son's to have played for the Birds, joining Bob and Terry Kennedy and Don and Damon Buford.

1994— Playing their first game in the Indians' new ballpark, the Orioles win a 7-6 thriller as Jeff Tackett's first home run of the year snaps a 6-6 tie in the eighth. Lee Smith mows down the side in the ninth for his 26th save.

June 28

1987— Just a day after earning his first American League win, 4-2, over Frank Tanana and the Tigers, Tom Niedenfuer allows three consecutive ninth inning solo homers to John Grubb, Matt Nokes and Bill Madlock as the Tigers overcome a 7-4 deficit to win 8-7 in 11 innings.

1989— The Orioles beat Toronto, 2-1, and open a 7½ game lead over the rest of the A.L. East, their biggest lead since the pennant winning 1983 season. Cal Ripken accounts for both runs, going 3-for-4 with a single, RBI double and game winning eighth inning homer. A crowd of 35,757 attend the Wednesday night game including a walk-up of 12,802.

1996— Arthur Rhodes beats the Yankees, 7-4, to run his record to 9-0, the second best start in Orioles history behind Dave McNally's 15-0 start in 1969.

Lee Smith

June 29

1994— The Orioles rebound from a 9-8 loss the day before as Chris Sabo delivers a game winning single in the 10th. The Birds win it, 7-6, at Cleveland as Mark Eichhorn pitches 4.2 innings of shutout relief and Lee Smith saves it in the 10th.

June 30

1987— The Orioles lose at Boston, 14-3, to complete a 5-23 month, the worst in club history. They lost 10 straight and 15 of 16 at one point. The 10 straight losses are the most since 1958 when they dropped 11 in a row.

1990— Bob Milacki hurls a three-hit shutout at Minnesota, beating future Oriole Scott Erickson, 6-0.

1992— Rookie catcher Jeff Tackett singles, doubles and homers to finish with five RBI in a 12-3 win over Milwaukee. It's the most RBI by an O's catcher since Dan Graham had six on July 21, 1980.

1993— Lefty Fernando Valenzuela becomes the only pitcher to shut out the World Champion Blue Jays during the regular season when he allows only six hits and no walks in a 6-0 win at Camden Yards.

1996— Mike Devereaux steals home on the front end of a double steal in a 9-1 win at New York. It was the first time an Oriole stole home since he did it on May 4, 1992.

1997— Mike Mussina beats the Phillies, 8-1, in Baltimore for his 100th career win. The victory gives Mussina a 100-43 career mark, the eighth fewest losses at 100 wins in history.

Mike Mussina

Mike Devereaux

JULY

July 1

1973— Eddie Murray signs his first professional contract with the Orioles after being selected in the June free agent draft.

1983— Todd Cruz, acquired the day before from Seattle, makes a spectacular Oriole debut with a career-high six RBI (three-run homer and three-run double) as the Orioles beat Detroit, 9-5, at Tiger Stadium.

1994— Eleven home runs, six by the Orioles, ties the major league record in the Orioles' season-high 14-7 rout of the Angels that launches a 10-game home stand with a bang. Mike Mussina ties Jim Palmer's club record by giving up five gopher balls.

July 2

1961— Jim Gentile hits his third grand slam of the season to beat Phil Regan and the Tigers, 6-3. With 17 RBI in his last six games and 27 in his last 14 outings, Diamond Jim led the league in RBI with 76. With 21 homers, he equalled his entire output of 1960.

1966— The Orioles sweep their second double-header in as many days, 6-5 and 3-2, over Minnesota. Russ Snyder's great diving catch of Bernie Allen's line drive ends the nightcap.

1970— Cleveland's Tony Horton becomes the first player to hit for the cycle at Memorial Stadium. Horton doubles in the first and triples in the fourth off starter Jim Hardin. Moe Drabowsky surrenders an RBI single to Horton in the seventh and in the ninth Horton completes the cycle with a solo homer over the left-field fence off Pete Richert. Despite Horton's heroics, the Orioles rally for three ninth inning runs to win, 10-9.

Eddie Murray

1975— Don Baylor hits three consecutive home runs at Detroit to lead the Orioles to a 13-5 rout over the Tigers. Baylor becomes the fifth O's player in history to hit three homers in a game. Coupled with the one he hit the night before in Boston, he had four in a row with a walk between the first and second.

1990— Stanford righthander Mike Mussina, the Orioles top choice in the recent June draft, signs his first pro contract.

1994— Is baseball a funny game? After 11 home runs the night before, only one run crosses the plate as the Angels win, 1-0. Ben McDonald, trying for his 11th victory, gives up just one run on four hits and has nothing to show for it.

1995— Armando Benitiez earns his first major league victory at Toronto when he pitches a shutout inning, striking out all three batters he faces in the Birds dramatic 9-7 come-from-behind win. Catcher Gregg Zaun, a nephew of former O's catcher Rick Dempsey, hits his first major league homer, a two-run shot off Toronto's Woody Williams.

July 3

1954— Vern Stephens hits the first inside-the-park homer at vast Memorial Stadium in a 5-3 win over Detroit. Bob Turley walked 11 batters in the nine-inning game. Whereas Stephens led the Birds in homers with the modest total of eight, Turley led the league in both strikeouts and walks.

1961— Milt Pappas blanks Jim Perry and the Indians, 5-0. Gus Triandos drives in three runs.

1965— Rookie Curt Blefary drives in four runs and goes 4-for-4 with two home runs in an 8-4 win over Cleveland.

1968— Tom Phoebus strikes out 12 White Sox and wins, 1-0, on Curt Motton's second-inning homer off Gary Peters.

1972— The Orioles win, 15-3, at Detroit with a club-record-tying 21 hits. The Birds score all their runs in the last four innings on 17 hits. They score six runs in the sixth, seven in the eighth, and two in the ninth after trailing, 2-0.

1973— In a scheduled twi-night doubleheader that took two days to complete, Jim Palmer makes his first relief appearance in more than four years and earns his first ever save as the Birds score six runs in the eighth to win, 9-7. The Brewers led the second game, 4-1, when the midnight curfew stopped play until the following day. The O's tied it with three runs in the eighth and won it, 6-4, on Elrod Hendricks' two-run homer in the tenth.

1974— Dave McNally, tossed out of the first game by umpire Hank Morganweck in the first inning after kicking his glove in the air in protest of two balks, is summoned in the ninth inning of the nightcap with one out and the bases loaded. Mac retires Carl Yastrzemski and Bernie Carbo to end the game. The Orioles swept both games at Fenway Park, 9-2 and 6-4.

Curt Blefary

1976— Mark "The Bird" Fidrych, the rage of the American League, beats the Orioles, 4-0, before over 51,000 fans at Tiger Stadium.

1982— Storm Davis makes his first major league start in Detroit and beats the Tigers, 8-3. At age 20, Davis is the youngest player in the majors.

1989— "Texas" Mike Smith, creamed for eight runs in the eighth inning in his big league debut three days before, hurls four scoreless innings and gains his first big league win in a 11-4 thumping of the Tigers.

1992— Mike Devereaux ties a club record with five hits in a 6-1 win at Minnesota. Mike Mussina ups his record to 9-3.

1994— The Orioles bounce back from a 1-0 loss the night before to blast the Angels, 10-3, as Cal Ripken delivers the club's only grand slam of the year. It comes off southpaw Brian Anderson. Chris Sabo matches a career high, scoring four runs.

1995— The Orioles beat the Twins, 9-4, at Camden Yards but Brady Anderson sees his consecutive steals streak end at 36 in a row as he's tossed out by Minnesota's Matt Walbeck. It's the first time Brady is thrown out since May 13, 1994 when he was also thrown out by Walbeck.

July 4

1932— For the second time in five weeks, Buzz Arlett hits four home runs in one game as the Birds beat Reading, 21-10, in the first game of a twin bill at Oriole Park. Arlett hit another home run, his fifth of the day, as the Orioles also won the second game, 9-8.

1934— In the first game of a doubleheader at Oriole Park, Art Jones of Albany pitches a no-hit game, beating the Orioles, 2-0. It is the only no-hitter ever pitched at Oriole Park, home of the International League Orioles from 1916 until it burned to the ground on July 4, 1944.

1944— Old Oriole Park, home of the International League Orioles for 28 years, is completely destroyed by fire. Nothing was saved, including valuable pictures and other mementos tracing Baltimore's baseball heritage. The pennant-bound Orioles were forced to move four blocks north to Baltimore Stadium, primarily used for football.

1962— Luis Aparicio's 2,000th hit is a homer as the Orioles beat Chicago, 7-3, at Comiskey Park.

Luis Aparicio

1971— Mike Cuellar notches his 10th straight win as he stops the Tigers on six hits, 3-2, with home run support from Boog Powell and Ellie Hendricks. Cuellar's record is a glittering 12-1.

1972— Ed Herrmann of the White Sox ties a major league record for catchers by participating in three double plays against the Orioles. Baltimore wins, 2-1, and moves into first place.

1977— In Mark "The Bird" Fidrych's first Baltimore appearance, a July 4th crowd of 45,339 watches the Orioles win, 6-4.

1986— Fred Lynn supplies the offensive fireworks with two homers and a double, driving in five runs in a 12-7 win in Minnesota.

1989— In their first game at the Skydome, the Orioles celebrate Independence Day by blanking the Blue Jays, 8-0. Dave Schmidt pitches six perfect innings before giving up a questionable bunt single to Tony Fernandez. The Orioles break it open with a five-run ninth.

1992— In the toughest loss of the season and longest game of the year, 15 innings, (4:40 to play) the Twins edge Baltimore, 3-2, before over 48,000 at the Metrodome. The Orioles tied the score 1-1 in the fifth, went ahead, 2-1, in the top of the 15th, but after Gregg Olson fanned the first two batters in the Twins' 15th, Chuck Knoblauch singled, as did Kirby Puckett. Kent Hrbek walked and Chili Davis hit a two-run single to win it.

1995— Cal Ripken scores two runs in a 6-3 loss to the Twins, becoming the Orioles all-time leader in runs scored, tying and passing Brooks Robinson with 1,233.

July 5

1961— Dick Hall, known more for his relief heroics, blanks the Senators, 2-0, on a four-hitter. Hall, striking out nine and walking none, has pitched 20⅔ scoreless innings against the Nats as the hot Birds win their 12th in the last 15.

1969— Cruising past Detroit, 9-3, the Orioles score four runs in the first and five in the eighth as Dave McNally wins his 14th straight.

1970— Jim Palmer tosses a three-hit shutout over the Tigers. Boog Powell drives in the only two runs of the game.

1982— Scott McGregor beats the Angels for the 12th straight time, 8-5, at Anaheim. Included in the streak is the 8-0 shutout in the fourth and deciding game of the 1979 playoffs.

1989— The Orioles reach the halfway mark with their best record since 1979 (47-34 and a 6½ game lead) by edging Toronto, 5-4. Gregg Olson saves his 13th game in 13 tries.

1997— Mike Mussina matches his career high and the Orioles club record by striking out 14 Tigers in Detroit. It's the fifth time that an Orioles pitcher strikes out 14 in a game, the second time for Mussina. Bob Turley, Connie Johnson and Mike Boddicker are the others.

1998— David Cone outduels Scott Erickson in a 1-0 Yankee win in New York. Brady Anderson sets a club record with four stolen bases.

Boog Powell

July 6

1954— The Indians score 11 runs in the first inning. Joe Coleman couldn't retire a batter, and the Tribe sends 16 men to the plate.

1966— Boog Powell drives in 11 runs against the Kansas City A's in a doubleheader in Baltimore. Boog hit a grand slam, two doubles, another homer, and a sacrifice fly, driving in four in the first game win, and seven in the extra-inning nightcap loss. Steve Barber wins his 10th straight in the 11-0 first-game victory.

1973— Enos Cabell's first major league homer, following a two-run blast by Merv Rettenmund, gives Dave McNally and the O's a 5-3 win over Oakland.

1992— Mike Devereaux's bases-loaded single in the 14th inning gives the Orioles a 4-3 win over the White Sox at Oriole Park. In his first at bat of the season, Rick Dempsey laid down a bunt and beat it out for his only hit of the season.

1993— Jamie Moyer, a non-roster invitee in the spring, shuts out Kansas City on four hits in a 8-0 win at Royals Stadium. It's his first shutout since June 3, 1988 with the Cubs. In a three-month span, between June 10 and September 12, Moyer wins more games than any lefty in the majors, going 12-3.

1996— Rookie pitcher Rocky Coppinger, who won his debut June 11 at Tiger Stadium, beats his boyhood idol Roger Clemens and the Red Sox, 4-3, becoming the first Oriole to win his first four major league decisions since Bill Dillman in 1967.

July 7

1961— Jim Gentile's pinch-hit grand slam gives the Orioles a 6-2 win over Kansas City. It is Gentile's fourth grand slam of the season, tying an American League record held by only seven others.

1964— Appearing in his eighth straight All-Star Game, Brooks Robinson triples home two runs in the sixth inning at Shea Stadium to tie the game, 3-3. The Nationals won, 7-4, to square the series at 17-17-1.

1970— Brooks Robinson's grand slam in the 10th off Lindy McDaniel gives the Orioles a 6-2 win over the Yankees at Memorial Stadium.

1973— The year's best crowd at Memorial Stadium, 42,180, sees the Birds pull off a triple play in a losing cause against Oakland. Gene Tenace hit into an around-the-horn triple play, from Roblnson to Grich to Cabell. The A's win, 5-4.

1995— Veteran righthander Scott Erickson is acquired from the Twins in exchange for pitcher Scott Klingenbeck and a player to be named later (Kimera Bartee).

1998— After suffering through an awful first half of the season in which they posted a 38-50 record, the Orioles sparkle in the 69th All-Star game. Game MVP Roberto Alomar, Cal Ripken and Rafael Palmeiro combine for six hits, four RBI and four runs scored as the American League hammers the National League in Denver, 13-8. Ripken's two-run double opened the scoring for the American League. Alomar added three hits including a solo homer, stole a base and scored twice while Palmeiro, a last minute replacement for Mo Vaughn, went 2-for-2 including an RBI single during the three-run ninth. The six hits were the most by teammates in an All-Star game since Cincinnati had seven in 1976. Alomar followed his brother Sandy as MVP and joined Brooks Robinson, Frank Robinson and Ripken as Oriole All-Star MVP's.

Brooks Robinson and Frank Robinson

July 8

1958— In the first All-Star Game played in Baltimore, the American League edges the Nationals, 4-3, and the pitchers steal the show. The American League attack consists of nine singles; the National League could muster only four singles. A crowd of 48,829 watches home-town favorite Billy O'Dell cop MVP honors by retiring nine straight batters on just 27 pitches.

1969— The Orioles score 10 runs in the fourth inning of the first game of a twin bill with New York, winning, 10-3. The Birds had nine hits in the inning, including seven straight. Mike Cuellar pitched a perfect game in the nightcap, except for Ron Woods, who collected all three Yankee hits on a homer and two singles and was the only Yankee to reach base. He hit .183 for the year.

1970— The Yankees were one strike away from an 8-7 victory. Loading the bases on no outs, Lindy McDaniel struck out two batters and had an 0-2 count on Don Buford. Buford singled to right, scoring two runs and winning the game, 9-8.

1971— Frank Robinson records his 2,500th hit, a three-run homer off Washington's Horacio Pina, as Mike Cuellar goes the distance to notch his 11th straight win and 13th of the season in 14 decisions.

1980— Steve Stone, picked by manager Earl Weaver to start for the American League in the All-Star Game at Dodger Stadium, retires all nine National League batters he faces in his three-inning stint, the first time that had been done since Denny McLain did it in the 1966 mid-season classic in St. Louis. Steve also fanned three, including Dave Parker and Dave Kingman.

1990— The Orioles play their final game at historic Comiskey Park in Chicago and win it, 6-4, on Mike Devereaux' two-out, two-run double in the 11th off ace reliever Bobby Thigpen. The Orioles were 127-146 lifetime at old Comiskey.

1997— The Orioles have four representatives, Roberto Alomar, Cal Ripken, Brady Anderson and Randy Myers in the All-Star Game in Cleveland. Jimmy Key would have made five but he declined Joe Torre's invitation because he was getting married. Alomar, Ripken and Anderson started with Ripken at third after 14 years at shortstop. Brady was elected to start and played the entire game going 2-for-4. Cal went 1-for-2 as the American League won, 3-1, on Sandy Alomar's seventh inning homer.

July 9

1954— Cal Abrams hits three doubles to pace the Orioles over Detroit, 7-5.

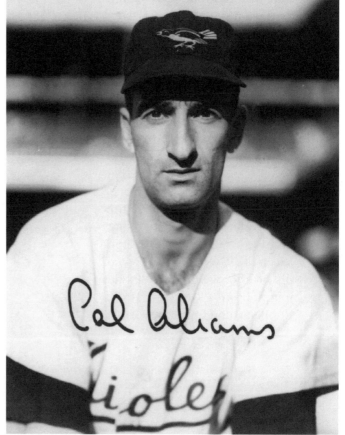

Cal Abrams

1959— After hitting .331 at Vancouver in 42 games, Brooks Robinson returns from the minors to stay. Milt Pappas and Jerry Walker blank Washington in a doubleheader, and Gus Triandos hit his 21st homer.

1961— Steve Barber's club-record fourth shutout, 8-0, over Kansas City, is the fourth shutout for the Birds in the past eight games.

1964— The Orioles sweep their sixth twin bill of the year, 4-3, and, 2-1, over the Indians, to move 3½ games in front of New York and 44½ in front of Cleveland. Boog Powell hit two homers in the opener and drives in all four runs. Sam Bowens' ninth-inning homer wins the second game against Sam McDowell as the Birds run their record in one-run games to 21-2.

1967— Brooks Robinson hits his 142nd homer to match Gus Triandos' club record. It was the margin of difference in a 2-1 win over the Yankees.

1971— Jim Palmer wins his 11th as the Orioles move four games in front in the east with a 4-1 win over Cleveland.

1976— Umpire Ron Luciano calls a press conference to apologize to O's skipper, Earl Weaver, for comments attributed to Luciano in a Chicago paper. The paper quoted Luciano as saying "I don't care who wins, as long as it's not Earl Weaver." That night in Anaheim, Weaver was ejected in the fifth inning of a 4-3 win over the Angels, by Bill Haller, not Luciano. The following day, Weaver was tossed out of the game in the third inning by Haller.

1989— The Orioles lose to Milwaukee, 7-2, but become one of just six teams to be in first place at the All-Star break after a last place finish the year before. The Orioles 48-37 record is an improvement of 21 games from the break a year ago, the greatest improvement ever by one team from one All-Star break to another.

1991— Cal Ripken becomes the fourth Oriole to win All-Star MVP honors by going 2-for-3 with a three-run homer off former teammate Dennis Martinez as the American League wins the 62nd All-Star Game, 4-2, at Toronto's Skydome. Cal becomes the first American League shortstop to start in an All-Star game eight years, surpassing Joe Cronin who started seven times for the Red Sox and Senators. In the home run hitting contest the day before, Cal incredibly hit 12 homers in 22 swings to lead the AL to a 20-7 pasting of the NL.

1992— Arthur Rhodes wins his first big league game, shutting down the World Champion Twins through 7.1 innings and winning, 4-2. The Orioles tied an American League record in the bottom of the first when newly named All-Star Brady Anderson and Mike Devereaux led off with back-to-back homers off Twins starter Scott Erickson.

1993— Down, 3-0, to the White Sox in the third, the Orioles score 14 runs from the sixth through the eighth inning and romp, 15-6.

1994— Jeffrey Hammonds homers into the left field seats leading off the bottom of the ninth to produce the Orioles' first "sudden death" win of the year, 8-7, over Oakland, as the Birds battle back from a 7-2 deficit to tie the game on Harold Baines seventh-inning single.

1995— Waivers are requested on pitcher Sid Fernandez for the purpose of giving him his unconditional release. In 26 starts Fernandez posted a 6-10 record with a 5.59 ERA.

1996— The Orioles have three starters in the All-Star game for the first time since 1972. Cal Ripken was named a starter for the 13th straight year while Robbie Alomar started at second for the seventh straight year. Brady Anderson started in right field for the injured Ken Griffey, Jr. The National League blanked the Americans, 6-0, at Veterans Stadium in Philadelphia.

1998— Losers of three straight and 11 of 12 before the All-Star break, the Orioles begin the second half with a 3-2 win over Boston at Camden Yards. Cal Ripken's looping two-out, two-strike single off reliever Jim Corsi in the eighth inning breaks a 2-2 tie and sends the crowd of over 48,000 home smiling. Red Sox skipper Jimy Williams had walked B.J. Surhoff intentionally to get to Ripken, who had been in a 6-for-38 skid. All-Star MVP Robbie Alomar led off the Oriole first by homering.

July 10

1960— Against Washington, Brooks Robinson collects hits his last three times up to begin a string of eight consecutive base hits.

1971— Dave Leonhard, in his first appearance after being recalled from Rochester four days earlier, pitches 8⅓ innings of one-hit ball in relief to beat Cleveland, 11-3. The only hit is a ninth-inning single by Chris Chambliss.

1973— Lee Stanton hits three home runs for the Angels at Memorial Stadium in a wild 10-8 California victory. His third homer, a two-run shot in the 10th, won the game after the Birds had scored five in the bottom of the ninth to tie it.

1983— Mike Boddicker pitches a five-hit, eight-strikeout shutout win over Seattle rookie Matt Young, who gives up only two hits and loses on two unearned runs. Another rookie, the Birds' Mike Young, is credited with his first major league game-winning RBI with a sac fly in the seventh. Boddicker's gem begins a six-game winning streak.

1984— Cal Ripken becomes the Orioles first All-Star starter since Ken Singleton in 1981 and is joined by Eddie Murray and Mike Boddicker at the game at Candlestick Park in San Francisco. Oriole manager Joe Altobelli manages the American League team and Cal Ripken Sr. serves as a coach. A record 21 batters struck out in the game, won by the National League, 3-1.

1987— Fred Lynn hits a pair of three-run homers off Bert Blyleven in a 13-12 win over the Twins at Memorial Stadium.

1990— Shortstop Cal Ripken and relief pitcher Gregg Olson represent the Orioles at the 61st All-Star game at Wrigley Field in Chicago. Cal batted fourth and went 0-for-2 before leaving in the sixth inning. Olson, the youngest Oriole All-Star since 22-year-old Chuck Estrada in 1960, didn't pitch in the 2-0 American League win. It is Cal's seventh straight All-Star start, two more than Brooks Robinson's five straight.

1993— Cal Ripken singles off Chicago's Wilson Alvarez for his 2,000th major league hit. Fernando Valenzuela and the Orioles blank the Chisox, 6-0, at Camden Yards. Fernando extends his string of scoreless innings to 24.2, the longest streak by an Oriole starter since 1978 when Jim Palmer (29) and Dennis Martinez (25.1) both had streaks.

1994— The Orioles, leading, 4-3, and just three outs away from first place at the All-Star break, are stunned by a Mark McGwire, two-run, ninth-inning homer off Lee Smith that results in a 5-4 loss to the

Athletics. Jamie Moyer had retired the last 17 batters he had faced, but for the fourth time, his lead and his win vanished after his departure.

1998— Subbing for the injured Harold Baines, Eric Davis homers off Red Sox ace Pedro Martinez with two down in the eighth to lift the Orioles to 3-2 win before over 48,000 at Camden Yards. Davis' 12th homer allows the Orioles to win consecutive games for the first time since June 19-20. Martinez hadn't lost since June 5 and had gone 7-0 on the road until tonight. Rookie Sidney Ponson pitches 6⅔ strong innings before Mo Vaughn homers in the seventh.

July 11

1967— In the longest ever All-Star Game, Brooks Robinson supplies the only American League run, a sixth-inning homer off Ferguson Jenkins at Anaheim Stadium. Tony Perez' 15th-inning homer off Catfish Hunter gives the National League a 2-1 win.

1968— With the Orioles floundering in third place, 10½ games out of first place, first base coach Earl Weaver replaces Hank Bauer as manager. Weaver immediately installs Don Buford as his lead-off man and left fielder. The Orioles go 48-34 the rest of the way to finish second to Detroit with a 91-71 record. In Earl's debut, the Orioles blank Washington, 2-0. It is the O's 10th win without a loss to the Senators.

1971— The Orioles reach the All-Star break with a 5½ game lead in the east, beating Cleveland, 7-1, as Pat Dobson wins his 10th. Brooks Robinson's bases-loaded triple is the key blow.

1975— Mike Torrez pitches a four-hitter and gains his first shutout as an Oriole as the Birds beat Vida Blue and the A's, 4-0.

1977— On All-America City night, a crowd of 42,605 watches the Yankees carry a 3-1 lead into the seventh. But Pat Kelly and Eddie Murray drive in runs to tie it, and after Al Bumbry triples in the ninth, Murray hits a one-out single off Dick Tidrow to win, 4-3. The O's had taken three of four with New York and drawn a record 154,835.

1985— Fred Lynn does it again. Lynn's two-out, three-run homer off Chicago's Mike Stanton in the bottom of the ninth caps a four-run rally and gives the Orioles a 7-6 win over the White Sox. It was Lynn's sixth ninth-inning homer of the year and his third sudden death game winner.

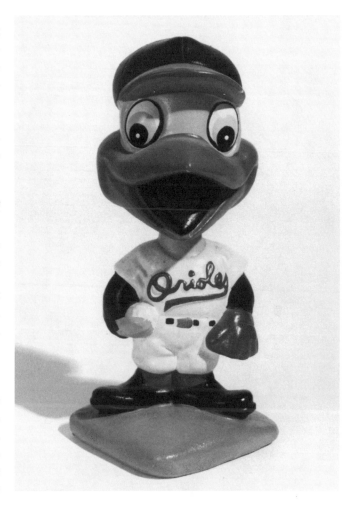

1987— For the first time in major league history two sons play for a team managed by their father as Bill Ripken makes his big league debut at second base, joining brother Cal and father Cal Sr. The Orioles lost that game, 2-1, to the Twins but went on to win their next 11 with the two Ripkens starting at the keystone combination for their father. It marked the first time three members of the same family have worn the same uniform in regular season play since Felipe, Matty and Jesus Alou were teammates on the 1963 Giants.

1988— Shortstop Cal Ripken is the lone Oriole representative at the All-Star game in Cincinnati. The American League wins, 2-1, as Cal plays 8½ innings going 0-3 with a walk.

1989— Cal Ripken, starting for the sixth straight year, joins Mickey Tettleton as the Oriole representatives in the 60th All-Star game at Anaheim. Ripken goes 1-for-3 while Tettleton strikes out in his only appearance but the American League wins, 5-3.

1995— Cal Ripken extends his American League record for shortstops with his 13th All-Star appearance, all consecutive. Cal, the O's lone All-Star representative, went 2-for-3 in the 3-2 loss to the National League at the Ballpark at Arlington.

1998— Scott Erickson pitches 8⅔ innings of four-hit baseball and the Orioles notch their third straight one-run win over the Red Sox, 2-1, at Camden Yards. Jesse Orosco needs only one pitch to coax Mo Vaughn into a ninth-inning ground out to end it as the Orioles beat 10-game winner Tim Wakefield.

The Ripkens—Billy, Cal Sr., and Cal Jr.

July 12

1966— Brooks Robinson, who played in 18 All-Star Games, is named All-Star MVP on a blistering hot day in St. Louis. Brooks had three hits, including a home run, and handled eight chances in the field, but the American League lost, 2-1.

1984— Storm Davis begins a streak of six straight wins, four of them complete games, by beating the White Sox, 2-1.

1987— Righthander Dave Schmidt pitches a two-hitter, blanking the Twins, 5-0, at Memorial Stadium and facing only one batter over the minimum.

1993— The scene is Camden Yards and the power hitters from both leagues put on a dazzling longball display in the All-Star home run hitting contest. Texas' Juan Gonzales was the winner, crushing several of the longest balls ever hit at Camden Yards including a ball off the facing of the third deck in left field. Ken Griffey, Jr. becomes the first player to hit the B&O Warehouse.

1994— Cal Ripken plays the entire game at shortstop, going 1 for 5, but Lee Smith blows the save opportunity as the National League rallies from a two-run ninth-inning deficit to beat the American League, 8-7, in Pittsburgh in the 65th All-Star Game. The win snaps a six-game NL losing streak. A Fred McGriff homer off Smith in the ninth forced extra innings and Moises Alou's double scored Tony Gwynn with the game winner in the 10th. It was Ripken's 12th straight All-Star performance.

1998— A pair of four-run innings and some solid relief work by lefty Doug Johns carry the Orioles to an 11-7 win over the Red Sox and a sweep of the four-game series. It's the first four-game sweep of the Red Sox in 18 years and the first in Baltimore since 1961. Eric Davis' 10th career grand slam keys the victory.

July 13

1962— Charley Lau ties a major league record and sets a club mark with four doubles to lead the Orioles to a 10-3 win over Cleveland.

1968— Tom Phoebus is the winner, 3-1, as the Orioles beat the Senators for the 12th straight time without a loss.

1969— Dave McNally wins his 13th of the season without a loss and 15th straight over two seasons, 6-3, over Boston.

1971— Earl Weaver manages the American League to its first All-Star win since 1962 and last until 1983. The final is 6-4 A's as Frank Robinson hit a two-run homer off Dock Ellis in the third inning that put the American League in front to stay. Frank is named the game's Most Valuable Player.

1974— Mike Cuellar out-pitches Wilbur Wood and the White Sox, 2-1

1983— Cal Ripken's grand slam in the fourth helps the O's beat the A's, 6-2, and complete a three-game sweep of Oakland.

1985— Gary Roenicke hits two homers, one a grand slam, and drives in six as the Orioles make up a 9-0 deficit with eight runs but fall short, 10-8, to the White Sox.

1989— Angel pitcher Bert Blyleven becomes only the 12th pitcher in 36 years to post 20 lifetime wins against the Orioles, winning, 13-5, in Baltimore. Blyleven also notches his 3,500th strikeout. Phil Bradley's string of seven straight hits is snapped but he's 14 for his last 19.

1990— On the disabled list since June 18 with a sore back and wrist surgery, Phil Bradley returns as a pinch hitter and belts an eighth-inning grand slam on his first swing against Minnesota's John Candlearia. It is the O's first pinch-hit slam since Ken Singleton did it in September, 1984 at Seattle. It is also Bradley's first major league pinch hit after going 0-for-12. The Orioles win, 8-5. The next day Bradley's 11th inning pinch single scores the game winner in a 3-2 Oriole win over the Twins in Baltimore.

1990— In the second game of a doubleheader, Dave Johnson retires 27 of the last 29 batters he faces in a complete game effort but loses, 3-1, to the Twins. John Moses' two-run first inning homer is the difference as Johnson throws 33 pitches in the first inning and only 83 over the last eight innings.

1991— The Orioles tie a Major League record for most pitchers used in a no-hitter, four, as they beat the Athletics in Oakland, 2-0, the Orioles' first no-hitter since Jim Palmer's gem against Oakland in 1969. Bob Milacki, Mike Flanagan, Mark Williamson and Gregg Olson combine for only the second four-pitcher no-hitter in major league history. The other was by Oakland in 1975 with Vida Blue, Glen Abbott, Paul Lindblad and Rollie Fingers sharing the honors. Milacki started for the O's but left after six innings when he was struck on the right hand by a ball hit by Willie Wilson. Flanagan, Williamson and Olson each worked an inning. It was the fifth no-hitter in club history and the first on the road.

1992— Cal Ripken is named the 22nd recipient of the Roberto Clemente Award, presented annually to the player who best exemplifies the game of baseball both on and off the field. Consideration is given to sportsmanship, community involvement and the player's contribution to his team and baseball. Ripken joins Brooks Robinson and Ken Singleton as Oriole winners.

1993— Baltimore hosts the All-Star Game for just the second time ever and first time in 35 years as a Camden Yards crowd of 48,147 watches the American League trounce the Nationals, 9-3, for their sixth straight win. The game climaxes baseball's first ever "All-Star Week" with the Fan Fest drawing over 111,000 visitors for the week and generating over $31 million. Cal Ripken is the only Oriole to play in the game, failing to get a hit in three trips, but getting a deafening ovation when introduced before the game. Mike Mussina warmed up in the ninth inning but failed to get into the game as manager Cito Gaston drew the wrath of the partisan Baltimore fans.

1995— Arthur Rhodes makes his first major league relief appearance after 59 big league starts. He doesn't get the decision in the Orioles' 9-8 loss to Kansas City but records a career-high 10 strikeouts in 7.1 innings pitched.

1998— The Orioles win their fifth in a row since the All-Star break, blanking the Blue Jays at Camden Yards, 5-0, behind a brilliant performance by rookie starter Nerio Rodriguez who took a perfect game into the sixth inning. Tony Fernandez singled to open the Toronto sixth. Lenny Webster fueled the attack with a two-run single and a two-run homer.

July 14

1963 — Jerry Adair is hit in the face by a John Buzhardt pitch in the second game of a twin bill in Chicago. It took 18 stitches to close the wound to Adair's left cheek and upper lip. He also broke a bone in the sinus area. In the next inning, Buzhardt beaned Brooks Robinson, who stayed in the game. Buzhardt left the game just as he was due to bat. Nellie Fox singled home two runs in the bottom of the ninth to win for Chicago, 3-2.

1970 — Eight Orioles, including manager Earl Weaver, are represented in the All-Star Game in Cincinnati (Cuellar, Johnson, McNally, Palmer, Powell, Brooks and Frank). Brooks went 2-for-3, hit a triple scored a run, and drove in two others, but the Nationals prevailed, 5-4, in 12 innings.

1972 — Doyle Alexander pitches a two-hitter and shuts out the White Sox, 3-0, to complete a sweep of a Memorial Stadium doubleheader.

1974 — The Orioles have 13 base runners but just two hits against the combined pitching of Stan Bahnsen and Goose Gossage, who walks 10 Orioles, but the Orioles still manage to escape with a 3-1 win at Comiskey Park.

1983 — Scott McGregor throws an 86-pitch masterpiece to silence the Angels for the 14th time in his last 16 decisions against them. It is Scotty's sixth win in seven outings since May 28.

1987 — Terry Kennedy joins Ted Simmons as the only two catchers in baseball history to have started an All-Star game for both leagues (Terry also started for the NL in 1985). He also became just the second Oriole catcher to start (Gus Triandos started in '58 and '59). The National League wins, 2-0, in Oakland in 13 innings. Cal Ripken becomes the first American League shortstop to start in four straight mid-summer classics.

1989 — Phil Bradley singles his first two times up to make it 16-for-21 and Gregg Olson records his 15th save in 15 tries as the Orioles hold off the Angels, 6-4.

1992 — Cal Ripken, playing in his 10th All-Star game, singles home a run in the American League's four-run, seven-hit first inning that sparks a 13-6 American League win at San Diego. It is the American League's fifth straight All-Star win. Playing in his first All-Star game, Mike Mussina pitches one perfect inning while Brady Anderson goes 0-for-3 but plays six innings in left field.

Scott McGregor

1998 — The Orioles send nine batters to the plate in the first inning, highlighted by Chris Hoiles' grand slam, and never look back in bashing Toronto, 11-5. Rafael Palmeiro, B.J. Surhoff and Joe Carter also homer as the Orioles win their sixth straight game and complete an undefeated homestand. Surhoff's blast completes a 4-for-4 night that gives him 11 hits in his last 12 times at bat.

July 15

1960— Brooks Robinson goes 5-for-5, becoming the only Oriole to hit for the cycle (homer, triple, double and single), and drives in three runs in a 5-2 win over the White Sox.

1963— Gary Peters, on his way to the American League ERA title, pitches a one-hitter against the Orioles in Baltimore, winning, 4-0. The only hit is a third-inning single by O's pitcher Robin Roberts.

1968— The Orioles win their fifth straight under new manager Earl Weaver, as Dave McNally and Moe Drabowsky combine to stop the Yankees on five hits, 8-2. It's the O's fifth straight over the Yanks at Memorial Stadium.

1983— The Orioles pound California, 10-4, at Memorial Stadium. Eddie Murray has four hits and four RBI, Mike Boddicker goes the distance and the Birds win their sixth straight.

1985— For the first time since 1972, the Orioles have two starters in the All-Star game. Eddie Murray starts for the first time in six appearances and Cal Ripken is a starter for the second time in three appearances. The Nationals win, 6-1, at the Metrodome in Minnesota, for their 13th win in the last 14 All-Star games.

1986— Oriole reliever Don Aase is called upon to protect a one-run lead in the ninth inning with one out and runners on first and third in the 57th All-Star game. Aase gets Chris Brown to hit into a game ending double play as the Americn League hangs on to beat the Nationals, 3-2, at the Astrodome. It is just the American League's sixth win in the last 33 All-Star games.

1989— Mike Devereaux's dramatic two-run homer just inside the left-field foul pole caps off a four-run, ninth inning comeback as the Orioles rally to beat the Angels, 11-9, in front of 47,393 fans. The Birds scored eight runs over the final three innings for their 50th win in 88 games on the season. The Orioles were outhit 19-9 and never led until Devereaux's homer. The other key blow in the game is Joe Orsulak's pinch two-run triple in the seventh.

1991— Chito Martinez hits a two-run homer with two out in the ninth inning off American League saves leader Bryan Harvey giving the O's a 2-1 win at California.

1993— Cal Ripken hits his 278th homer as a shortstop, surpassing Hall of Famer Ernie Banks' previous record of 277. Cal connects off Minnesota's Scott Erickson in a 5-3 win over the Twins.

1996— Manny Alexander starts at shortstop in an 8-6 win against Toronto, becoming the first person other than Cal Ripken to start at shortstop for the Orioles since Lenn Sakata on June 30, 1982. Cal started at third for the first time since '82, after 2,216 consecutive starts at shortstop.

1998— The Orioles parlay a season high 19 hits into a 14-3 shellacking of the Rangers in Arlington for their seventh straight win. They break a 10-game road losing streak in the process. Six players had two RBI apiece as Rafael Palmeiro hits his 299th career homer in the fifth.

July 16

1958— Jack Harshman becomes the first Oriole pitcher to hit two home runs in one game, versus the White Sox at Memorial Stadium. Harshman, who began his career as a first baseman, hit six home runs in 1958, a club record for a pitcher.

1963— Boog Powell, Jim Gentile, Brooks Robinson and Bob Johnson hit homers as the Birds beat Detroit at Tiger Stadium. Brooks and Johnson hit back-to-backers in the ninth off Mickey Lolich. That gave the Birds 11 homers in four games at Tiger Stadium.

1968— Jim Hardin wins his fifth straight (upping his record to 11-5), and the O's win their seventh straight (six under Weaver), 4-2, over the White Sox.

1973— Left-hander Don Hood makes his big league debut, pitching four scoreless innings in relief to win, 7-5, over the A's in Oakland before 43,571 Family Night fans.

1976— In his last big offensive show as an Oriole, Brooks Robinson goes 3-for-3 off Nolan Ryan, including a two-run homer, as the O's edge the Angels, 5-4, at Memorial Stadium. It is Brooks' third and last homer of the year. Earlier, on April 27, Brooks had broken up a Ryan no-hitter with a seventh-inning RBI triple.

1987— Billy Ripken's first major league hit is a double off the left field fence in Kansas City. The drive off Charlie Liebrandt misses being a home run by about a foot. The Orioles win, 5-4. Three days later, also in Kansas City, Billy connects for his first major league home run, a three-run shot off Bud Black in a 5-1 Oriole win.

1989— Angel manager Doug Rader, still protesting Mike Devereaux' homer down the line the night before, is ejected before the game even starts for continuing to protest. Rader isn't around to see Mickey Tettleton's hit to right in the 11th that scores Cal Ripken from first and gives the O's a 3-2 win.

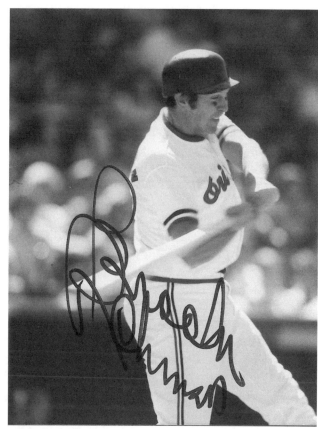
Brooks Robinson

1998— The sizzling Orioles win their eighth straight, 9-3, in Texas as Scott Erickson wins his 10th game. The Orioles send 10 batters to the plate in the third inning, scoring four runs, two on Lenny Webster's two-out double that gives Erickson a 4-1 lead.

July 17

1969— For the second straight game, Brooks Robinson accounts for the winning runs as he belts a two-out, two-run homer in the ninth off Stan Williams for a 3-2 win over Cleveland.

1975— Elrod Hendricks lofts a three-run homer into the right-field seats in the 12th inning to give the O's a 6-3 win over Bill Campbell and the Minnesota Twins.

1978— Doc Medich of the Rangers saves the life of a 61-year-old fan who suffered a heart attack just before the game. The man survived thanks to the heart massage Medich, a medical student, administered until help arrived. Medich had beaten the Orioles 11-1 two days before and, as one writer put it, he left Baltimore with "a win and a save."

1982— Twenty-year-old Storm Davis beats 43-year-old Gaylord Perry as the Birds defeat Seattle, 8-4.

1983— After Dennis Martinez had lost the night before to end the winning streak at six, Alan Ramirez pitches the Orioles to an 11-1 romp over the Angels. Jim Dwyer led the 16-hit attack with four hits and four RBI and Ramirez won his third without a loss.

1989— Pete Harnisch earns his first big league win with an 8-4 win over Seattle. It wasn't pretty as Harnisch pitches 8.1 innings, walking six and giving up eight hits.

1991— Sam Horn has a game he'd love to forget, striking out six times in an extra-inning game to tie a big league record. The Orioles blow a 7-0 lead and lose to Kansas City in 15 innings, 9-8.

1992— Mike Mussina dominates the Rangers in tossing his first career one-hitter in blanking Texas, 8-0. Kevin Reimer's fifth-inning double is the only hit Mussina allows as he strikes out 10. It's the 29th one-hitter in club history.

1995— Relief pitcher Mark Lee tosses one shutout inning to record the win in the Orioles, 3-2, 13-inning victory at Texas. It is his first major league win since September 16, 1991 with Milwaukee.

1996— Rocky Coppinger gets the win in an 11-10 thriller over Toronto, running his record to 5-0. It is Rocky's only relief appearance of the season. He joins Jerry Walker as the only two Orioles to win their first five major league decisions.

1997— Recently acquired outfielder Geronimo Berroa matches his career high with five RBI, including a three-run homer off Aaron Sele, in a 12-9 loss to Boston at Camden Yards.

1998— Rafael Palmeiro hits his 300th career home run at Anaheim in a 4-1 win over the Angels. Raffy now has hit 30 or more homers in each of the last four seasons and five of the last six.

July 18

1944— In the first night game played at Baltimore Stadium, where the Orioles were forced to move after Oriole Park was destroyed by fire, Stan West pitches a no-hitter for the Birds in defeating Jersey City, 5-0.

1955— Tiger pitcher Babe Birrer hits two home runs versus the Orioles as Detroit thumps Baltimore, 12-4.

1963— Stu Miller, who has either won or saved the Orioles' last eight wins, saves this one, 8-6, over Detroit.

1971— Brooks Robinson's grand slam (fifth of career) off John "Blue Moon" Odom propels the O's to a 7-3 win over Oakland.

1972— A Brooks Robinson single up the middle in the 15th inning scores Bobby Grich in a 2-1 win over Texas.

1975— Elrod Hendricks, the hero the day before with an extra-inning game-winning homer, hits a grand slam homer off Dave Goltz as the O's score eight runs in the fourth inning and win, 9-6, over the Twins. Lee May added a three-run homer in the same inning.

1989— Oriole Magic plays a big role in a 4-3 win over Seattle. With two out and Greg Briley on first in the eighth, Gregg Olson gives up a hit to left center by Darnell Coles. Briley scores the tie run but the ball bounces over the fence for a ground rule double, meaning Briley has to go back to third. Craig Worthington follows with a great play at third to nip the slow footed Dave Valle by a hair at first and the O's win to up their lead in the east to 7½ games.

1992— Ben McDonald follows Mike Mussina's one-hitter the day before with a two-hit performance in blanking the Rangers, 7-0. The Birds hold Texas to three hits in 18 innings. Leo Gomez hits his second three-run homer in four games and drives in a career high four runs.

July 19

1960— Umpire Bob Stewart rules that a Bud Daley pitch hit Walt Dropo to load the bases in the top of the 10th. Daley, the A's, and the fans contended the ball hit Dropo's bat. The Birds went on to score six runs. In the bottom of the 10th, a fan named Boyd Owens vaulted onto the field, sprinted to home plate, popped umpire Stewart on the side of the head and flattened an usher. Umpires Soar, Flaherty, and Hurley jumped into the melee, but Owens fought fiercely for another 10 minutes before police dragged him off to jail.

1971— Pat Dobson wins his ninth straight, 4-2, over Oakland, with home-run help from Paul Blair and Dave Johnson.

1973— Mark Belanger breaks up Nolan Ryan's bid for consecutive no-hitters with an eighth-inning single at Anaheim Stadium. The O's win 3-1 in 11 innings as Ryan goes 16 straight innings without allowing a hit. Mike Cuellar went the route, striking out 12.

1975— Paul Mitchell, pitching for the first time in Baltimore, gains his first win in the big leagues by edging Vida Blue and the A's, 3-2.

1994— Before the Kingdome gates open, a 25-pound ceiling tile, 32 inches by 48 inches, comes crashing down on the seats below forcing postponement of the game that night and the one the day after. No one is hurt in the incident. The Orioles leave Seattle playing just one game and losing, 7-5, on July 18.

1998— Angel pitcher Troy Percival walks four batters in the ninth inning to force home the go-ahead run and Cal Ripken follows with a two-run single to give the Orioles a 7-4 win in Anaheim. Eric Davis hits two home runs as the Orioles win their 10th in the last 11 games.

Pat Dobson

July 20

1966— Moe Drabowsky is brilliant in relief, retiring all 12 hitters he faces and fanning eight, including five straight, as the Orioles top the Tigers, 10-7. Boog Powell's two-run homer in the sixth, which cleared the hedge in dead center on one hop, put the Birds on top, 8-7.

1968— Dave McNally hits a two-run homer, his first hit of the season in 42 at bats, as the Orioles beat Detroit, 5-3.

1970— Elrod Hendricks cracks a grand-slam homer as the Orioles demolish Chicago, 14-5, at Comiskey Park.

1974— Trailing, 2-1, to the Angels in the ninth, Brooks Robinson ties the score with a hit, and Mark Belanger, using a 32-ounce bat, hits a three-run homer, his fifth of the season as the Birds win, 5-2.

1976— Reggie Jackson and Lee May hit back-to-back 450-foot homers off Larry Gura as the O's smash the Royals, 10-3, in Kansas City.

1983— Dan Ford comes off the disabled list and hits three home runs as the O's complete a three-game sweep of the Mariners with a 4-2 win at the Kingdome. Ford had missed over a month with an injured knee. The win put the O's back into a tie for first place.

1990— The Orioles acquire slugger Ron Kittle from the White Sox for outfielder Phil Bradley. They also beat the White Sox, 3-2, in 10 innings as Mark Williamson runs his record to 8-1. It was Williamson's seventh straight win, the most since Jim Palmer won 11 straight in 1982.

1991— Relief pitcher Jim Poole, claimed on waivers from Texas in May, strikes out six batters in 3.1 shutout innings at Seattle in his Orioles debut.

1993— Ben McDonald pitches the 30th one-hitter in Oriole history and the first of his career, blanking the Royals and David Cone, 7-0. Gary Gaetti's fourth-inning single is the only hit McDonald allows.

July 21

1935— Moe Drabowsky is born in Ozanna, Poland.

1954— Oriole pitcher Don Larsen hits two triples and a single, but loses, 6-5, to Camilo Pascual and the Senators on Jim Brideweiser's ninth inning error. Larsen finished with a 3-21 record in 1954.

1972— Boog Powell hits a homer off Bruce Dal Canton that clears the right-field fence at Kansas City's old Municipal Stadium and

Reggie Jackson

The Orioles come to Baltimore

The Baltimore Sun welcomes the Orioles

The first game

The first scorecard

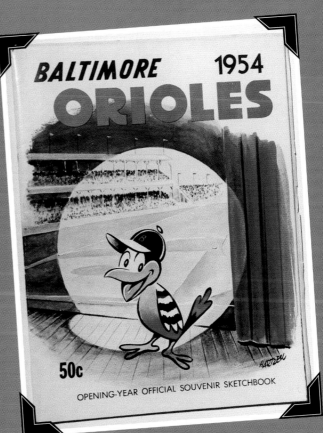

The first yearbook

All-Star Games in Baltimore

Photo by Rich Riggins

1958 at Memorial Stadium

Photo by Rich Riggins

1993 at Camden Yards

Brooks Robinson

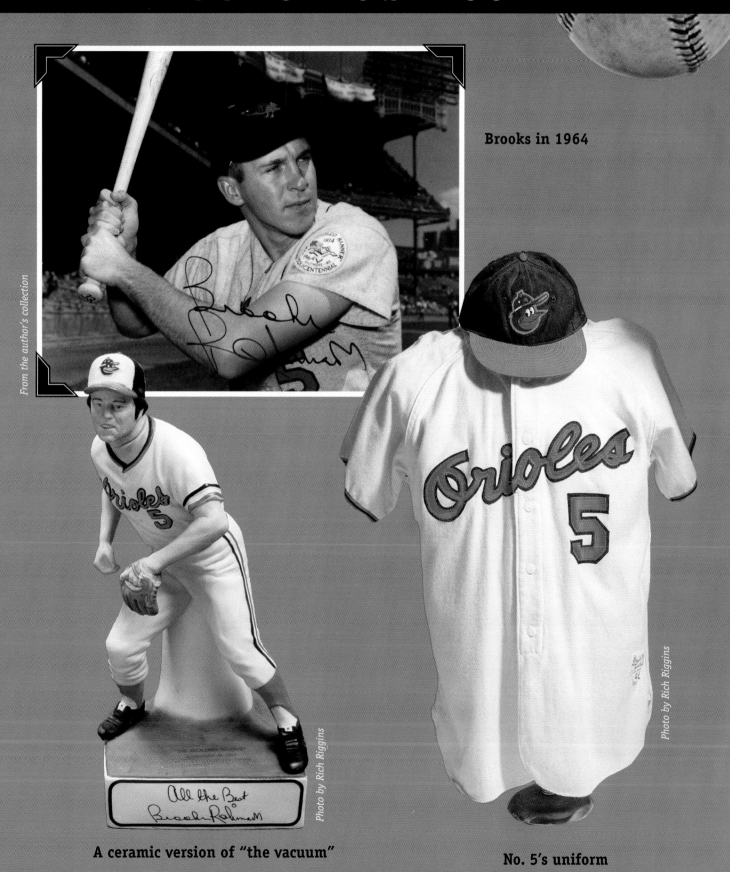

Brooks in 1964

From the author's collection

Photo by Rich Riggins

Photo by Rich Riggins

A ceramic version of "the vacuum"

No. 5's uniform

Frank Robinson

In addition to his playing career, Robinson managed the Orioles from 1988-91.

Frank Robinson was inducted into baseball's Hall of Fame in 1982.

Photo by Rich Riggins

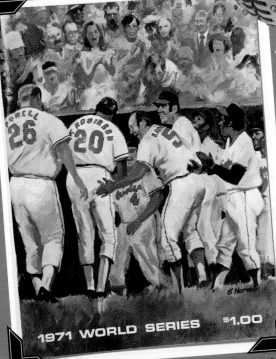

No. 20 was featured on the cover of the 1971 World Series program.

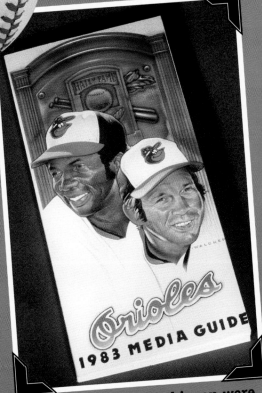

Frank and Brooks Robinson were coverboys for the Orioles' 1983 Media Guide.

Homes of the Orioles

From the author's collection

From 1954 to 1991, Baltimore's Memorial Stadium was the scene of many historic moments.

The Orioles' home since April 3, 1992.

From the author's collection

Oriole All-Stars

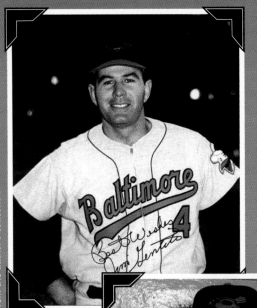

From the author's collection

"Diamond Jim" Gentile

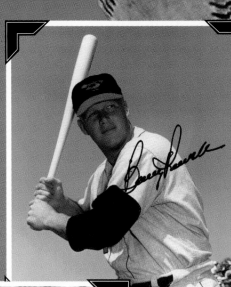

Boog Powell was selected as the Orioles' greatest first baseman in 1991.

Dave McNally posted four consecutive 20-win seasons.

From the author's collection (both photos)

Jim Palmer figured prominently in three Orioles' World Series championships.

Photo by Rich Riggins

Eddie Murray hit more home runs as an Oriole than any other Baltimore player.

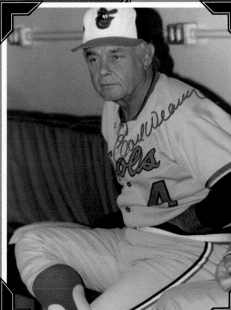

Earl Weaver directed Oriole teams to four American League Pennants.

Cal Ripken, Jr.

Ripken was a two-time American League MVP.

This collectible honored Baltimore's iron man.

Cal Ripken, Jr. eclipsed the seemingly unbreakable consecutive games record of Lou Gehrig.

Ripken was as wholesome as the product he endorsed.

Wheaties honored Cal for his record-breaking feat.

Baltimore's World Series Press Pins

1966

1969

1970

1979

1971

1983

lands on Brooklyn Ave. Only a handful of players accomplished the feat in 17 seasons of major league baseball there, and Boog's was the last. The Royals moved to Royals Stadium the next year.

1975— Lee May sparks the O's to their fifth win in six games, hitting his fifth homer in the last six games as the Birds top Oakland, 6-2.

1980— Spearheaded by Dan Graham's first career grand slam, the Orioles win the second game of a doubleheader in Minnesota, 12-5. Graham, a former Twin, wound up driving in 13 runs in the last three games of the series, all won by the Orioles.

1989— Arguably the toughest loss of the season. The O's rally with two in the eighth to lead Oakland, 2-1, as Bob Milacki gives way to relief ace Gregg Olson in the ninth. Olson walks four, throwing a wild pitch that ties the game as the A's come back to win, 3-2, on Rickey Henderson's game ending single off Mark Williamson. It's the eighth time Milacki has allowed two or fewer runs and been dealt a loss or no-decision.

1990— Ben McDonald, making his first big league start, pitches a four-hitter and blanks Jack McDowell and the White Sox, 2-0. Both went the distance with nobody on either side reaching base after the fourth inning. McDonald becomes the fourth Oriole to pitch a shutout in his first start, joining Charlie Beamon, Dave McNally and Tom Phoebus. McDonald becomes the first Oriole ever to win his first five major league starts and six major league decisions.

1993— Reliever Gregg Olson bats and strikes out against Billy Brewer in a 8-6 loss to the Royals. Olson is the first Bird hurler to bat in a regular season game since the designated hitter rule came into effect in 1973. The O's are the last team to have a pitcher bat after the DH rule.

1995— Utility infielder Bret Barberie collects a career high five RBI in a 10-6 win at Kansas City. Barberie connects for a grand slam off Melvin Bunch, the first grand slam of Bret's career.

Moe Drabowsky

1996— All-time Oriole great Eddie Murray, who left Baltimore on a sour note after the disastrous 1988 season, is reacquired in a deal with the Indians for pitcher Kent Mercker.

1998— The red hot Rafael Palmeiro hits his 30th homer and Scott Erickson goes the distance for a league leading seventh time in a 7-1 win over Oakland at Camden Yards. Before the game Oriole management announces they would keep the team intact for a possible wild-card stretch drive. Palmeiro, one of the players on the trading block, responds with a three-run homer. Eric Davis and Cal Ripken also homer.

July 22

1970— Chico Salmon's bunt single in the 13th scores Dave Johnson with the winning run as the Orioles chalk up their 19th straight over the Royals, 4-3.

1973— Brooks Robinson drives in five runs with three hits, including a homer, to key the Orioles over the Angels, 8-2, as Jim Palmer wins in Anaheim.

1987— Outfielder Ken Gerhart homers off Scott Nielson and Bob James at Comiskey Park to spark the Orioles to a 10-5 win over the White Sox. John Habyan allows only one base runner in the 6.2 innings he works, retiring the last 19 batters he faces.

1992— While the Orioles are in Chicago, Sam Hulett, the next-to-youngest of Tim and Linda Hulett's four sons, is struck by an automobile near his Baltimore area home and dies the following day. Sam was six years old.

1998— Rafael Palmeiro's homer off Mike Fetters with two outs in the bottom of the ninth inning lifts the resurgent Orioles to a 5-4 win over the Athletics. It's the Orioles ninth straight win at home and Palmeiro's 31st homer of the season.

July 23

1958— Trailing, 4-2, entering the ninth in Chicago, the Orioles score four times to win, 6-4. Bob Boyd supplies the big hit, putting him 48 for 120 (.400 pace) in his last 28 games.

1970— Jim Palmer wins his 14th and the Orioles win their 20th straight over Kansas City, 5-4.

1971— Pat Dobson, who came over from San Diego in a big offseason trade, wins his 10th straight and pitches his seventh consecutive complete game and ninth in his last 10 starts as the O's edge the Angels, 4-3. Pinch hitter Elrod Hendricks singled sharply past first with the bases loaded and none out in the ninth to win it.

1972— Don Baylor hits a two-run homer in the first and Terry Crowley hits a grand slam in the seventh as the Orioles beat Kansas City, 8-4.

1976— Reggie Jackson ties the American League record for home runs in consecutive games with his sixth in as many gannes. His roundtripper was not enough to beat the Brewers; Milwaukee won, 4-3, in Baltimore.

1990— Mike Devereaux' grand slam off Clay Parker in Detroit, helps propel the Orioles to a 13-3 win at Tiger Stadium. Devereaux had homered the previous two nights and capped it with six RBI on the 23rd. For his efforts Devereaux is named A.L. Player of the week.

1998— Lenny Webster's two-run ninth-inning homer off Mike Fetters caps a four-hit, six-RBI night and a 9-7 win over the Oakland A's to make it 13 wins in the last 14 games and a three-game sweep of the Athletics. The win evens the O's record at 51-51 as they reach the .500 mark for the first time since

Bob Boyd

May 15. Fetters had given up a ninth-inning game winning homer the night before to Rafael Palmeiro. Joe Carter, who contributed an RBI and scored the winning run on Webster's homer, was traded to the Giants after the game for minor league pitcher Darin Blood. Carter hit only .247 in his half-season in Baltimore. All 11 of his home runs were solo shots.

July 24

1964— Dave Vineyard makes his major league first victory a memorable one by throwing a two-hitter against Washington, 7-2. Vineyard had a no-hitter until Mike Brumley and Don Lock hit back-to-back doubles in the seventh.

1968— Don Buford opens the game with a triple and Boog Powell drives him in for the only run of the game as Dave McNally shuts out Cleveland on six hits.

1975— The Brewers hit five home runs, but the Orioles and Wayne Garland win, 10-7, at County Stadium. All the Milwaukee homers were solo shots. Tommy Davis got his 1,000th career RBI when he drove in two runs in the eighth.

1982— Floyd Rayford hits his first big league home run to beat Oakland and Bob Owchinko, 5-4, in 13 innings at Memorial Stadium.

1993— Harold Baines collects his 2,000th career hit, an infield single at Minnesota off future Oriole Scott Erickson, in a 9-2 Oriole win.

1994— In a heart-crusher in Oakland, the Orioles lead, 6-0, in the last of the seventh before Mark McGwire clouts a two-run homer off starter Jamie Moyer, who once again leaves with a lead only to see the opposition rally for a 7-6 win.

1998— And the beat goes on. The Orioles win their fifth in a row and 14 of 15 since the All-Star break, beating Seattle, 7-4, before 48,148 fans at Camden Yards. Rafael Palmeiro homers twice and unheralded rightfielder Rich Becker drives in four with a two-run homer and bases loaded double that is inches from being a grand slam. Palmeiro's second homer with one aboard travels 418 feet, becoming the 19th shot in Camden Yards history to land on Eutaw Street between the park and the B&O warehouse. Mike Mussina pitches 7⅔ solid innings as the O's pull to within seven of Boston in the wild-card race. The 14 of 15 is the Orioles best streak since taking 17 of 18 in 1982 when they nearly overtook Milwaukee.

July 25

1958— The Orioles score seven runs in the third inning (a season high) and beat the Kansas City Athletics. Gene Woodling hits a three-run homer and Gus Triandos a two-run blast in

Harold Baines

the big inning. Arnie Portocarrero, the O's first 15-game winner, wins his 10th. It is his sixth straight win and sixth straight complete game.

1969— Reliever Dick Hall pitches out of a tight jam in the eighth to preserve Dave McNally's 14th straight win (16 over a two-year span). The final is 4-2, Baltimore, the Orioles' 16th straight win over the White Sox.

1971— Dave Johnson hits an inside-the-park homer against the Angels, but the Orioles lose, 6-2, to Andy Messersmith at Memorial Stadium.

1977— Dave Criscione, a 25-year-old catcher who had bounced around the Texas Ranger organization for seven minor league seasons, hits an 11th-inning, sudden-death home run off Sam Hinds to give the Orioles a 4-3 win over Milwaukee. Criscione, called up when Rick Dempsey broke a bone in his hand, spent 34 days with the Orioles and went 3-for-9 with the one homer and run batted in. It was to be his lone experience in the major leagues.

1979— Seattle wins its first game ever at Memorial Stadium, snapping a string of 14 straight Mariners' losses in Baltimore.

1983— The Orioles lose to the Angels at Anaheim and fall into a four-way tie for first place with New York, Detroit and Toronto while Milwaukee sits 2½ back in fifth and Boston 5½ back in sixth place.

1996— Robbie Alomar homers from both sides of the plate in a 10-7 loss to Cleveland. It's the second time Alomar has homered from both sides. He did it in 1991 against the White Sox, while playing for the Blue Jays.

July 26
1959— Gene Woodling drives in all the Oriole runs and Milt Pappas throws his third shutout to snap the Birds' losing streak at six. Woodling singled home a run in the first, then hit a three-run homer in the sixth as the O's blanked Chicago, 4-0.

1969— Boog Powell's bases-loaded single drives in both runs as the Orioles nip Chicago, 2-1, at Memorial Stadium. Tom Phloebus raises his record to 10-3.

1970— The Orioles have 16 hits in an 11-1 win over the Twins. All but one are singles. The lone extra-base hit is a grand slam home run by Boog Powell that breaks the game wide open.

1973— Dave McNally is hit above the left ear by a line drive off the bat of Cleveland's Chris Chambliss. McNally suffered abrasions of

Robbie Alomar

the ear and a hairline fracture of the jaw, but missed just one start. The Orioles won the game, 8-4, on Bobby Grich's second career grand slam and Boog Powell's solo homer, his 1,000th career run batted in.

1975— Mike Cuellar pitches his second one-hitter of the season, 4-0, against Milwaukee. The lone hit is a single by George Scott leading off the eighth. It is Cuellar's fourth Oriole one-hitter.

1979— The O's conclude an 8-2 home stand with a 12-1 win over Seattle. Lee May hits his second grand slam of the season and 11th lifetime.

1980— Steve Stone wins his 14th straight game, one shy of Dave McNally's club record and longest in the league since Gaylord Perry's 15 straight in 1974, as the Birds top Milwaukee, 4-1.

1983— Dennis Martinez, jerked from the starting rotation 10 days before, allows only one run over the last six innings as the O's edge the Angels, 5-4. Eddie Murray hit a two-run homer in the fifth to break a 3-3 tie.

1991— Dwight Evans' pinch grand-slam homer helps erase a 9-3 deficit to the Athletics, who eventually win, 12-9. Rickey Henderson's streak of 25 straight steals against the Orioles is snapped by catcher Bob Melvin. Rick Dempsey had been the last O's catcher to nab Henderson in June, 1986.

1993— Fittingly, on an off-day, Kelly Ripken gives birth to the couple's second child, Ryan Calvin Ripken. The next day Cal hits a three-run homer in the eighth inning off Toronto's Duane Ward in a game won by the Blue Jays, 6-5.

July 27

1959— Gene Woodling drives in all five Oriole runs on his first ever grand slam and eighth-inning single as the Birds top Detroit.

1966— The Orioles increase their lead to 12½ games over second-place Detroit with a 7-1 win over Cleveland. Larry Haney homered in his second major league at bat with one on in the second.

1969— The Orioles set a club record for margin of victory, shutting out Chicago, 17-0, at Memorial Stadium. The total base count of 39 also set a club mark.

1971— Pat Dobson strikes out 13 A's and wins his 11th straight, 1-0. Brooks Robinson's dramatic two-out, two-run homer in the ninth completed the sweep, 6-4. Brooks connected off Rollie Fingers.

1973— Jim Palmer fires a one-hitter and beats Cleveland, 9-0. George Hendrick spoiled Palmer's bid for a second no-hitter.

1975— In one of the most stirring comebacks in club history the Orioles score six runs in the ninth inning to tie the game, and five in the 10th to beat the Brewers, 11-6, in Milwaukee. The Birds scored the six runs in the ninth inning before a batter was retired, the big blow a three-run homer by Al Bumbry. In the 10th, Tommy Davis hit a grand-slam home run. Davis got his 2,000th career hit in the first game win, 7-4.

1976— Slugger Reggie Jackson is struck in the face by a pitch from Dock Ellis at Memorial Stadium. The incident happened in the eighth inning; in the top of the ninth, Jim Palmer hit Mickey Rivers in the back with a pitch. Reggie suffered no broken bones, but missed several games. He homered on his first at bat upon returning to the lineup July 31 against Detroit.

1983— The O's break open a tight, 5-3, game with five runs, in the top of the ninth to beat the Angels, 10-4. Alan Ramirez won his fourth in five decisions, Cal Ripken had four hits and the Birds were alone in first place.

July 28

1960— Steve Barber throws a one-hitter, shutting out the Kansas City A's, 5-0, while striking out 10.

1961— Hal "Skinny" Brown throws a 4-0 masterpiece at the Yankees. Gus Triandos hit a two-run homer and Jackie Brandt connects for a solo shot, both off Bud Daley.

1962— Steve Barber pitches a 3-0 shutout over KC and is now 9-0 with five lifetime shutouts against the A's.

1968— The Orioles end a nine-game losing streak against Mickey Lolich by beating the Tigers, 5-1. It is the O's first win off Lolich since May 6, 1964.

1971— In a game Brooks Robinson would like to forget, the Hall of Famer has his worst day in the field as an Oriole, committing three errors, all in the fifth inning versus Oakland. Coupled with the fielding blunders, Brooks grounded into two double plays and fouled out to the catcher. Frank Robinsons's three-run homer in the bottom of the ninth off Rollie Fingers gave the Birds a 3-2 win. Frank connected on Fingers' first pitch.

1986— Don Aase breaks the Oriole club record with his 27th save in a 4-3 win at Texas. The record was 26 set by Tim Stoddard in 1980. Aase, named the Most Valuable Oriole for 1986, finished with 34 saves, the most ever by a pitcher on a last place team.

1988— Pitcher Oswald Peraza, the only Oriole to win three straight starts in '88, stops Julio Franco's 22-game hitting streak, longest in the American League in '88, with a 5-2 win at Cleveland in his lone complete game.

1989— The Orioles snap an eight-game losing streak by edging Kansas City, 4-3, in 13 innings. Once again Gregg Olson fails in relief as Jeff Ballard leaves with a 3-1 lead in the ninth. The Birds win it on Bob Boone's

Hal "Skinny" Brown

throwing error. He throws a perfect strike to second trying to nail Jim Traber but nobody is covering and the winning run scores.

1990— Cal Ripken sets a major league record for most consecutive errorless chances for a shortstop, 431, before making an error in Kansas City. The streak began on April 14 and breaks the mark of 383 set by Buddy Kerr of the New York Giants in 1946-47. In the process Cal also sets a major league record for errorless games by a shortstop, 95, breaking the record of 72 held by Eddie Brinkman of Detroit in 1972.

1994— Armando Benitez makes his major league debut a memorable one, entering the game against Cleveland in the seventh inning with two on and one out. Benitez strikes out Albert Belle and gets Eddie Murray to fly to left but the Tribe prevails, 7-2. Benitez would pitch 9.1 scoreless innings to begin his career during his two weeks with the club.

1995— The Orioles acquire slugging third baseman/outfielder Bobby Bonilla and pitcher Jimmy Williams from the Mets for highly touted outfield prospect Alex Ochoa and outfielder Damon Buford.

1998— Red hot Eric Davis, who a year earlier had undergone surgery for a cancerous tumor in his colon, hits a three-run homer as the Orioles overcome a five-run deficit to beat

Eric Davis

the Tigers, 6-5, in Detroit. Lenny Webster also homers as the Orioles run their record to 15-3 since the All-Star break. Davis has hit in 15 straight games with a .408 average, seven home runs and 25 RBI since the All-Star break.

July 29

1966— Jim Palmer shuts out the Twins, 3-0, as the top three American League RBI men each knock in a run. Brooks Robinson doubled in the fourth, Frank Robinson hit his ninth homer in 10 games in the seventh and Boog Powell drove in a run in the eighth. The O's took their biggest lead to date, 13½ games over the Tigers.

1972— Brooks Robinson belts a home run with two outs in the 11th and two strikes on him to beat Cleveland, 4-3.

1983— Eddie Murray's two-run single off Victor Cruz and a sacrifice fly by John Lowenstein, both in the three-run eighth inning, gives the O's a comebacking 8-6 win over the Rangers at Memorial Stadium.

1992— Arthur Rhodes tosses his second straight complete game and his first career shutout in blanking the Yankees, 6-0, at Yankee Stadium. Both Billy Ripken and Mike Devereaux homer. It's the Orioles first shutout in Yankee Stadium since Scott McGregor beat Tommy John, 1-0, on September 25, 1981.

1997— DH Harold Baines, who played for the Orioles from 1993-1995, returns to Baltimore via a trade with the White Sox for a player to be named (infielder Juan Bautista).

1998— Chris Hoiles hits a pair of two-run homers and drives in six runs and Cal Ripken hits his first triple in almost two years to highlight a 14-2 rout of the Tigers in Detroit. Brady Anderson homers and scores three runs as Mike Mussina runs his lifetime record to 13-2 against the Tigers.

July 30

1954— Bob Kennedy drives in six runs on a 3-for-3 day as Don Larsen wins his first game since May 30 after eight straight losses. The Orioles blank the Yankees, 10-0.

1961— At Yankee Stadium, the Orioles have their biggest day of the season by sweeping a pair from the Yankees. Steve Barber's fifth shutout notches the first game as Hank Foiles hits two home runs. In the second game, Milt Pappas led, 2-1, in the ninth when the Yanks loaded the bases with none out. With a 2-1 count on Clete Boyer, Dick Hall is summoned from the bullpen. Hall got Boyer on a disputed called third strike and got Hector Lopez to ground into a game-ending double play. Yankee manager Ralph Houk had come out of the dugout with fist cocked after Boyer was called out. The Major made token contact with umpire Ed Hurley and was suspended five days and fined $250.

1969— Dave McNally wins his 17th straight game, a 4-2 decision in Kansas City, and ties two American League marks in the process. McNally tied Johnny Allen of the 1937 Cleveland Indians for consecutive wins and most wins (15) to start a season.

1979— Steve Stone pitches perhaps the finest game of his life, a one-hit shutout for 8.2 innings at Milwaukee against one of the top-hitting clubs in baseball. His only mistake was a third-inning home run ball to Charlie Moore, but that was offset by Al Bumbry's two-run shot in the sixth off Jim Slaton. With two down and none on in the Brewer ninth, Stone walked Don Money. At that point, Earl Weaver summoned Tippy Martinez, who got Cecil Cooper on a routine fly ball to preserve the 2-1 victory.

1983— Trailing Texas again in the late innings, the O's rally for four runs in the seventh as Scott McGregor wins his 13th and fifth in a row with help from Tim Stoddard, who finished with two perfect innings. The final was Baltimore 7, Texas 4.

1984— Floyd Rayford becomes just the second catcher in Oriole history to start in the leadoff spot, and first since Curt Blefary in 1968, when he leads off in Texas.

1985— The Orioles snap Toronto's club record nine-game winning streak with a 10-inning, 4-3 win, capped by Lee Lacy's sacrifice fly.

Don Larsen

1988— The Orioles acquire outfielder Brady Anderson and pitcher Curt Schilling from Boston for pitcher Mike Boddicker, whose 79 wins rank ninth on the Oriole's all-time list.

1990— The brothers Stottlemyre, Mel Jr. and Todd, combine to shut out the Orioles for 10.2 innings over a two-day period (July 29-30). Mel, pitching for Kansas City, blanks the O's for six innings the first day in a game the Orioles score early and win, 4-1, and Todd for 4.2 innings the following evening as Toronto wins, 9-2.

1994— Harold Baines hits the longest home run ever by an Oriole at Oriole Park against Toronto's Todd Stottlemyre. The drive soars to a stop in the center field bleachers, 442 feet from home plate. It's the third longest ball hit at the three year old park, behind Eric Davis of Detroit who hit a 452-foot blast off Arthur Rhodes in 1993 and Juan Gonzales' 450 foot shot off Mike Mussina in '92. The Orioles win the game, 7-5.

1998— Eric Davis continues his offensive heroics as the Orioles complete a three-game sweep of the homestanding Detroit Tigers with a 6-4 victory. Davis' second homer of the game, a two-run shot in the seventh inning, snaps a 4-4 tie and helps the Birds collect their 17th win in 20 games since the All-Star break. Davis' third multi-homer game of the season extends his hitting streak to 17 games. He's hitting .423 since the break with nine homers and 28 RBIs.

July 31

1960— Brooks Robinson's first of six career grand-slam homers helps the Orioles to a 6-5 win over Gary Bell and the Indians.

1961— Facing Sandy Koufax of the Dodgers, Brooks Robinson delivers his first All-Star Game hit, a single at Fenway Park in a game called after nine innings because of rain, tied, 1-1.

1989— The globe circling Orioles who have gone from Baltimore to Oakland to Minnesota to Kansas City to Boston on this 15 day trip, lose in Boston for their 11th loss in the last 12 games. The Oriole lead is down to three games, still the biggest lead of all four major league divisions.

1994— Brady Anderson and the Blue Jays' Devon White deliver spectacular plays in center field but the biggest ovation of the day is reserved for Cal Ripken, who plays in his 1999th consecutive game. Since the Orioles would be on the road for number 2,000, the fans pay tribute today with an emotion filled ovation and stirring salute on the video board as he takes the field in the top of the fifth inning. Juan Guzman beats Ben McDonald, 6-4. Little did anyone know that they were watching the last home game of 1994.

1998— With the trade deadline looming at midnight, the Orioles make a move to bolster their starting staff, acquiring 31-year-old righthander Juan Guzman from the Toronto Blue Jays for rookie pitcher Nerio Rodriguez and 19-year-old outfield prospect Shannon Carter. Guzman was only 6-12 in 1998 but has a 76-62 lifetime record and has pitched in three Championship Series and two World Series with the Blue Jays in eight big league seasons.

AUGUST

August 1

1966— In a rare double play against Cleveland, center fielder Paul Blair makes a putout at second base. In the sixth inning, Chico Salmon hit a blooper to short center, with Blair and second baseman Dave Johnson in pursuit. Johnson caught the ball and threw to Blair who was still running toward the infield. Blair beats Rocky Colavito, who had been running to third, to the bag for the force out.

Paul Blair

1970— The Orioles beat the Kansas City Royals, 10-8, at Baltimore for their 23rd straight win over the Royals (over two years), a major league record for consecutive victories against one team. KC won the first game ever played between the two clubs (May 9, 1969), but the Orioles won the next 23. The streak ended April 30, 1971, when KC eked out a 5-4 victory.

1975— For the second time in less than a week, Tommy Davis hits a grand-slam home run as Jim Palmer beats the Brewers, 6-4.

1979— On the same day that Thurman Munson is killed in an Ohio air crash, Oriole board chairman Jerry Hoffberger announces the sale of the club to Washington attorney Edward Bennett Williams at a stadium press conference. Williams announces that, contrary to speculation, the Orioles would remain in Baltimore as long as the city supported the ball club.

1989— The 1989 season, filled with so many highs, hits rock bottom as the Birds drop two in Boston to go 1-12 on the road trip and 1-13 in their last 14 games. Baltimore native Dave Johnson, just up from Rochester, makes his first major league start in the second game and loses, 6-2. The once healthy division lead is down to one game.

1993— Popular all-time Oriole broadcaster Chuck Thompson is inducted into the broadcasting wing of the Hall of Fame in Cooperstown. Reggie Jackson, who spent the 1976 season in an Oriole uniform, is the lone player to be enshrined.

1994— The fans of Minnesota give Cal Ripken a warm salute when he comes to bat in the top of the first of his 2,000th consecutive game. Arthur Rhodes delivers the Orioles' first shutout of the year, winning, 1-0.

August 2

1989— Down, 6-0, in the sixth and well on their way to a 14th loss in 15 games, the Orioles score nine runs in the sixth, seventh and eighth and stun the Red Sox, 9-8. Randy Milligan's three-run homer ties it in the seventh and Cal Ripken's RBI double wins it in the eighth. The brothers Ripken combine for seven hits, four by Billy.

1991— The Orioles set a club record for most pitchers used in a shutout, five, in blanking the White Sox, 3-0, at Comiskey Park as Ben McDonald notches the win, with relief help from Mike Flanagan, Mark Williamson, Jim Poole and Gregg Olson.

1993— Rookie outfielder Jack Voigt doubles in the seventh and homers in the eighth to help turn a 5-3 deficit into a 7-5 win over Milwaukee at Camden Yards.

1994— After 102 games without a shutout the unpredictable Orioles toss their second in a row. This 10-0 whitewash in Minnesota is a collaborative effort by Mike Mussina, Mark Eichhorn and Alan Mills.

1995— Mike Mussina wins his eighth straight game over nine starts, a four-hit, 1-0 win over Toronto. The Orioles muster only one hit, a solo homer by Harold Baines off Paul Menhart. In the midst of the streak, Mike suffered through the shortest outing of his career but did not receive the decision in the 9-8 loss to Kansas City on July 13. Mussina allowed six runs in ⅔ of an inning.

Orioles broadcaster Chuck Thompson

August 3

1961— Hal Brown sets a club record of 32 consecutive scoreless innings with his third straight shutout as the Birds blank Minnesota, 3-0. Jack Fisher had set the record of 29⅓ the year before. Brown did not give up a run for 5½ weeks and walked only one batter in the process.

1966— Despite a record-tying five home runs, the Orioles lose to Cleveland, 9-6. Frank Robinson and Boog Powell each hit two homers, which was the first time two Orioles hit a pair of homers in the same game.

1969— Rich Reese's pinch hit grand slam in the seventh with two out gives Minnesota a 5-2 win and stops Dave McNally's 17-game winning streak (15 in 1969). In the streak, McNally pitched 189.2 innings and allowed only 55 earned runs with 10 complete games, five shutouts and a 2.62 ERA.

1979— On the day after Thurman Munson's death, Scott McGregor and Tippy Martinez combine to beat the Yankees, 1-0, in a game no one wanted to play. John Lowenstein's home run off Luis Tiant accounted for the only run of the game.

August 4

1955— Eddie Lopat celebrates his 37th birthday by winning his first start as an Oriole, 8-1, over Kansas City.

1961— Dave Philley ties the American League record for most pinch hits in a season, 20, set by Ed Coleman with the St. Louis Browns of 1936. Philley is now 20-for-48 with 17 RBI, six doubles and three walks as a pinch hitter.

1975— Don Baylor ties a club record by going 5-for-5 and scores four runs to tie another mark as the O's overcome a 6-1 Boston lead and win, 12-8, at Fenway Park.

1979— Trailing, 4-0, to Catfish Hunter and the Yankees through seven, the O's score five times in the eighth off Jim Kaat and Goose Gossage. Dave Ford wins in relief on three scoreless innings, 5-4, and Tippy again came on to save it, fanning Graig Nettles and Oscar Gamble to end it. The Birds go 40 games over the .500 mark and are 15-3 since the all-star break.

1989— Texas beats the Orioles, 6-4, as Charlie Hough wins his first game at Memorial Stadium in his sixth try. In the game Oriole leftfielder Phil Bradley equals a major league record and sets an American League mark by reaching base three times on errors. It's been accomplished just three times in major league history and just once in the last 53 years, by Jerry Grote of the Mets in 1975.

1991— Mike Mussina makes his major league pitching debut in Chicago against knuckleballing Charlie Hough and allows the only run of the game on Frank Thomas' sixth-inning homer. Mussina works 7.1 innings, giving up four hits.

1992— Rick Sutcliffe, winless in July at 0-5, wins for the first time in five weeks as the Orioles top Detroit, 6-3, for their fifth straight victory. It is Sutcliffe's 150th major league win.

1995— Former Cy Young winner Mike Flanagan, former pitching coach George Bamberger and broadcaster Chuck Thompson are the latest inductees into the Orioles Hall of Fame.

1996— Earl Weaver, who managed 17 seasons in Baltimore, finishing 17th on the all-time win list and fifth in winning percentage (.583), winning four pennants and one World Series, is inducted into the Baseball Hall of Fame in Cooperstown. Joining Earl are legendary Oriole from yesteryear, Ned Hanlon, former Negro League pitcher Bill Foster and Detroit and Phillie pitching great Jim Bunning.

Don Baylor

1998 — Mike Mussina loses his bid for a perfect game with two outs in the eighth inning and settles for a two-hitter, leading the Orioles past visiting Detroit, 4-0. Mussina retires the first 23 batters before rookie Frank Catalanotto lines a double into the right-field corner. Eric Davis homers to extend his hitting streak to a career high 21 games as the Orioles improve to 19-5 since the All-Star break.

August 5

1968 — Boog Powell and Brooks Robinson hit back-to-back homers leading off the 10th to beat the Yankees, 5-3.

1969 — Brooks Robinson unloads a two-run homer off Galen Cisco in the last of the 10th to give the Orioles a 7-5 win over Kansas City.

1975 — Jim Palmer shuts out the Red Sox, 3-0, on two hits. It's Palmer's seventh shutout to set a personal high and the 33rd of his career, tying Dave McNally for the most career shutouts by an O's pitcher.

1977 — Brooks Robinson bats for the 10,654th and last time in the majors at California.

1983 — Some 39,544 turn out on a rainy night to welcome Brooks Robinson back from Cooperstown. Those who stayed saw one of the most exciting finishes in the O's 30 Baltimore seasons. With two outs, none on in the ninth and the O's trailing the White Sox, 4-2, the uprising begins. Cal Ripken singles, and so does Eddie Murray. John Lowenstein's hit scores Ripken and then Ken Singleton ties it with a hit to left. Dick Tidrow relieves Dennis Lamp and serves up the game-winning single to Rich Dauer to win the same, 5-4. Five straight hits with two outs produced three runs and a victory. Oriole Magic at its finest.

1989 — Bob Milacki snaps a 16 game winless streak for the Oriole starters by pitching 8⅓ solid innings in a 5-2 win over Nolan Ryan and the Rangers. Ryan is now 5-15 lifetime and 0-8 against the Birds since he last won on April 20, 1976.

1990 — Jim Palmer is inducted into the Baseball Hall of Fame in Cooperstown, New York, joining slugging second baseman Joe Morgan as the only 1990 inductees. Palmer, elected on the first ballot, receives the highest percentage of votes (411 out of 444 votes cast or 92.5%) than any pitcher except Bob Feller (93.75%). Palmer becomes the seventh modern Oriole to be chosen and the sixth in the last seven years.

1994 — After a pair of losses, including the sixth in which Jamie Moyer left with a lead, Ben McDonald fires a one-hit, 4-0 shutout over

Jim Palmer

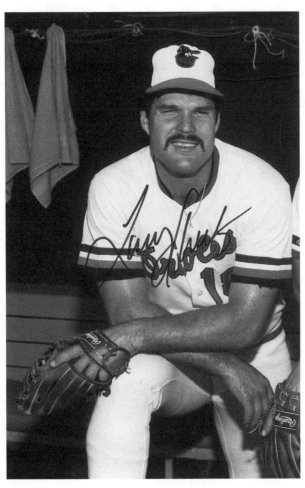

Larry Sheets

Milwaukee to give the O's their third shutout in a week.

1998— Newly acquired Juan Guzman pitches seven innings of four-hit ball in his Oriole debut and Rafael Palmeiro hits his fifth career grand slam to key a 6-1 win over the Tigers on a sunny Wednesday afternoon in Baltimore. The Orioles take the season series, 10-1, their best single-season record against Detroit in franchise history. The O's move three games over the .500 mark for the first time since April 26.

August 6

1959— The Orioles and White Sox play to an 18-inning 1-1 tie before the game is halted at 12:13 AM because of the curfew. Billy Pierce and Turk Lown pitched for Chicago while Hoyt Wilhelm pitched the last 8.1 innings in relief of Billy O'Dell.

1975— In the second game of a doubleheader sweep of the Tigers, Don Baylor goes 4-for-4 and ties a club record with three stolen bases. Baylor swiped 13 bases in 16 attempts in four games.

1979— After delivering an emotional eulogy at the funeral of his friend and teammate, Thurman Munson, Bobby Murcer returns to Yankee Stadium and almost singlehandedly beats the Orioles, 5-4. Murcer drives in all the Yankee runs and hits his first home run in Yankee Stadium since September 28, 1973.

1982— Terry Crowley becomes only the eighth pinch hitter in history to record 100 pinch hits, in a losing effort against Kansas City. Crowley finished tied for seventh at year's end, with 103.

1986— The Orioles and Texas Rangers set a major league record by combining for three grand slams in the Rangers' 13-11 win at Memorial Stadium. Jim Dwyer and Larry Sheets hit slams for the Orioles, both in the fourth inning. It was just the fifth time in major league history that one club has hit two grand slams in a single inning. Toby Harrah hit Texas' grand slam. The loss, in which the Orioles trailed, 6-0, then led, 11-6, sent the club spiraling downward from second place, 2½ behind Boston, to losing 42 of their last 56 games.

1989— Mike Devereaux homers in the 10th off Jeff Russell to beat the Rangers, 3-2, after Randy Milligan ties the game in the ninth with a one out single. Pete Harnisch goes 8.1 innings, marking the first time since April that O's starters have gone eight or more innings in back-to-back starts.

1993— Don Buford, the best leadoff man in Oriole history, becomes the 24th player or manager to be inducted into the Orioles Hall of Fame.

1993— Jack Voigt doubles three times in a 8-1 win over Cleveland.

1994— Arthur Rhodes tosses his second straight shutout, 5-0, in Milwaukee, lowering the club's ERA on game six of the road trip to 1.75. Still, the second-place Orioles are a season-high 10 games behind the Yankees.

August 7

1960— The Orioles hit five homers against Cleveland to set a club record, with Jim Gentile hitting two, but it isn't until Jack Fisher's belt in the eighth that the Birds win, 8-6.

1969— Dave McNally helps his own cause with a two-run homer in this second inning as the Birds blast KC, 10-2. McNally is now 16-1,

1971— The Orioles get only two hits, but one is a two-run homer by Dave Johnson off Mike Kekich to give Jim Palmer an 8-1 win over the Yankees.

1987— Larry Sheets, who hit a club high 31 homers and was named "Most Valuable Oriole" of the '87 season, homers twice in a 9-2 win over Texas. Sheets homers twice the following night against the Rangers in a losing cause and two days later has another two homer game against Cleveland.

Jack Voight

1989— Cal Ripken Jr. is ejected for the second time in his career after a called strike two in the first inning by plate umpire Drew Coble. The next eight innings are the only ones he misses all year. The Twins win, 4-2.

1990— Randy Milligan, among the league leaders in five offensive categories, barrels into catcher Ron Hassey in Oakland and suffers a separated shoulder as he scores from first on Sam Horn's double in a 3-2 loss. Milligan misses the next 48 games as the Orioles try seven players at first base.

1992— It had been more than 13 years since the Orioles had hit into a triple play but Brady Anderson actually flew into one against the Indians at Camden Yards. With the bases loaded, Brady flies to center field. Kenny Lofton throws Leo Gomez out at the plate trying to score. Meanwhile Tim Hulett tries to go from second to third and is tossed out by Sandy Alomar. The Indians win, 5-4, in 13 innings.

1993— In one of the season's most poignant moments, Cleveland lefty Bob Ojeda, who suffered a severe head injury in the March 22 boating accident that killed teammates Steve Olin and Tim Crews, makes his first appearance of the season to a standing ovation at Camden Yards. Ojeda works two innings, giving up two runs, one a solo homer to Cal Ripken, as the Orioles win, 8-6.

1994— Mike Mussina's 16th and last win in the strike-aborted season is a 6-3 triumph over the Brewers in Milwaukee.

1998— Despite Scott Erickson allowing five runs in the first inning, the Orioles still rout the hapless Twins, 16-9, as sore-armed Jimmy Key notches his first win since April 30 in his first relief appearance since 1986. Brady Anderson breaks a 7-for-48 skid with five hits including two home runs and two doubles. Cal Ripken adds a three-run homer in the eighth as the Birds climb to within 7½ games of the Red Sox for the wild-card spot. Harold Baines homers and drives in five runs and Eric Davis singles in the eighth to extend his hitting streak to 23 games.

August 8

1956— Earl Weaver begins his managing career at Knoxville of the Sally League.

1961— Steve Barber hurls his sixth shutout of the year to lead the majors, and blanks Kansas City, 7-0. It's his third whitewash of the A's in '61.

1969— Paul Blair hits an inside-the-park homer against Minnesota at Memorial Stadium. It was the 11th in club history and the sixth at home but the first since Billy O'Dell's back in May of 1959.

1989— Dave Johnson, a graduate of Overlea High School and resident of Middle River in Baltimore County, goes the route in beating the Twins, 6-1, for his first major league victory. It's the first complete game win for an Oriole since Jay Tibbs beat Toronto on June 27. Some 30 family members and hundreds of friends are on hand to watch the 29-year-old Johnson realize his boyhood dream.

1990— The Orioles pull off the 10th triple play in club history at Oakland. It's started by pitcher Jeff Ballard who was facing the A's Willie Randolph with Terry Steinbach on second and Walt Weiss on first in the seventh inning. Randolph lined to Ballard who threw to Cal Ripken to double off Steinbach. Cal then threw to Sam Horn at first to force Weiss. The Orioles won, 4-1. Ballard was also on the mound when the O's executed their last triple killing, the season before at home against the Yankees. He and Mike Cuellar are the only Orioles pitchers to be involved in a triple play.

1992— Cleveland's Charles Nagy pitches a one-hitter to beat the Orioles, 6-0, at Camden Yards.

1993— Jack Voigt singles as a pinch-hitter in the eighth inning and scores the tying run to bring the Orioles back from a 5-2 deficit to a 7-6 win over the Indians.

August 9

1937— The Orioles crush Buffalo, 12-3, at Oriole Park, but the big story is Smokey Joe Martin, the Oriole third baseman who hit home runs his first two times up to give him five consecutive home runs over two games. He hit circuit blows in his last three at-bats the day before as the Orioles beat Toronto, 6-2, in the second game of a twin bill.

1960— Chuck Estrada notches his first career shutout, blanking the Tigers, 3-0, as Brooks Robinson hits a three-run homer off Frank Lary.

1970— The Yankees and Orioles use a total of 21 pitchers to tie an American League record in a double-header at Yankee Stadium. New York uses 12 pitchers and the Birds nine as they split the twin bill. Both games went 11 innings and there were 31 runs, 48 hits and seven errors during the day.

1975— Bobby Grich draws a club-record five walks in a losing cause against the White Sox.

1981— The 50-day players' strike is over and baseball returns with the 52nd All-Star Game in Cleveland.

Ken Singleton put the American League into the lead, 1-0, with a second inning homer off Cincinnati's Tom Seaver. The National League win their 10th straight All-Star Game, 5-4.

1992— One day after his wife Capri gives birth to their first child, a six pound, 14-ounce baby girl, Mark McLemore goes 2-for-4 and scores the winning run in the 10th inning as the Orioles edge the Indians, 3-2.

1996— Cal Ripken collects his 2,500th career hit, a single off Bill Simas at Comiskey Park in a 4-3 White Sox win.

1998— The Twins halt a seven game losing streak and snap the Orioles' five-game win streak with a 5-4 win over Mike Mussina and the Orioles in Minnesota. It's Mussina's first loss in eight starts dating back to June 27. Eric Davis singles in the third to break Rafael Palmeiro's four-year old record for the club's longest hitting streak by hitting safely in his 25th consecutive game. Roberto Alomar and B.J. Surhoff homer to make it a club record 20 straight games with at least one home run.

Mark McLemore

August 10

1961— Dave Philley, 41 years old, sets an American League record with his 21st pinch hit of the season, breaking the old record set by Ed Coleman of the 1936 St. Louis Browns. Milt Pappas and the Orioles shut out Kansas City.

1963— John "Boog" Powell becomes the first Oriole ever to hit three home runs in one game. Boog hits two off Bennie Daniels and one off Steve Ridzik, all with the bases empty, as the Washington Senators win, 6-5, at D.C. Stadium.

1965— The Orioles yield a club-record 12 runs in the fifth inning to the Red Sox in a 15-5 loss. Boston bangs out eight hits, and benefits from four walks and two Oriole errors.

1969— Mike Cuellar takes a no-hitter into the ninth inning against Minnesota, but gives up a lead-off single to Cesar Tovar and settles for a one-hit, 2-0 win. Cuellar had retired 35 batters (11 from his previous start) without allowing a hit.

1971— Harmon Killebrew hits his 500th and 501st career home runs, both off Mike Cuellar, but the Orioles beat the Twins, 4-3, in 10 innings at Minnesota. The homers were Harmon's 64th and 65th off Oriole pitching. No other player has hit as many.

1976— Jim Palmer hurls the fourth one-hitter of his career when he beats the Twins, 2-0, at Memorial Stadium. The lone hit is a second inning single by Mike Cubbage.

1980— Trailing, 5-4, in the ninth, the Orioles rally to beat Tommy John as Rick Dempsey and Eddie Murray drive in runs to complete an exhilarating three-game sweep of the Yankees in New York.

1981— Exactly four months after defeating the Royals on opening day at Memorial Stadium, the O's beat them again, 3-2, when the season resumes after an 8½ week shutdown due to the players' strike.

1982— Luis Aparicio and Mike Cuellar join Frank and Brooks Robinson, Dave McNally, Boog Powell and Gus Triandos in the Orioles Hall of Fame. Earl Weaver and Mark Belanger were inducted in 1983.

1983— Lary Sorenson follows Rick Sutcliffe and Neal Heaton, as all three Cleveland starters go the distance in a three-game sweep and give the Indians their second straight season-series edge over the Orioles.

1987— The Orioles execute a club record-tying five double plays, all the ground ball type, while edging the Indians, 4-3, at Memorial Stadium.

1994— In what turns out to be the last game of the strike-abbreviated season, Ben McDonald and the Orioles beat the Yankees, 8-1, handing Jimmy Key just his fourth loss against 17 wins. McDonald now stands, 14-7, and Rafael Palmeiro's four hits and five RBI in the victory boost his average to .319, the fourth best in club history. The Orioles and Red Sox were rained out the following night and the work stoppage began on August 12. The Orioles played only 112 games with a 63-49 record, seven games behind the Yankees. Their pitching had really jelled in August as they allowed only 24 runs, fewest in the majors.

1998— The Orioles swing a deal with Cincinnati, sending talented but oft-injured outfielder Jeffrey Hammonds to the Reds for outfielder/third baseman Willie Greene. Juan Guzman then pitches the Orioles to a 2-1 win over Tampa Bay as Eric Davis extends his hitting streak to 26 games.

August 11

1963— With the Orioles leading the Senators, 3-2, in the ninth, Ron Kline hits Bob Johnson, knocks Jackie Brandt down (he then singles), and hits Jerry Adair in the mouth. Stu Miller then delivers a three-run triple to ice the verdict.

1966— Sam Bowen's two-out single in the 11th, with Luis Aparicio aboard on a double, wins it, 6-5, over the Yankees at Yankee Stadium, but this game will be remembered for Frank Robinson's great game-saving catch. With one out in the bottom of the 11th, Clete Boyer hit a long drive to right that Frank caught as he crashed into the fence, his glove hand going into the seats.

1970— Mike Cuellar ups his record to 16-7, 7-0, over California, as Paul Blair and Brooks Robinson unload two-run homers in the first and Frank Robinson caps it off with a homer in the eighth.

1972— Mike Cuellar strikes out 13 Red Sox and Bobby Grich homers, leading off the ninth for a 2-1 win.

1980— At Kansas City, the Orioles, behind Dennis Martinez, who is just off the disabled list, beat the Royals and Larry Gura, 2-1, to extend their winning streak to 10 games.

1983— Lenn Sakata breaks an 0-for-66 lifetime hitting drought against the White Sox by getting a base hit, but the Orioles lose their sixth straight, 9-3. It took Sakata, who came up in 1977 seven seasons to get a hit against the White Sox.

1986— Mike Flanagan takes a one-hit shutout into the ninth against Toronto in Baltimore and, with help from Don Aase, finishes with a combined two-hit, 3-1 win.

1989— In the second game of a doubleheader, Pete Harnisch pitches his first major league complete game, beating the Red Sox, 4-1, on a three-hitter. It's the O's first complete game win over Boston since June 20, 1986, a span of 48 games.

1991— Chicago's Wilson Alvarez throws the sixth and last no-hitter in Memorial Stadium history, blanking the Orioles, 7-0. The 24-year-old rookie is the youngest to toss a no-hitter since Oakland's Vida Blue in 1970. Cal Ripken reached on a throwing error by catcher Ron Karkovice in the seventh inning, the closest the Orioles came to a base-hit.

1993— Catcher Jeff Tackett is called upon to pitch in a 15-5 loss at Detroit, the first Orioles position player to pitch in a game since Todd Cruz at New York in September, 1984. Tackett faces five batters and throws 20 pitches, allowing a single and walk but retires the side on a ground out and two fly balls.

1997— Rex Barney, former Brooklyn Dodger righthander, and the Orioles beloved public address announcer for over 20 years, dies unexpectedly at his home at the age of 72. The Orioles paid tribute during a ceremony the following night and by keeping his PA spot in the press box empty for the remainder of the '97 season. Rex made famous such phrases as "Give That Fan A Contract" and "Thank Youuuu," at Memorial Stadium and Camden Yards.

Mike Flanagan

August 12

1973— Jim Palmer wins his eighth straight, 10-6, over Kansas City, and ups his record to 16-6.

1978— In a game marked by the first power failures in the history of Memorial Stadium, the Orioles defeat the Yankees, 6-4. Circuit breakers in two malfunctioning light towers caused a total delay of one hour and 16 minutes.

1983— A season low point, the O's drop their seventh straight, 6-4, to Chicago, as Lamarr Hoyt out-duels Mike Flanagan. Joe Altobelli is ejected for arguing balls and strikes, and his ballclub drops to fourth place, but only one game out of first.

1985— Larry Sheets and Wayne Gross hit back-to-back pinch home runs off Cleveland's Jerry Reed, tying a major league record. The last time the Orioles did it was on August 26, 1966 when Boog Powell and Vic Roznovsky both homered in pinch-hit roles off Boston's Lee Stange.

1990— Utility player Jeff McKnight, who hit only .200 in 75 at bats, bangs out four hits and scores four runs in an 11-6 win at California.

1992— Mike Devereaux drives in five runs on two at bats with a bases loaded single and bases loaded double in an 11-4 rout of the Blue Jays at the Skydome. "Devo" is now 10-for-16 (.625) with 25 RBI with the bases loaded. Joe Orsulak drives in three runs, two on a double that bounces high off the plate and then caroms into right field past an on-rushing Roberto Alomar.

1993— The Tigers complete a three-game sweep of the Orioles with a 17-11 win in Detroit. In the previous two games the Tigers had won, 15-1 and 15-5, collecting 48 hits, 10 home runs and three grand slams in the process. The 47 runs scored by Detroit are the most ever scored against the Orioles in three consecutive games. The 32 scored in the last two games are the most ever the O's have yielded in back-to-back games.

1998— Scott Erickson, roughed up in his two previous starts, pitches a masterful five hit, 7-0 shutout over the Tampa Bay Devil Rays for his eighth complete game as Eric Davis extends his hitting streak to 27 games.

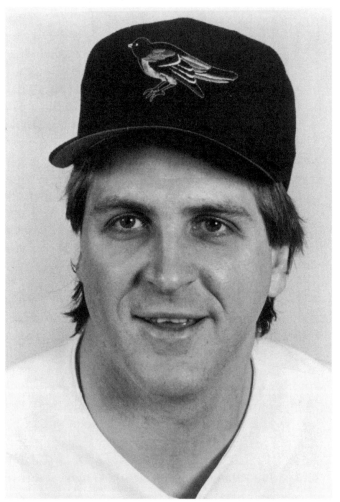

Joe Orsulak

August 13
1961— Steve Barber ties a record for a pitcher by walking 11 Red Sox. He also strikes out 11, throws 195 pitches and hits two batters, but he prevails, 6-5, in 11 innings.

1969— Jim Palmer pitches an 8-0 no-hitter against the Oakland A's at Memorial Stadium just four days after coming off a six-week stretch on the disabled list. Palmer strikes out eight and walks six in besting Chuck Dobson to record the only no-hitter in the American League in 1969.

1973— Don Baylor begins a string of eight consecutive hits against the Texas Rangers. He had five straight hits on the 14th and reached base 10 consecutive times. He went 12-for-14 and 15-19 in a five-game stretch.

1975— Jim Palmer pitches to only 28 men in two-hitting Kansas City, 3-0. It is his second two-hit shutout in his last three starts as Palmer becomes the first 17-game winner in the majors.

1978— The Orioles squeeze in a 3-0 win over New York in a game called after six innings because of wet grounds at Memorial Stadium. The Yankees scored five runs in the top of the seventh, but then the rains came and, after a wait of 38 minutes, the game was called, thus reverting to the last full inning of play and enabling the Birds to come away with a win.

1983— The O's begin a seven-week, 34-10 stretch that would culminate in the eastern title as rookie Bill Swaggerty makes his big league debut and holds the White Sox to two runs in six innings. Sammy

Stewart and Tippy Martinez held off Chicago, and Cal Ripken hit a two-run homer in the eighth to win it, 5-2, and beat Jerry Koosman for the sixth straight time.

1984— Mike Boddicker tosses the 25th one-hitter in Orioles history, beating the Blue Jays in Toronto, 2-1. Rance Mulliniks doubles and scores in the third for the only Toronto hit. Lenn Sakata's two-run homer off Jim Clancy accounted for the Oriole runs.

1988— Orioles Chairman and President Edward Bennett Williams passes away at the age of 68 after a long and courageous fight against cancer. Owner of the club since August, 1979, it was Williams who gave the fans a lengthy formal commitment to keep the Orioles in Baltimore. On the same day, Jeff Ballard, celebrating his 25th birthday, hurls his first major league shutout, three-hitting the Brewers, 5-0, at County Stadium.

1989— Baltimore area native Dave Johnson goes the route for the second straight start and beats the Red Sox, 6-1. For his efforts Dave is named American League "Player of the Week," the first rookie to win the honor since Boston's Al Nipper in 1985.

1991— The Orioles use 13 pitchers (seven in game one and six in game two) in a sweep of visiting Texas, tying a major league record for most pitchers used in a twinbill. The doubleheader consumed 7:45 and didn't end until 12:52 a.m. The scores were 4-3 in 12 innings, and 8-7.

1998— Rafael Palmeiro hits his 37th home run of the season with two on in the top of the 12th off Steve Reed as the Orioles beat the Indians, 7-4, at Jacobs Field. Raffy surpasses the 100 RBI level, making him only the second Oriole ever to have four consecutive 100+ RBI seasons. Eddie Murray did it from 1982-85. Eric Davis, who extended his hitting streak to 28 games with a double in the sixth, lined a single before Palmeiro homered. The O's are a major league best, 25-7, since the All-Star break.

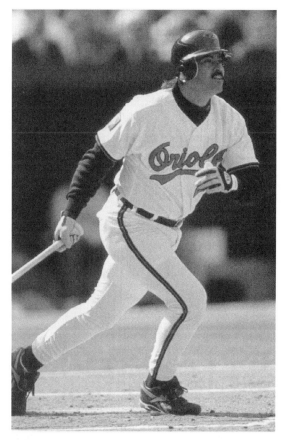

August 14
1930— Earl Weaver is born in St. Louis, Missouri.

1979— Steve Stone pitches 10 tough innings, striking out 10 White Sox. Al Bumbry's 12th-inning single gives reliever Tippy Martinez a 2-1 win at Memorial Stadium.

1983— Chicago leads, 1-0, in the fifth at Comiskey Park, when, with one man aboard, Carlton Fisk hits a line drive deep to left that reaches the left-field stands. Third base umpire Greg Kosc calls it a home run. The Orioles argue that a fan reached down below the top of the wall and caught the ball, thus helping it into the seats. The umpires confer and change Kosc's ruling, crediting Fisk with a double. Rudy Law, the base runner, is forced to return to third. An irate Tony La Russa is ejected after pulling third base out of the ground and heaving it. When play resumes,

Rafael Palmeiro

Scott McGregor intentionally walks Tom Paciorek loading the bases, then escapes the jam by getting Greg Luzinski to pop out foul and striking out Ron Kittle. Joe Nolan's ninth-inning single off Richard Dotson gives the Orioles a 2-1 lead. The White Sox load the bases with nobody out in the bottom of the ninth and Tim Stoddard comes in and fans Fisk, gets Paciorek looking and gets Luzinski to bounce into a game-ending force. Hard luck Richard Dotson, who had earlier lost a one-hitter to the Orioles, gives up just three hits but loses, 2-1.

1989— Deciding to rest his starters against tough Jack Morris in Detroit, Frank Robinson throws four relief pitchers and gets away with it as the O's win, 4-1, in 10 innings. Morris has a two-hitter going into the 10th but Craig Worthington hits a one-out three-run homer into the upper right-field stands to keep the O's 2½ games in front in the A.L. East.

1991— Rookie Mike Mussina earns his first major league win on his third try, fanning 10, while fellow rookie Chito Martinez hits two homers as the Orioles beat Texas, 10-2.

Earl Weaver

1998— Chris Hoiles enters the history books, becoming just the ninth major league player, and the first catcher, to hit two grand slams in one game. Hoiles finishes with eight RBIs and three hits in the 15-3 pasting of the Indians. Hoiles connects first off loser Charles Nagy in the third and five innings later yanks a towering homer inside the left-field foul pole off lefty Ron Villone. With his mom, wife, kids and other family members from nearby Bowling Green, Ohio looking on, Hoiles joins former Orioles Jim Gentile and Frank Robinson in the two-grand-slam club. Eric Davis' third inning single extends his hitting streak to 29 games, five games more than the previous club mark set by Rafael Palmeiro. Davis breaks a tie with Anaheim center fielder Garret Anderson for the longest hitting streak in the majors this season.

August 15

1952— In a night game at Memorial Stadium, Dick Marlowe of Buffalo beats the Orioles, 2-0, on a perfect game. Marlowe, who was a 10-10 pitcher that year, threw only 84 pitches and just 18 were called balls.

1966— Boog Powell sets a club record with 13 total bases at Boston as his three home runs provide all the Orioles' runs in a 4-2 win in 11 innings. Boog went 4-for-5, raising his average to .298 with 79 RBI in 79 games.

1969— Mike Cuellar wins his sixth straight and 16th of the season, 2-1, over Seattle, as Boog Powell drives in both runs to up his league-leading total to 106.

1975— Earl Weaver ties a major league record for the quickest ejection in the history of the game, getting the thumb before the second game even started, during the pregame lineup exchange. Weaver had been tossed out of the first game of the doubleheader with Texas. Texas won the first game 10-6 as all 18 starting Oriole and Ranger batters hit safely. The O's won the nightcap, 13-1.

1979— Edging toward the pennant, the Orioles find another way to win when Eddie Murray steals home with two out in the 12th inning, giving the Birds a 2-1 win over Chicago at Memorial Stadium.

1989— Bob Milacki loses his no-hit bid with one out in the seventh and finishes with a two-hit, 2-0, shut-out win. Joe Orsulak and Cal Ripken homer off long-time nemesis Doyle Alexander. Milacki is now 3-0 lifetime at Tiger Stadium, allowing only one earned run and six hits in 25.1 innings.

1993— Don Buford, arguably the greatest leadoff hitter in Oriole history, is inducted into the Oriole Hall of Fame in pre-game ceremonies.

1998— Closer Armando Benitez lets an 8-6 ninth-inning lead slip through his fingers when he issues three walks and a base hit but center fielder Brady Anderson comes to the rescue by hammering Doug Jones' first pitch of the 10th inning for a home run as the Orioles beat Cleveland for the third straight time in Cleveland, 9-8. Eric Davis runs his hitting streak to 30 games, a level reached only 35 times in baseball history as he bangs out four consecutive singles.

August 16

1969— Chico Salmon, obtained from Seattle a week before the season opened, goes 4-for-4 with two home runs and six RBI to lead the Orioles to a 15-3 thumping of the Pilots. The game is highlighted by Boog Powell's inside-the-park homer. It is the 12th inside-the-parker in club history and second in eight days.

1996— Rafael Palmeiro matches his single-game career high with six RBI in the first game of a double-header in Oakland, won by the O's 14-3. Raffy has 57 RBI in his last 59 games and goes on to set a new club record with 142, topping Jim Gentile's 1961 record by one.

1998— The Orioles lose, 5-3, in Cleveland, coming within three innings of their first four-game road sweep of the Indians in 27 years. Eric Davis, facing Indian starter Jaret Wright and reliever Steve Reed for the first time, strikes out three times to end his hitting streak at 30 consecutive games. The Orioles are seven games behind Boston for the wild-card spot with 23 of their last 39 games at home.

August 17

1972— Because of a previous postponement, the White Sox make a one day trip to Baltimore and knock off the Birds, 6-1. Rain fell all morning and delayed the game 35 minutes. It was played in a semi-fog before the club's all-time smallest crowd of 655 fans.

1980— Scotty McGregor, the big-game specialist, beats the Yankees, 1-0, before a national television audience. He throws only 102 pitches giving up six hits. Terry Crowley's sixth-inning double drives in the only run of the game.

1983— Mike Flanagan, in his third start since coming off the disabled list, wins his first game since May 11, 4-2, in Texas in 10 innings. Tim Stoddard saved his third game in four days. Doubles by Dan Ford and Cal Ripken each drove in runs in the decisive 10th inning.

1984— Eddie Murray begins a streak of hitting safely in 22 straight games, breaking Doug DeCinces' single season record of 21 set in 1978. It is the longest hitting streak by an American League switch-hitter in history.

1989— Cal Ripken Jr., playing in his 1208th straight game, moves into third place on the all-time consecutive game list ahead of Steve Garvey. To celebrate, Cal hits a two-run homer in the eight-run fourth inning as the Birds thump the Blue Jays, 11-6.

August 18

1962— The umpires hold up the game twice to make Cleveland pitcher Pedro Ramos change his clothing. First he changed his shirts, then his pants and hats, because the umpires suspected Pete of using a foreign substance on the ball.

1969— Baltimore scores eight runs in the second, with Mark Belanger getting two doubles in the inning, in a 12-3 win at Seattle. Belanger had five RBI for the game.

1972— The Orioles obtain Tommy Davis from the Cubs in a straight waiver deal for Elrod Hendricks.

1979— The O's beat Kansas City, 9-2, behind Scott McGregor and set a new single-season attendance record, breaking the 1,203,366 of 1966.

1980— Jim Palmer out-duels Ron Guidry, 6-5, at Memorial Stadium, capping a series of five games on consecutive days that saw the Birds win three and draw 249,605 fans, the largest turnout for a single series in the history of baseball.

1988— Lefty Jeff Ballard beats Oakland at home, 10-1, on a four hitter, his second consecutive complete-game win. Ballard becomes only the second Oriole in three seasons to toss consecutive complete-game wins. He won a three-hit, 5-0 game at Milwaukee on August 13.

1998— Eric Davis explodes for two home runs and drives in four runs as the Orioles rip the Twins, 7-1, before over 44,022 fans at Oriole Park. Davis, rested the night before after his 30 game hit streak was snapped at Cleveland, went three-for-four and has hit in 33 of 35 games since the All-Star break. Twenty-one-year-old rookie Sidney Ponson gets the win and is now 6-0 since July 2.

August 19

1961— Billy Hoeft throws a one-hitter against Washington to notch his first major league shutout since 1957.

1980— Steve Stone beats the Angels, 5-2, at Anaheim to become the earliest 20-game winner since Wilbur Wood of the White Sox won his 20th on July 30, 1973. It is also the earliest in Oriole history, beating Dave McNally in 1970 by six days.

Mark Belanger

1983— Two weeks to the day after they had beaten Chicago with five straight two-out hits in the ninth (and then lost five straight home games), the O's, with one on, two out and trailing, 4-2, in the ninth, lash out four straight singles, tying it on Ken Singleton's hit and winning on Lenn Sakata's sudden death hit. The achievement was made more notable since the victim was Dan Quisenberry, the top relief pitcher in baseball, who hadn't lost since April 23. The Birds won, 5-4, and beat the Royals, 3-1, in the nightcap to give the O's their first ever doubleheader sweep over Kansas City.

1984— Rick Dempsey homers twice in a 10-4 win over California at Memorial Stadium. Dempsey had 10 total homers for the year.

1990— Anthony Telford, making his major league debut, holds the American League champion Oakland Athletics to one hit over seven innings. Terry Steinbach, who had singled in the fifth inning on August 8 to break up Ben McDonald's no-hit bid, also singles in the fifth. Telford beats Scott Sanderson, 3-2, at Memorial Stadium, with the save going to Gregg

Rick Dempsey

Olson. Mark McGwire becomes the first batter ever to hit a home run off Olson at Memorial Stadium after 52 games and 72.1 innings. Incidentally, Telford is one of 48 players and 22 pitchers used by the Orioles in the season, which ties for second behind the 54 Orioles who played in 1955.

1992— Brady Anderson sets a club record for RBI by a leadoff hitter in a season with 69 and Mike Devereaux, Leo Gomez and Brady all homer with one on, but the Mariners prevail, 10-8, at Oriole Park. The O's set a club record for attendance at 2,575,744 in only 58 dates.

1998— The Orioles, 30-8 since the All-Star break, continue to pressure the Red Sox for the wild-card spot as they beat Tampa Bay, 6-4, behind Mike Mussina's gutty pitching performance. Mussina strikes out 10 and induces 10 ground-ball outs in winning his 12th game. Shortstop Mike Bordick's three-run homer off Devil Rays starter Rolando Arrojo is the difference.

August 20

1967— Frank Robinson chases umpire Emmett Ashford all over the Comiskey Park outfield after Emmett rules that Tommy Agee caught a ball that Frank had hit to center (Frank and the O's were convinced Agee had trapped it). The White Sox won, 2-1.

1973— Brooks Robinson's 2,500th career hit is a run-scoring single off Bill Hands and the Minnesota Twins.

1989— Dave Stieb remains winless lifetime in Baltimore (0-5) as the Orioles withstand the Blue Jays' challenge for first place by winning, 7-2, to remain a half game on top in the east.

1991— Glenn Davis, in his second game back from a four month stint on the disabled list, homers off Dennis "Oil Can" Boyd and drives in five runs in an 8-6 win at Texas.

1992— Mike Devereaux drives in both runs in a 2-1 come-from-behind win over Seattle at Camden Yards. With the O's trailing, 1-0, after seven innings, Devo triples in one run in the eighth and wins the game with a sacrifice fly in the 10th.

1995— Arthur Rhodes strikes out 10 Athletics in Oakland in just 4.2 innings of relief in an Oriole 6-3 defeat.

1998— Cal Ripken drills his 380th career home run to tie him with Brooks Robinson atop the Orioles all-time hit list with 2,848, but Tampa Bay prevails, 4-2. The wild-card deficit remains seven games behind the Red Sox, who also lost. Cal's consecutive games streak is now at 2,605, 489 games more than the combined total of the current playing streak of the other 14 players whose streaks include every game in 1998.

August 21

1962— Bidding for his 298th career victory, Chicago's Early Wynn gives up five runs in the first inning as Robin Roberts wins his 242nd game. Boog Powell hits a grand-slam homer and, with a double his last time up, Brooks Robinson begins a string of eight consecutive hits over three games.

1975— Jim Palmer holds the Rangers to five hits and one unearned run in 12 innings in a game the O's eventually win in 14 innings, 4-2.

1985— The Orioles tie a club record by scoring 10 runs in the third inning at Seattle and then hang on to win, 11-8.

1989— The Brewers come to town having won nine of their last 10 to trail the O's by just ½ game. Jeff Ballard hurls his second career shutout, becoming the first Oriole to pitch a shutout while neither walking or striking out a single batter. Cal Ripken hits his 200th lifetime homer, a three-run shot, in the Orioles' 5-0 win.

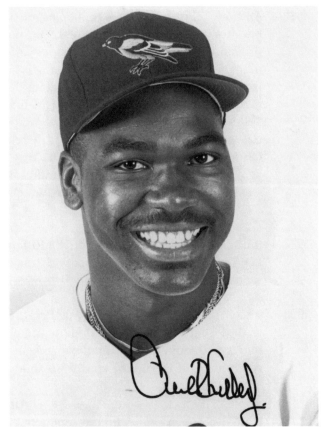

Arthur Rhodes

1992— Leadoff hitter Brady Anderson reaches base four times in four tries with a homer and three walks, scores twice and steals his 41st base in a 4-2 win over the Athletics at Oriole Park.

1993— Mike Pagliarulo, obtained from the Twins six days earlier, hits a grand slam off Nolan Ryan in his first at bat as an Oriole at Camden Yards. The Orioles win, 6-5, in 12 innings. "Pags" homered four times in his first 31 at-bats with the O's after hitting only four homers in his last 459 regular season at bats with the Twins. Ryan exits with a pulled muscle after the third inning, finishing with a 10-17 career record against Baltimore.

1997— Randy Myers sets the Orioles single season save record with his 38th save at Kansas City in a 4-3 win. Myers surpasses Gregg Olson's mark of 37 set in 1990. Myers goes on to lead the league with 45 saves, blowing only one all year when he allows a two-run homer to Jason Giambi in the ninth on May 3 in Oakland. Myers is voted Oriole MVP at season's end.

1998— Cal Ripken becomes the Orioles all-time leading hit leader when he singles to right in the seventh inning off Cleveland's Jaret Wright for his 2,849th career hit, breaking the record of Hall of Fame third baseman Brooks Robinson. The crowd of 48,374, the largest ever for a regular season game at Camden Yards, gives Cal a long standing ovation. Ripken shook hands with rookie Indians first baseman Richie Sexson, then acknowledged the fans by removing his helmet and waving. Ripken's record breaker comes in his 2,671st game, 225 fewer than Brooks. The Indians won the game, 6-3, to drop the Birds eight games back in the wild-card chase with 34 to play.

August 22

1969— Curt Motton's pinch homer in the 10th gives the Orioles a 4-3 win over the A's in Oakland as Jim Palmer wins his 10th straight en route to a 16-4 season.

1976— Reggie Jackson, scratched from the starting lineup after fouling a ball off his ankle the night before, enters the game in Chicago with the score tied, 2-2, in the ninth inning. Reggie belts a pinch grand-slam homer to give the O's a 6-2 victory.

1993— Texas' Butch Davis, a former Oriole, hits the first inside-the-park home run at Camden Yards as the Rangers wallop the Birds, 11-4. It's only the third inside-the-parker hit by a visiting player ever in Baltimore and the first in 33 years since 1960 when Washington's Lenny Green hit one.

1997— Recuperating outfielder Eric Davis returns to Baltimore for the first time since beginning chemotherapy treatments to begin workouts with the team. Eric is in uniform in the dugout for the game with the Twins and receives a standing ovation from the fans.

August 23

1961— Dave Philley ties Sam Leslie's major league record, set back in 1932, for most pinch hits in a season. Philley's 22nd pinch hit helps the Orioles beat Kansas City in 12 innings.

1964— The Orioles cap a 3-for-4 weekend in Chicago by splitting a doubleheader. Brooks Robinson drove in the key runs in all three wins as the O's took over first place by 1½ games.

1978— Posting his sixth shutout of the season and the 51st of his career, Jim Palmer tosses a three-hitter, hurling the Orioles to an 11-0 romp over the A's in Oakland.

1980— Steve Stone gains his 21st victory while pitching the Orioles to a 4-2 victory over the A's at Oakland.

1981— Mike Flanagan's streak of 157 straight starts without missing a turn is snapped when he tears a muscle in his left forearm. "Flanny" didn't pitch for 26 days after not missing an assignment in more than four years.

1985— Held scoreless on one hit by Oakland's Jose Rijo and Steve Mura through eight innings, the Orioles score seven times in the top of the ninth to beat the A's and their relief ace Jay Howell, 7-2.

August 24

1959— Gus Triandos drives in seven runs with four hits, including a grand-slam homer, as the Birds bomb Detroit, 11-0.

1969— Light-hitting Ted Kubiak, 0-for-8 in the game, singles home the winning run to give Oakland a 9-8 win in the 18th inning of a twinbill nightcap. The game lasted five hours, eight minutes.

1973— The Orioles win their 11th in a row to tie a club record for most consecutive wins in a single season. Bobby Grich has four hits and three RBI. Dave McNally shuts out Kansas City, 6-0.

1977— The Orioles pound out a season-high 19 hits in a 10-5 thumping of the Chicago White Sox at Baltimore. Every Oriole starter hits safely and scores at least one run.

1980— Mike Flanagan's 3-0 shutout over the A's in Oakland spoils Billy Martin Day but gives the Birds 26 wins in their last 32 games and brings them to within a half game of the Yankees' lead in the American League east.

1982— Joe Nolan's first career grand slam beats the Blue Jays in 10 innings, 7-3, at Memorial Stadium. Nolan's victim is Joey McLaughlin.

1983— Reliever Tippy Martinez picks off three Toronto Blue Jays in the 10th inning (the first was labeled a caught-stealing) as the Orioles down Toronto, 7-4, on Lenn Sakata's three-run homer. Sakata, who had committed two costly errors the

Gus Triandos

night before, caught the 10th inning while John Lowenstein played second and Gary Roenicke played third. The O's had trailed, 3-1, with two down in the ninth, but came back to tie on RBI singles by Benny Ayala and Al Bumbry. But in the top of the 10th Cliff Johnson hit Tim Stoddard's first pitch over the left-field fence to put the surprising Blue Jays up by one. Tippy then came in to pick off the side without retiring a batter. Sakata was catching for the first time since Little League. In the bottom of the 10th, Cal Ripken led off with a game-tying homer, then after two walks and two outs, Sakata did his thing. The extra-inning loss was the first for Toronto in exactly one year, when the O's had beaten Joey McLaughlin (who also lost this game). During the interim, the Blue Jays had won 12 straight extra-inning games.

1984— Mike Flanagan extends his career record at the Oakland Coliseum to 10-0 with a 4-2 victory over the A's. In 13 lifetime starts in Oakland, Flanagan has hurled six complete games, compiling a 1.88 ERA, beating Rick Langford four times and Matt Keough three.

1989— Jeff Ballard comes within one out of his second straight shutout, fanning Don Mattingly three times, and beating the Yankees, 3-1. Gregg Olson rescues Ballard in the ninth and records his 20th save.

1992— At home against the Angels, the Orioles pull the 11th triple play in club history. With runners on first and third, Gary Gaetti lines out to third baseman Leo Gomez, who steps on the bag at third for the force and throws to first to "triple up" Chad Curtis. The Orioles win, 9-1, as Rick Sutcliffe beats Bert Blyleven. It's a courageous effort for Sutcliffe, who flew home two days earlier to Kansas City where his mother died, flew back to pitch and then flew back to KC the next morning for the funeral.

1993— The Orioles and Jamie Moyer beat Chuck Finley and the Angels, 1-0, at Camden Yards, managing only two hits off the Angel southpaw. It's the fewest hits in an Oriole win since they mustered just two in a 4-2 Opening Day win over Texas in 1985.

August 25

1960— The Orioles score six runs with two out in the eighth to break a 3-3 tie vs. Detroit. Gus Triandos hits his second grand slam in five days, and Chuck Estrada fans 12 Tigers.

1961— Journeyman Dave Philley sets a major league record with his 23rd pinch hit of the season with a base hit against Minnesota. He finished with 24 pinch hits for the season.

1962— Hoyt Wilhelm picks up a win and a save on the same day as the Orioles sweep a day-night, separate-admission' doubleheader from the Yankees.

1968— In the longest game (by time) in Oriole history, five hours and 27 minutes, Brooks Robinson's single in the 18th inning scores Boog Powell with the winning run in a 3-2 win over Boston. The Orioles set another record of dubious distinction, leaving 21 men on base.

1970— Dave McNally becomes the first American League pitcher since Bob Lemon in 1952-'53-'54 to record three consecutive 20-win seasons as the Orioles down Oakland, 5-1.

1973— The Orioles set a club record for most wins in succession in a single season as they down the Royals, 7-1, for their 12th in a row.

1979— The game in Comiskey Park is called for the second straight day because of the unplayable mess the field is in due to several rock concerts and heavy rains. Lee MacPhail flew in to personally inspect the field on Saturday.

1983— The O's and Blue Jays are tied 0-0 after nine innings, but Bobby Bonnila homers with two down in the 10th. With one out and two on in the bottom of the 10th, Dan Ford lines a drive past Lloyd Moseby in right center that scores Joe Nolan and Al Bumbry with the tying and winning runs.

1960— Cal Ripken Jr., baseball's all-time iron-man, is born in Havre de Grace, Maryland.

1988— The Orioles come from behind in their last at bat to win both games of a doubleheader at home against Seattle, both by 4-3 scores with the second game going 12 innings. It marks their first doubleheader sweep since September 24, 1984. They had gone 16 straight doubleheaders without a sweep. Larry Sheets' dramatic two-run, two-out homer off Mike Schooler wins the first game.

1990— Cal Ripken celebrates his 30th birthday by driving in three runs including the game winner on an 11th inning sac fly as the Orioles edge Cleveland, 5-4, at Memorial Stadium.

1992— What a birthday present! Cal Ripken signs a five-year $30.5 million contract, plus $500,000 per year for four years as a front office executive at the end of his career. The announcement is made to the crowd before the start of the game, won by the Angels, 5-2.

1993— Cal Ripken's single drives in the only run of the game in a 1-0 win over Chuck Finley and the Angels at Oriole Park. Jamie Moyer gets the win. It's just the second 1-0 game in Camden Yards history and Cal has won both with singles. The first was June 5, 1992 against Toronto.

August 26

1954— Bob Turley beats Boston, 5-3, and ends the Orioles' club-record, 14-game losing streak.

1962— The Orioles cap a five-game sweep of the pennant-bound Yankees as Robin Roberts pitches a brilliant five-hitter and out-duels Whitey Ford. The final is 2-1, Baltimore, on solo homers by Brooks Robinson and Jim Gentile. Tony Kubek homers for New York's only run.

1968— Dave McNally pitches and bats his way to an 8-2 win over Oakland. McNally hits a grand-slam homer in the seven-run first inning and wins his ninth straight to tie a club record.

1973— Paul Blair hits an inside-the-park grand-slam homer against Kansas City at Memorial Stadium as Amos Otis and Steve Hovley collide while going after the drive to right center. The pitcher was Paul Splittorff. The Orioles win, 10-1.

Bob Turley

1979— On a field far from playable, the O's sweep two from Chicago, winning the first, 12-7, as Doug DeCinces hits a grand slam. Umpire Ron Luciano thumbed Earl Weaver for questioning the umpire's competency. Gary Roenicke wins the second game with a 13th-inning homer off Ed Farmer. The Birds' lead in the east grows to 6½.

1983— Mike Boddicker pitches his fourth shutout, a three-hit, 9-0 win over the Minnesota Twins at Memorial Stadium. The win keys a three-game sweep in which the Birds outscore the Twins, 25-7.

1985— In one of the greatest hitting performances in club history, Eddie Murray drives in nine runs on four hits including three homers, one a grand slam, as the Orioles blast the Angels, 17-3. The Orioles club seven total homers in the game.

1989— Joe Orsulak, batting cleanup before a nationwide TV audience, hits two home runs, both off Walt Terrell,

Mike Cuellar is congratulated after the Orioles beat Oakland in the 1971 ALCS playoffs.

scores four runs and drives in three, including the game-winner in a 6-4 win over the Yankees. Bob Geren's seventh inning homer off Dave Johnson breaks a string of 81 straight homerless innings for O's pitchers.

1992— The Orioles hit five home runs, including three in one inning to erase a 4-1 deficit and beat the Angels, 6-4. Randy Milligan, with just one homer in his last 55 games, hits two and so does Mike Devereaux.

1993— Jack "Roy Hobbs" Voigt's pinch single in the eighth inning breaks a 4-4 tie and sparks the Orioles to an 8-4 win over the Angels.

1995— Kevin Brown snaps a six-game losing streak with his first win since June 2, beating the Angels, 5-2, in Anaheim. During the losing skid, Brown made 12 starts and had a 5.07 ERA without a win.

August 27

1970— Mike Cuellar wins his 20th as Frank Robinson hits two home runs in a 6-4 win over Oakland.

1975— Mike Torrez notches his 16th win, 4-2, over Kansas City, to match his career high. Ken Singleton was ejected for the first time in his career, by Russ Goetz, for beefing about a called third strike.

1977— The Kansas City Royals' club-record, 10-game winning streak is stopped by the Orioles, 4-2, at Baltimore.

1995— Mike Mussina pitches a complete game shutout and strikes out 11 Angels in winning, 4-0, at Anaheim.

1997— Rafael Palmeiro homers twice, including a game winning grand slam, driving in five runs in a 7-3 win over Kansas City at Camden Yards. It's Raffy's third two-home run game of the season and 18th of his career.

August 28

1957— After being humiliated by the Cleveland Indians with just 11 wins against 55 losses in their first three years in the American League, the Birds gain a measure of revenge with a 19-6 win in Cleveland. Gus Triandos sparked the 19-hit attack with two home runs as the Orioles set a club record that still stands for runs in a game.

1960— The Orioles are leading Chicago, 3-1, behind Milt Pappas in the top of the eighth when Ted Kluszewski hits an apparent three-run homer to put the Chisox in the lead. However, third base umpire Ed Hurley had called time an instant before the pitch because Earl Torgeson and Floyd Robinson were playing catch outside the prescribed bullpen area. A violent argument ensued, to no avail, and Klu lined to center to end the inning. Hoyt Wilhelm came on in the ninth to fan Torgeson and get Luis Aparicio on a fly to center with the bases full. The Orioles win, 3-1.

1973— Texas' 5-3 win at Baltimore breaks an Oriole club record of 14 straight victories in one season. The loss was also the first for Dave McNally to the Rangers since September 12, 1968, after he had won 17 straight against them.

1980— Eddie Murray, Rich Dauer and Gary Roenicke each have four hits to lead the Orioles to a club record 26-hit attack, as the Birds outslug the California Angels, 13-8, at Memorial Stadium. The O's also tied club records for most doubles in a game (eight), and for most hits in one inning (nine) in the fourth.

1981— The Orioles record 21 hits and beat the Angels, 13-8.

1984— Scott McGregor's realistic shot at 20 victories ends in the bottom of the first inning in Anaheim when a line drive off the bat of Brian Downing breaks his left ring finger ending his season abruptly at 15-12. The run McGregor allowed made him a loser in Anaheim for the first time in six seasons after 10 straight wins including the pennant clincher in 1979.

1986— Don Aase, who had a hand in 55% of the Orioles victories, becomes the first pitcher in club history to lose twice in one day, Oakland winning both games in the ninth inning, the first on a two-out, two-run homer by Dave Kingman, and the second a two-out, two-run triple off the bat of Carney Lansford.

1987— Fred Lynn hits a dramatic "sudden death" homer in the ninth to beat Chuck Finley and the Angels, 6-5. The homer snaps a scoreless streak of 17.1 innings by Finley against the Orioles.

August 29

1970— Dave McNally wins his 21st, 6-1, over Milwaukee, and helps his own cause with three hits and three RBI. It is McNally's ninth straight win.

1972— Bobby Grich drives in five in a 9-4 win over Minnesota. Rich Coggins doubles in his first two major league at bats.

1974— The Birds knock off Texas, 6-2, as Ross Grimsley wins his 15th, a career high.

1977— Pat Kelly's grand-slam homer in the seventh inning off Nolan Ryan propels the Orioles to a 6-1 triumph over the Angels in Baltimore. It is the Angels who rack up the milestones; Nolan Ryan striking out 11 to eclipse the 300-strikeout mark for the fifth time, and Bobby Bonds stealing his 30th base, marking a record fourth season of 30 steals and 30 homers.

1978— The Orioles, for only the second time in American League history, win all their games with another club; the Birds beat Oakland, 6-2, at Memorial Stadium for a season record of 11-0. In 1970, Baltimore also beat Kansas City 12 times without a loss.

1979— After going homerless in his career against the Twins (26 games), Eddie Murray hits three home runs and drives in all seven runs in a 7-4 win over Minnesota. Eddie hits two off Geoff Zahn and one off Mike Marshall.

Pat Kelly

1983— John Shelby hits his first career grand slam and Scott McGregor (16-5) goes the route to beat Gaylord Perry, 9-2, at Royals Stadium. The Birds increased their lead to 24½ games in the east.

1992— Arthur Rhodes, Todd Frohwirth and Gregg Olson combine to blank the Mariners, 4-0, the first of three straight shutouts. Randy Milligan paces the O's attack with four hits and two RBI.

1993— The Orioles play their final game at Arlington Stadium and beat the Rangers, 6-3, giving them an 81-46 record there since the Rangers moved from Washington after the 1971 season.

1996— Bobby Bonilla hits his 20th home run of the year against Seattle in a 9-6 loss, giving the Orioles seven players with 20 or more homers, a new major league record.

1996— The Orioles acquire Todd Zeile and Pete Incaviglia from the Phillies for pitchers Garrett Stephenson and Calvin Maduro.

August 30

1961— Paul Richards, who announced his resignation earlier in the day, manages his last game as an Oriole, at old Wrigley Field in Los Angeles. The Birds, behind five home runs, wallop the Angels, 11-5. Luman Harris took over as manager, and Richards returned to Texas to become general manager of the new Houston franchise.

1975— For the fifth time in six years, Jim Palmer becomes a 20-game winner with a 4-2 win over the White Sox. Palmer had dipped to a 7-12 record the year before.

1979— Before the Orioles and Twins meet, new owner Edward Bennett Williams announces, contrary to many reports, that all 81 home games in 1980 will be played at Memorial Stadium. Then Mike Flanagan went out and won his 19th game and fifth straight, 5-4. Ken Singleton drove in two runs and became the sixth player in O's history to drive in 100 runs in a season.

1983— The O's bomb KC, 12-4, and Storm Davis wins his 11th as the O's finish with a winning record on the Royals carpet, 4-2, for the first time since 1974.

1989— The Birds jump on Greg Swindell for seven runs in the first inning and that's the ballgame as the Orioles win in Cleveland, 7-4. Outfielder Phil Bradley ties a major league record by doubling twice in the same inning. Jeff Ballard ups his record to 15-6 and the Orioles hold onto first place by a game over Toronto.

1991— Joe Orsulak ties a club record with five hits in a game in a 11-5 win at Minnesota.

1992— The Orioles are involved in their third triple play of the season and second in five days. With Randy Milligan on first and Brady Anderson on second at Seattle, Mike Devereaux lines out to right fielder Jay Buhner who makes a great catch while hitting the wall in right center. Both runners, thinking the ball wouldn't be caught, took off. Buhner tossed the ball to second baseman Harold Reynolds who flipped it to shortstop Omar Visquel who stepped on second to get Anderson and then tagged Milligan who had passed Anderson on the base paths and was out anyway. The Orioles win 2-0 as Rick Sutcliffe wins his 14th.

1996— Pete Incaviglia becomes the first Oriole ever to hit a grand-slam homer in his first game in an Oriole's uniform as the Orioles win, 5-2. "Inky's" slam is the 165th in club history. It is also Inky's 200th career home run. The Orioles and Mariners break the major league record for grand slams in a season with 11 each. Since 1980 the Birds have bashed 84 grand slams, more than any other major league team.

1998— Three more names join the list of greats in the Orioles Hall of Fame. In pre-game ceremonies, former general manager Lee MacPhail, second baseman Bobby Grich and first baseman/DH Lee May are enshrined. For MacPhail, it comes on the heels of his induction at Cooperstown a few weeks earlier. MacPhail's astute trading, including the famed Frank Robinson acquisition for Milt Pappas, helped the Orioles to their first pennant and World Championship in 1966. Grich set several fielding records and was a solid performer at the plate, making three of his six All-Star trips while an Oriole and winning all four of his Gold Gloves. In six seasons as an Oriole, May hit 123 homers and drove in 487 runs and helped young Eddie Murray adjust to the majors in 1977.

August 31

1935— Frank Robinson is born in Beaumont, Texas.

1955— Cleveland beats Baltimore, 5-1, scoring all five runs in the first inning before a man is out. Hal Skinny Brown then relieved Bill Wight and did not give up a hit the rest of the game (eight innings). The teams set a major league record for fewest total assists, five (Baltimore 3, Cleveland 2).

1960— After Dick Stigman knocks him down with a high inside pitch, Gene Woodling hits a grand-slam home run to overcome a 3-0 Cleveland lead. Hal Brown relieves Steve Barber and pitches shutout baseball for the last 8⅓ innings to get the win.

1966— On his 31st birthday, Frank Robinson has a home run and three hits in a 5-1 win at Cleveland.

1968— Dave McNally sets an Oriole club record for consecutive wins in one season with his 10th straight, breaking Hoyt Wilhelm's record of nine in 1959. Paul Blair's three-run homer helped McNally to a 5-1 win over Detroit.

1983— Toronto's Jim Gott gives up seven runs before retiring a batter in the first inning as the O's roll to their eighth straight win, 10-2. Todd Cruz hits a three-run homer as the Birds increase their lead to 3½ in the east.

1984— Mike Flanagan surrenders the first grand-slam home run of his career to Jim Presley but the Orioles prevail at the Kingdome, 11-7.

1988— The Orioles obtain catcher Chris Hoiles from Detroit along with pitchers Robinson Garces and Cesar Mejia in exchange for outfielder Fred Lynn.

Davey Johnson

1992— Mike Mussina runs his record to 13-5 in pitching the Birds to their third straight shutout, 4-0, over the A's in Oakland. The string of consecutive scoreless innings is now up to 29. Cal Ripken collects career RBI 1,000 with a two-run single off Kelly Downs. In the first inning, the A's announce a blockbuster deal. Jose Canseco, who started the game in right field, is pinch hit for in the bottom of the first. Athletics General Manager Sandy Alderson holds an in-game press conference revealing Canseco has been dealt to Texas for Ruben Sierra, Bobby Witt and Jeff Russell. The Orioles make a deal just before midnight, acquiring Craig Lefferts from San Diego for a pair of minor leaguers.

1993— Mike Mussina strikes out six straight batters in the fourth and fifth innings, one shy of the club record of seven by Sammy Stewart in 1978, in an 8-2 win at California.

1997— In ceremonies before the Orioles play the Mets, former second baseman and current manager Davey Johnson, fan favorite Rick Dempsey and former general manager Harry Dalton, are inducted into the Orioles Hall of Fame.

1998— The free-fall continues. The Orioles drop their eighth straight game and 10th in 11 games, 4-1, to the White Sox to fall 12 games behind Boston in the wild-card hunt.

SEPTEMBER

September 1

1961— Lum Harris replaces Paul Richards as interim manager. Harris wins 17 and loses 10 for a .630 winning percentage in September.

1974— Bobby Grich's 18th homer in the fourth inning is the game's only run. Ross Grimsley beats Boston's Luis Tiant, both pitching three-hitters.

1978— Sammy Stewart sets a major league record for most consecutive strikeouts in a rookie's debut, fanning seven in a row to feature the Orioles' 3-0 and 9-3 twi-night doubleheader sweep over the White Sox at Baltimore. The former record for most consecutive strikeouts by a rookie in his first game was six, shared by Karl Spooner of the 1954 Dodgers and Pete Richert of the 1962 Dodgers.

1984— Ken Singleton's pinch hit grand slam, the only pinch slam of the season, is still not enough as the Orioles lose, 10-9, in Seattle.

1989— After 98 days on top, the Birds drop to second place for the first time since May 25 as the White Sox rough up Bob Milacki and Mickey Weston to the tune of a 10-1 win at Comiskey Park. The Orioles have now been outscored, 21-1, in their last two games.

1992— The Orioles come within one out of their fourth straight shutout as they beat Oakland, 5-1. Bob Milacki, returning from a lengthy stay at Rochester, pitches shutout ball through eight innings that extends the Orioles scoreless string to 37 consecutive innings. Oakland scores a ninth inning run off Pat Clements and Todd Frohwirth.

September 2

1957— Connie Johnson ties Bob Turley's club record by striking out 14 batters in a 6-1 win over the Yankees at Memorial Stadium.

1960— Milt Pappas begins the most exciting and successful weekend the Orioles have ever experienced by throwing a three-hit shutout at the Yankees and beating Whitey Ford, 5-0. Jack Fisher shut out the Yanks, 2-0, the next night, and Chuck Estrada and Hoyt Wilhelm teamed up for a 6-2 win on Sunday. The Yankees went 25 scoreless innings against Oriole pitching.

1964— Milt Pappas has a no-hitter for 7½ innings until Voilo Versalles singles sharply between short and third with two out in the eighth. Milt settles for his first one-hitter and a 2-0 win over the Twins.

Milt Pappas

1974— In the opener of a Labor Day doubleheader, Ross Grimsley beats Luis Tiant and the Red Sox, 1-0, as both pitch three-hitters. Bobby Grich's homer in the fourth is the difference. In the nightcap, Mike Cuellar pitches a two-hitter, also winning 1-0, over Bill Lee, as the Birds move to within two of the eastern lead.

1983— Mike Flanagan wins the first 1-0 game in the history of the MetroDome, winning his 14th straight over the Twins. Ken Singleton supplies the only run with a ninth-inning homer.

1956— Trailing the Red Sox, 8-0, after 2½ innings at Fenway Park, the Orioles engineer the greatest comeback in their history by scoring three runs in the top of the ninth inning to win, 11-10. Bob Nieman's single drives in the winning run. Billy Loes is the winner.

1988— Gregg Olson, the Orioles' top draft pick in the June draft, wins at Seattle, 4-3, in his major league debut. The "Otter" is the first Oriole to win in his debut since Don Welchel in 1982. Bob Milacki later did it on September 18 of 1988.

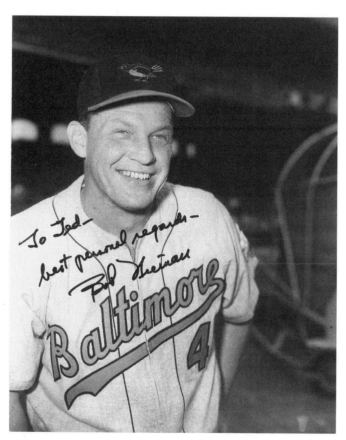

Bob Nieman

1992— Starter Ben McDonald and relief pitcher Alan Mills combine to toss a two-hitter as the Birds edge the A's, 2-1, in Oakland. Mills didn't allow a hit in the four innings he worked. Randy Milligan's 10th-inning double wins it as the Orioles move to 17 games over .500 for the first time since 1983.

1993— Mike Devereaux breaks a 2-for-40 drought with a 2-for-4 game off California's Chuck Finley, including a two-run homer in the O's 4-3 win, completing their first sweep in Anaheim since August of 1987.

September 3

1960— The Orioles move into first place as Jack Fisher blanks the Yankees on a seven-hitter and Brooks Robinson drives in both Baltimore runs. It is the second straight shutout for Fisher and the Birds.

1971— Dave McNally ups his record to 17-4 and wins his 11th straight as the Orioles knock off Washington, 4-2.

1973— Paul Blair hits two three-run homers, and an inside-the-parker, as Baltimore beats Boston, 13-8, at Fenway Park.

1979— The Birds sweep Toronto, 2-1 and 5-1, at Memorial Stadium, as Mike Flanagan, on his way to the Cy Young Award, becomes the majors' first 20-game winner in the nightcap. Flanagan becomes the Orioles' 20th 20-game winner in the last 12 years, and the O's reach the 90-victory plateau for the 10th time in 12 Earl Weaver seasons.

1980— Steve Stone wins the 100th game of his career, 5-1, against Seattle at Memorial Stadium. In his 10th full season in the majors, over one third (36) of his victories came in two seasons in a Baltimore uniform.

1983— The Orioles bombard the Twins, 13-0, on 18 hits. Cal Ripken has five hits (to tie a club mark), hit his 22nd and 23rd homers (to break Ron Hansen's record for an Orioles shortstop), hit his 37th and 38th doubles (to tie Brooks Robinson's one-season record) and accumulates 13 total bases (to tie a club record). The six Oriole homers are the most ever hit against the Twins since moving from Washington in 1961.

1984— Outfielder Mike Young's first career grand slam off Detroit's Aurelio Lopez with two-outs in the eighth inning breaks a 3-3 tie in the Oriole's 7-4 win at Detroit.

1988— Jose Bautista, the first Oriole rookie to lead the staff in innings pitched since Tom Phoebus in 1967, loses, 1-0, to Mark Langston and the Mariners in Seattle. It is the shortest game of the season in the majors in '88, one hour and 45 minutes. Bautista allows only four hits, but two are back to back doubles by Jim Presley and Mickey Brantley in the sixth.

1993— David Segui homers off Dennis Eckersley in the 13th inning at Oakland giving the Orioles a 5-4 win. It's the O's only extra-inning home run all year and their first win over Eckersley since September 6, 1987.

September 4

1960— Chuck Estrada has a no-hitter until Bill Skowron singles with two out in the seventh. The Yankees score twice in the inning, ending an Oriole's scoreless string of 33 innings (25 against the Yanks). Estrada and Hoyt Wilhelm combine on a 6-2 win to run the Birds' winning streak to seven.

1968— Dave McNally wins his 11th straight and hits his third homer of the year as the Orioles beat New York, 6-3. Stan Bahnsen loses his fourth straight to the Orioles in 1968.

1969— Frank Robinson, Boog Powell and Brooks Robinson hit consecutive home runs in the ninth to tie the Tigers, 4-4, in Detroit. The Orioles win it on Mark Belanger's ground out.

1970— Brooks Robinson goes 5-for-5, including two home runs at Fenway Park in an 8-6 win over the Red Sox. It is the second time in his career that Brooks has five hits in a game. The first was more than 10 years earlier, July 15, 1960, against the White Sox.

1973— Jim Palmer and Luis Tiant match pitches for 12 innings before Ben Oglivie's homer wins it, 2-1, for Boston, at Fenway Park.

1974— The Birds blank the Red Sox for the third straight game on Jim Palmer's three-hitter. Earl Williams blasts two homers in the 6-0 win. In the series, Boston is held to eight hits, all singles, in 27 scoreless innings.

1989— Tim Hulett, playing at Memorial Stadium for the first time since being called up from Rochester, hits a two-out ninth inning homer

Tim Hulett

off Rod Nichols, who had retired 15 straight batters, as the Orioles edge Cleveland, 5-4.

September 5

1965— Curt Blefary, the American League Rookie of the Year, breaks a 5-5 tie with a grand-slam homer off Cleveland's Bob Tiefenauer. It is Blefary's second homer of the game and first grand slam by an Oriole since Luis Aparicio connected off Jim Grant in September, 1963.

1969— Mike Cuellar becomes the third pitcher in Oriole history to win 20 games in a season as the Birds beat Detroit, 8-4. Steve Barber (1963) and Dave McNally (1968) were the first two Orioles to win 20.

1989— Bob Milacki wins his 10th and Gregg Olson notches his 24th save, setting an American League record for a rookie, in a 3-1 win over the Indians. Cal Ripken becomes the first shortstop to hit 20 or more homers for eight straight seasons, but Cleveland's Brad Komminsk steals the spotlight by jackknifing over the left field fence with Cal's drive in his glove. The ball falls out when he lands on the other side. Later, teammate Joe Carter called it "the greatest catch never made."

1992— The Orioles win their seventh straight, 4-1, in Anaheim as Mike Mussina pitches eight strong innings to notch his 14th win against just five losses. In six of the seven straight wins, O's pitchers allowed a total of only three runs. They would never again be as close to first place as they were after this game (½ game behind Toronto).

1995— The impossible is finally at hand. Cal Ripken ties baseball's "Iron Man," Lou Gehrig by playing in his 2,130th consecutive game. In the days leading up to the magic event, a banner was unfurled from the warehouse signifying the number of consecutive games Cal had played. The fifth inning ceremony, when the number 2,129 gave way to 2,130, brought a huge ovation from the fans. A specially designed baseball emblazoned with the "Streak Week" logo was used in the tying and record breaking games, marking the first time ever that a special ball was used to honor an individual. In the 8-0 win over the Angels, the Orioles tied a club record for most homers in a game in Baltimore with six. They tied another team mark by hitting four homers in one inning when Chris Hoiles, Jeff Manto, Mark Smith and Brady Anderson went deep in the second inning. Cal himself homers in the sixth inning to add the frosting on the cake and set the scene for the record breaker the following night. Ceremonies afterward featured Henry Aaron, Ernie Banks, Johnny Unitas, Frank Robinson, David Robinson, Tom Selleck and others. Former pitcher Jim Gott

Cal Ripken Jr.

gave Cal the game ball from the first game of the streak in 1982. It was from Gott's first major league win with Toronto.

1997— The Orioles and Yankees combine to play a four-hour, 22-minute game at Yankee Stadium, breaking by one minute the record for longest nine-inning game in major league history. The Orioles win, 13-9, with the game ending at midnight. It breaks by a minute the mark set April 30, 1996 at Camden Yards between the same two teams.

September 6

1974— The Orioles set an American League record by stretching their consecutive shutout string to five games after blanking Cleveland in both ends of a doubleheader. Dave McNally pitches a three-hitter in the opener to win, 2-0, and Enos Cabell hit his first home run. Mike Cuellar, with the pressure mounting, pitches a five-hitter to win his second 1-0 decision in a row.

1979— Dennis Martinez, who hasn't won a game in five weeks, pitches a five-hit shutout, defeating Toronto, 5-0. It is the O's 14th straight win over Toronto in two seasons.

1982— Benny Ayala's two-run pinch homer, off Dave LaRoche at Yankee Stadium, is the 11th pinch homer of the year by the O's, setting an American League record.

1983— Jim Palmer wins the 267th game of his career as the Orioles pound Dennis Eckersley and the Red Sox, 8-1, at Memorial Stadium. The Orioles up their division lead to four games.

1987— Jim Dwyer hits a pinch-hit, two-run homer in the bottom of the ninth off Dennis Eckersley giving the Orioles a 7-6 win over the A's. Oakland had wiped out a 4-1 Orioles lead with five runs in the seventh. Cal Ripken's eighth-inning homer off Eckersley made it 6-5, setting up Dwyer's heroics.

1995— It was out of a Hollywood script. Lou Gehrig's invincible record of 2,130 consecutive games, held for 56 years until the evening before, officially fell at 9:20 p.m. when the Orioles left the field in the middle of the fifth inning. Cal, who had homered the previous two nights, homered in the record breaker as the Orioles led, 3-0. When the number 2,131 was unfurled with a musical fanfare, fireworks erupted throughout the ballpark amidst the black and orange balloons and confetti. As Cal's parents looked on, along with the President and Vice President of the United States and the "Yankee Clipper" Joe DiMaggio, Cal removed his jersey and handed it to his two-year-old son Ryan. Despite numerous curtain calls, the crowd refused to stop applauding and Cal, at the urging of several teammates, took a victory lap around the park, shaking hands with fans, security guards, groundskeepers, bullpen pitchers, umpires and members of the visiting Angels. The ovation lasted over 22 minutes before the Orioles and Angels resumed action. The Orioles won, 4-2, as Rafael Palmeiro homered twice, and Cal and Bobby Bonilla one apiece.

Postgame ceremonies featured DiMaggio, who had played with Gehrig, and several members of the 1982 Orioles. Cal paid tribute to Lou Gehrig, saying, "I know that if Lou Gehrig is looking down on tonight's activities, he isn't concerned about someone playing one more game than he did. Instead, he's viewing tonight as just another example of what is good and right about the great American game."

1996— One year to the day that Cal Ripken broke Lou Gehrig's consecutive games streak, Eddie Murray hits his 500th career home run, in Baltimore, off Detroit's Felipe Lira in a 5-4 loss. With the blast, Eddie becomes the 15th player with 500 home runs and only the third, along with Willie Mays and Henry Aaron, to have 500 homers and 3,000 hits.

1998— Pitching for the first time since the birth of his first son, Mike Mussina pitches eight solid innings, striking out 10 in the 5-2 win over Seattle at the Kingdome. Eric Davis, Mike Bordick and Roberto Alomar homer as the O's win for just the second time in the last 13 games.

September 7

1956— Bob Nieman sets a club record by hitting in his 20th straight game.

1958— The Orioles use 24 players out of the 25-man roster in a loss to Boston.

1971— Dave McNally picks up his 12th straight win to up his record to 18-4 as the O's beat Cleveland, 3-1. McNally hits a two-run homer off loser Sam McDowell.

1974— The winning streak reaches 10, but the consecutive scoreless innings string is stopped at 54, a new league record, when Ross Grimsley, leading, 3-0, in the ninth, gives up a two-run homer to Charlie Spikes. The previous American League record of 47

Dave McNally

consecutive scoreless innings was set by the 1948 Cleveland Indians. The Birds fell two shy of the major league record of 56, set by the 1903 Pittsburgh Pirates.

1975— Jim "Catfish" Hunter becomes the third pitcher in American League history to win at least 20 games in five straight seasons with a 2-0 win over the Orioles and Jim Palmer. Catfish was the second biggest winner against the Orioles with 26 career wins, four behind Whitey Ford. He was the biggest loser with 24.

1988— Curt Schilling, obtained in a trade with Boston on July 30, is recalled from AA ball and makes his major league debut in a 4-3 win over the Red Sox. Schilling works seven innings in his first appearance above AA. The Orioles win the game in the ninth despite a shift employed by Bosox manager Joe Morgan. With Cal Ripken up and the scored tied at 3-3, Morgan brings Mike Greenwell in from left field to play between shortstop Jody Reed and the second base bag. Ripken hits a bouncer to Reed who flips to second baseman Marty Barrett to start a double play. Todd Benzinger can't handle the relay to first and the winning run scores. The Sox lost for the first time all season when leading going into the ninth. They had been 71-0.

1989— In the first of two with Texas, Nolan Ryan strikes out 10 but loses, 8-3, as Mike Devereaux drives in a career-high five runs. Ryan is now 5-16 lifetime against the Orioles. The Orioles win the nightcap 9-5 for just their second sweep since September, 1984.

1996— Mike Mussina blanks the Tigers, 6-0, at Camden Yards for the Orioles' only shutout of the season. It comes in the 142nd game to tie an American League record. The O's become the fourth American League team to throw only one shutout in a season, matching Chicago (1924), Washington (1956) and Seattle (1977). The previous club record for fewest shutouts in a season was four in 1994.

1998— Mark McGwire hits his 61st home run off former Oriole Mike Morgan and later on this Labor Day, Ken Griffey hits his 49th and 50th home runs in Seattle's 11-1 rout of the Orioles at the Kingdome. Griffey hits the 50 home run level for the third time, hitting a grand slam off Jimmy Key and driving in six runs.

September 8

1960— After a scoreless tie for the first six innings, the Orioles erupt for nine runs in the seventh inning to set a club record as the Orioles beat Cleveland on Jack Fisher's third straight shutout. The Birds muster only four hits, including a three-run homer by Gene Woodling and Marv Breeding's bases-clearing triple. Cleveland pitchers walk six as 13 O's bat in the inning.

1968— Dave McNally becomes the second 20-game winner in club history, joining Steve Barber, and wins his 12th straight in the process. McNally's 3-2 win over Chicago ties Moe Drabowsky's club record for consecutive wins.

1976— Jim Palmer becomes a 20-game winner for the sixth time in seven years, beating Cleveland, 3-1, at Memorial Stadium. He becomes the first 20-game winner in the American League in 1976.

1985— The Orioles (20) and Angels (23) combine to use 43 players, a record for an Oriole game, as the Angels score three runs in the 11th to win, 7-4.

Gene Woodling

1992— Led by Danny Tartabull's two homers and nine RBI (a record for RBI by one player against the O's), the Yankees bludgeon six Oriole pitchers for 20 hits and win 16-4 at Camden Yards. Chito Martinez sets an O's fielding record with 10 putouts in right field.

1998— On the night in which Mark McGwire slugs his record-breaking 62nd homer against the Cubs, the Orioles beat the A's in Oakland, 5-2, to reach the .500 mark before the smallest crowd of the season, 7,924, at the Coliseum.

September 9

1954— Enos Slaughter's bad-hop single in the eighth over Bobby Young's head deprives Joe Coleman of a no-hitter, but Joe wound up with a one-hit, 1-0 win over the Yankees.

1962— The Orioles, who had no hits and trailed, 3-0, with two down in the seventh, tie it in the eighth, and Brooks Robinson's homer in the 14th wins it 4-3 over L.A. Hoyt Wilhelm works five perfect innings, striking out five.

1967— Frank Robinson hits his 400th homer off Minnesota's Jim Kaat, but the Twins win, 3-2.

1970— Mike Cuellar wins his 22nd of the season, 1-0, over the Yankees. Brooks Robinson drives in Frank Robinson with the only run of the game.

1974— Paul Blair's game-saving catch in the 11th helps preserve a 6-5 win in Milwaukee. George Scott smashes a screaming line drive to deep center, and Blair races back and catches the ball just a few feet from the fence. His momentum carries him through the fence that led to the bullpen.

1977— Terry Crowley's pinch-hit, grand-slam homer in the eighth inning enables the Orioles to defeat Cleveland, 7-1, at Memorial Stadium.

Terry Crowley

1983— Scott McGregor loses his first on the road after 13 straight wins away from home, 5-3, to the Yankees. Graig Nettles' two-run homer in the eighth erases a 3-2 Orioles' lead.

1986— The Orioles announce that Earl Weaver will not return as manager in 1987. He would finish out the '86 season and would be succeeded by third base coach Cal Ripken, Sr.

September 10

1965— Brooks Robinson, Curt Blefary and Jerry Adair hit consecutive home runs, the first off Fred Talbot and the last two off John Wyatt, in a 5-2 win over Kansas City at Memorial Stadium.

1979— The Orioles explode for 16 hits and rout the Red Sox, 16-4, at Fenway Park. Rick Dempsey hits his first grand slam ever (and a club-record-tying seventh for the O's).

1982— Eddie Murray's home run in the 13th off Dan Spillner beats the Indians, 3-2, in Cleveland. Murray's clout is one of a club-record 30 game-winning RBI for Eddie in 1982.

1983— The O's and Yanks are tied, 2-2, in the ninth when the Birds erupt for six runs. John Lowenstein hit a grand slam off Goose Gossage. Mike Boddicker wins his 13th in the nightcap, 3-1, and Tippy Martinez saves his 16th as the Birds lead the east by 5½.

1989— Phil Bradley homers in the first inning, making him the first Oriole ever with double figures in doubles, triples, homers and steals in one season but the Rangers score six in their half of the first off Dave Schmidt and roll, 8-1.

September 11

1959— Two 20-year-olds from the Orioles' "Kiddie Corps," Jack Fisher and Jerry Walker, toss shutouts in a doubleheader sweep of the White Sox at Memorial Stadium. Fisher had a perfect game until Nellie Fox singled with one out in the seventh (19 batters in a row), and Walker went 16 innings until the O's scored the only run of the game on a Brooks Robinson single. It remains the longest pitching stint in Oriole history.

1974— Boog Powell's pinch single in the bottom of the 17th gives Baltimore a 3-2 win over New York and ties the two teams for first place.

1975— Jim Palmer sets a club record with his 22nd complete game, collecting his 21st victory, 10-2, over Cleveland.

1989— Jeff Ballard (17-7) becomes the first American League pitcher in '89 and first Oriole since Steve Stone in 1980 to beat every opponent in one season as the Orioles dump Chicago 6-3.

1992— Cal Ripken suffers a twisted right ankle running out a double against the Brewers in a 3-2 Oriole win. Manny Alexander is quickly recalled from Rochester but Ripken doesn't miss another inning for a week. At season's end Ripken had played in 1735 consecutive games, 395 games shy of Lou Gehrig's 2130.

1996— Scott Erickson pitches his league-high 10th complete game of the season, beating the Angels, 8-3, at Camden Yards. Eric Davis hits his 27th homer, a three-run shot, and drives in five runs. Rafael Palmeiro follows Davis with his 42nd homer of the season.

September 12

1962— Washington's Tom Cheney sets a major league record by striking out 21 batters in going the route to beat the Birds, 2-1, in 16 innings at Memorial Stadium. Ten different players went down on strikes. Snyder, Gentile, Nicholson, Breeding and Hall all struck out three times.

1964— Baltimore's Frank Bertaina beats Kansas City's Bob Meyer, 1-0, with each pitcher allowing only one hit. It is Bertaina's first major league win.

1973— Jim Palmer becomes a 20-game winner for the fourth consecutive year, beating Milwaukee, 4-1, at Memorial Stadium.

1987— Eddie Murray supplants Boog Powell as the Orioles' all-time home run leader, hitting his 304th lifetime homer off Boston's Bruce Hurst in a 4-3 Red Sox win at Fenway Park.

1988— A year to the day when he became the Orioles' all-time home run leader, connecting off Bruce Hurst in Boston, Eddie Murray records his 2,000th career hit, again at Fenway Park and again off Hurst, in a 6-1 loss to the Red Sox.

1990— Ben McDonald tosses his second complete game, a three-hitter and a 2-1 win over Jack Morris and the Tigers at Memorial Stadium. Jeff McKnight hits his first major league homer off Morris to tie the score and Cal Ripken plates the game winner with a bases loaded single.

1991— In a 6-5 loss in Cleveland, Joe Orsulak ties a club record by throwing out three base runners from leftfield.

1992— Cal Ripken ends his home run drought at 73 games (291 at bats) with a solo homer in the sixth inning in the Orioles' 2-1 win over the Royals. Cal has three hits and his diving catch of a liner ends the game.

1993— Mike Devereaux enjoys his biggest game of the season, going 3-for-4 with five RBI in a 14-5 win over Oakland. "Devo" then went 5-for-38 (.132) the rest of the season.

1998— Trailing, 2-0, to the Angels in the ninth, the Orioles come storming back. Mike Bordick fouls off five pitches with the count full before hitting a two-run homer off closer Troy Percival to tie the game. Brady Anderson then singles, steals second and scores on Eric Davis' hit up the middle to give the O's a 3-2 win. Form was working against the Birds. They were 1-68 when trailing after eight innings and the Angels were 72-1 when leading after eight.

September 13

Ben McDonald

1969— The Orioles clinch the division championship as Detroit loses, 11-6, to Washington in the afternoon. The Birds went out and capped the day by belting Cleveland, 10-5, behind the pitching of Tom Phoebus, who won his 14th against six losses.

1971— Frank Robinson hits home runs number 499 and 500 in a doubleheader against Detroit at Memorial Stadium. In the first game, Frank connects off Mike Kilkenny as Dave McNally notches his 13th straight win, 9-1. In the ninth inning of the second game, after most of the fans had left the ball park, Frank joined 10 other sluggers by hitting his 500th, off Fred Scherman. It was 11:47 p.m. and most of the fans had departed when Frank flied out in the eighth, the O's trailing 10-1, thinking he wouldn't bat again. But the Birds rallied for four runs in the ninth and Frank made it a memorable night.

1973— Doug DeCinces' first big league hit drives in the winning run as the Orioles beat Milwaukee, 7-6, in 10 innings.

1976— Utility infielder Tony Muser hits his first home run in over two years, a 10th-inning game winner off Bill Castro in Milwaukee, to complete a four-game sweep. Muser had gone to bat 626 times and played in 312 games since his last home run on June 16, 1974, while with the White Sox. Ironically he hit that one in Baltimore off Jesse Jefferson, whom the Birds traded a year later to Chicago to get Muser.

1983— The Orioles sweep their third straight doubleheader, 7-4 (12 innings) and 7-1, over Boston. Jim Dwyer won the first game with a bases-loaded double off Bob Stanley, and Gary Roenicke's grand slam in the second game helped Bill Swaggerty pick up his first major league win.

1990— Jose Mesa beats Dave Steib and the Blue Jays, 5-3, at Toronto for his second major league victory, 1,077 days since his first one, September 30, 1987 at Detroit.

1992— All-time favorite catcher Rick Dempsey becomes the oldest player to ever play for the Orioles as he celebrates his 43rd birthday.

September 14

1954— A new era begins when Paul Richards signs for 1955 as manager/general manager, replacing manager Jimmie Dykes and general manager Arthur Ehlers.

1976— Trailing the Tigers, 6-0, after 2½ innings, the Orioles score five runs in the third and four in the seventh to gain a 9-7 win. The victory in relief went to a young right-hander making his major league debut, Dennis Martinez.

1982— Cal Ripken hits his first career grand slam off Mike Morgan and the Yankees in a 5-3 win at Memorial Stadium. It was win number three in a memorable five-game sweep of New York.

1983— Dennis Martinez starts for the first time in 5½ weeks and earns his first win since July 26 as Dennis and Sammy Stewart combine to shut out Boston, 5-0, at Fenway Park. Gary Roenicke hits a two-run homer off John Tudor for the O's sixth straight win.

1987— The low point of the season comes at Toronto when the Blue Jays hit a major league record 10 home runs off Baltimore pitching in an 18-3 bombardment. The game also marks the end of Cal Ripken's remarkable consecutive innings streak at 8,243. Ron Washington replaces him at shortstop in the bottom of the eighth inning. The streak had begun on June 5, 1982, five games after the start of his consecutive games streak. Ripken's streak of consecutive innings had run for 5½ seasons. He was the first to play every inning for at least two seasons since Rudy York in 1940-41.

1991— The bells were ringing in the 10th inning of a 6-5 loss to Cleveland as Baltimore's Juan Bell hit a pitch from former Oriole Eric Bell to left field where it is caught by Albert Belle.

1993— Harold Baines hits a 449-foot homer into the centerfield bleachers at Fenway Park in a 11-3 win over the Red Sox. It's the longest ball hit at Fenway Park this season. Baines connects off Danny Darwin and the ball lands 12 rows up. The Orioles trail, 3-2, in the sixth before exploding. Chris Hoiles hits a two-run homer in the seventh and Tim Hulett delivers a pinch-hit bases-loaded double.

1994— The Commissioner's office makes it official. After over a month of no baseball due to the strike, the baseball season is over. No pennant race, no new wild card berth, no LCS and no World Series. The game had hit the depths and it would take several seasons to heal all the wounds the strike inflicted.

1998— Continuing to play the spoiler role, the Orioles blank the Rangers, 1-0, at Camden Yards for their sixth straight win. The O's touch reliever Xavier Hernandez for the lone run in the eighth inning on pinch hitter Eric Davis' one-out sacrifice fly that scores B.J. Surhoff. Juan Guzman, with help from Alan Mills and Armando Benitez, outduels Aaron Sele. Coupled with the Red Sox, 3-0, defeat to the Yankees, their ninth loss in 11 games, the Orioles have pulled to within 6½ of Boston in the wild card chase.

September 15

1963— Milt Pappas, attempting to bunt in the Orioles two-run fifth inning, taps a soft liner to Norm Cash, who throws to McAuliffe at second (doubling Al Smith), who relays to Don Wert, covering first (tripling Bob Saverine). It was the first triple play in the league since 1960 and first by Detroit since 1951. The O's and Pappas win, 2-1.

1966— Hometown boy Tom Phoebus breaks in with a bang, shutting out the Angels, 2-0, on four hits at Memorial Stadium.

1970— Dave McNally's 23rd win, 3-2, over Washington, reduces the Orioles' pennant-clinching magic number to two.

1972— Two walks and a Boog Powell homer give Jim Palmer a 3-1 win over New York. Palmer reaches the 20-win circle for the third straight year.

1977— Down, 4-0, in Toronto in the fifth, the Orioles forfeit the game to the Blue Jays when Earl Weaver removes the O's from the field. Weaver demanded that a tarpaulin covering a mound in the left field corner be removed, contending it was a hazard. The tarp remained and when Weaver refused to return the Orioles to the field after 15 minutes, umpire Marty Springstead awarded the game to Toronto.

B.J. Surhoff

1979— Bob Watson becomes the first player to hit for the cycle in both leagues. Having first performed the feat with the 1977 Houston Astros, Watson singled, doubled, tripled and homered (in that order) to pace Boston over the Orioles, 10-2.

1990— Cal and Billy Ripken both homer in a 4-3 loss at Toronto, becoming the first set of brothers to homer in the same game since Graig (New York) and Jim Nettles (Detroit) did it on September 14, 1974. Both Bill and Cal homered in the fifth inning off David Wells. It was the 15th time brothers have homered in the same game and fifth time it was done in the same inning (first since Hank and Tommy Aaron did it for Milwaukee on July 12, 1962). Cal's homer was his 214th, setting an American League record by a shortstop. The previous record of 213 was held by Vern Stephens, who played with the Browns, Orioles, Red Sox and White Sox in the 1940s and 1950s.

1996— Catcher Mark Parent homers against the Tigers in a 16-6 Oriole win. It's the 241st homer by the Birds in '96 eclipsing the record 240 hit by the 1961 Yankees. Cal Ripken Jr. homers twice with his second coming immediately after Bobby Bonilla connects, marking the 16th time the Orioles have hit back-to-back homers this year, tying a major league record. The Orioles finished with 251 homers, a new major league record. Seven Orioles hit at least 20 homers, led by Brady Anderson's 50 and Rafael Palmeiro's 39.

1997— The Orioles beat Cleveland, 6-5, in the first game of a doubleheader and become the first team in the majors to clinch a playoff spot. The Orioles become the third American League team and the sixth in major league history to win a title by leading from the first day of the season to the end. They join the '27 Yankees and the '84 Tigers in going wire-to-wire in the American League. Both the Yankees and Tigers went on to win the World Series. Before the game the Orioles activate Eric Davis from the disabled list due to cancer surgery and he starts in the first game against the Indians. In the game, Jeffrey Hammonds smashes a 460-foot homer, the second longest homer in the six-year history of Camden Yards.

September 16

1973— In the fastest game of the year (one hour, 39 minutes) Jim Palmer makes it look easy, blanking the Yankees on two hits and winning his 21st of the year, 8-0.

1983— Mike Boddicker pitches another complete-game masterpiece as the O's batter six Milwaukee pitchers for 17 hits and an 8-1 win.

Jeffrey Hammonds

1985— The Orioles set a club record for total bases in one game (41) at Detroit, downing the Tigers, 14-7. Dennis Martinez is the beneficiary of the 19-hit attack that features four doubles and six homers. Three of the homers come in succession in the eighth inning when Fred Lynn, Cal Ripken and Eddie Murray go deep to tie a club record.

1990— The Orioles lose in Toronto, 6-5, their third straight loss in "sudden death" to the Blue Jays. It is the first time the Birds have lost three in a row in the final inning since August, 1965, when they dropped three straight to the Washington Senators.

1991— Mike Mussina goes the distance for the first time in his brief major league career, beating the Red Sox, 9-2, at Fenway Park. It is the Orioles' first complete game win at Fenway since Mike Boddicker turned the trick in 1986. Randy Milligan homers twice to lead the offense.

1992— Mike Mussina pitches his eighth complete game and fourth shutout in winning his fifth straight decision, allowing only four hits in a 3-0 shutout of the Royals. The Birds complete a three-game series sweep despite scoring a total of seven runs. It's the fewest runs scored in a Baltimore three-game sweep since July 4-6, 1972 when they beat the White Sox, 2-1, 1-0, 2-1, at Chicago.

September 17

1955— Brooks Robinson goes 2-for-4 in his major league debut, a win over Washington. Brooks' first hit was off Chuck Stobbs. He went 0-for-18 the rest of the year.

1970— The Orioles win by losing. As they stepped off the team bus at RFK Stadium in Washington, the Orioles found that the Yankees had lost, thus clinching the division title for the second straight year. The O's then played the fastest game of the year (one hour, 48 minutes), losing, 2-0, to Dick Bosman and the Senators, but the loss did not temper the customary postgame celebration.

1970— Dick Bosman, who would serve as Johnny Oates' pitching coach in Dallas, allows manager Johnny Oates' first major league hit at RFK Stadium in Washington when Oates was breaking in with the Orioles and Bosman was pitching for the Senators.

1974— Winning just his seventh game against 12 defeats, Jim Palmer shuts out the Yankees, 4-0, behind Paul Blair's three-run homer to pull Baltimore to within 1½ of the division lead.

1983— Mike Flanagan wins his fifth straight, upping his record to 12-3, as the O's edge Milwaukee 5-4, reaching the 90-win level for the 17th time in the last 23 years. The win stretches the Birds' lead in the east to seven games.

1995— Kevin Brown combines with Jesse Orosco in a four-hit, 2-0 shutout over the Yankees at Oriole Park. The win gives Kevin a 12-3 career record against the Yankees, the best all-time winning percentage against New York (.800).

September 18

1960— The Yankees cap a four-game sweep of the Orioles, who trailed by just .001 in the standings when the crucial series began by taking both ends of a doubleheader before 53,876 at Yankee Stadium. The Yanks win, 7-3 and 2-0, to crush the Orioles' hopes for their first pennant.

Brooks Robinson

1963— Steve Barber becomes the first modern Oriole to win 20 games, beating L.A., 3-1, with relief help from Dick Hall. It is Barber's third try for the magic 20th.

1964— On Brooks Robinson Night at Memorial Stadium before 35,845 fans, MVP-bound Brooks drives in his 100th run for the first time in his career as the Orioles top the Angels, 10-8.

1968— Roger Nelson puts on an outstanding pitching show at Fenway Park. He had a no-hitter for six full innings and struck out 13 over the first six. But he weakened in the seventh and lost, 4-0.

1969— Cy Young-bound Mike Cuellar wins his 23rd as the Birds come from behind to beat Boston, 6-4.

1970— Don Baylor, playing his first major league game, is the star as he collects two hits and drives in three runs, including the game winner, in a 4-3 win over Cleveland.

1974— Mike Cuellar wins his 20th for the third time as the Orioles score seven runs in one inning to beat the Yankees, 10-4.

1977— An Oriole-record, regular-season crowd of 51,798 attend Thanks Brooks Day to pay tribute to the most beloved Oriole of them all. Robinson had retired one month earlier. Sixteen new Gold Gloves were presented in ceremonies to replace the originals that he had given away. In a classic gesture, third baseman Doug DeCinces rips the third base bag out of the ground and hands it to Brooks.

1978— Gary Roenicke's first major league grand slam highlights the Orioles' 10-3 victory over the Indians in Cleveland.

1983— Trailing, 7-3, in the eighth, the Orioles explode for six runs, the big blow an Eddie Murray grand-slam homer, to take a 9-7 lead over the Brewers. Milwaukee ties it in the ninth, but the Orioles win in their half on John Stefero's single to right, scoring Glenn Gulliver.

Mike Cuellar

1984— Third baseman Todd Cruz makes his major league pitching debut at Yankee Stadium, facing three batters and retiring the side on seven pitches in the eighth inning of a 10-2 loss. It is the first time that Cruz, who has one of the strongest infield arms in baseball, has pitched since high school.

1988— Pitcher Bob Milacki makes his major league debut in Detroit, combining with Tom Niedenfuer on a one-hit, 2-0 win, the 28th one-hitter in Oriole history. In his third start on September 28, he shuts the Yankees out on three hits to all but knock New York out of the pennant race. Milacki's big league beginning (2-0, 0.72 era, nine-hits, 25 innings pitched and two earned runs) is the best Oriole debut since Dave McNally won his first three starts in '62-'63 and Tom Phoebus tossed shutouts in his first two starts in 1966.

1991— Cal Ripken becomes the fourth shortstop to hit 30 homers in a season when he connects in a losing cause off Mike Gardiner at Boston, joining Ernie Banks, Vern Stephens and Rico Petrocelli. Boston wins the game, 7-5.

1995— Jimmy Haynes, in his second big league start, earns his first major league victory, beating the Tigers in Detroit, 6-2. Haynes strikes out 11 batters, the most by an Orioles rookie since Mike Boddicker struck out 14 on October 6, 1983 in the ALCS against the White Sox. It was the most K's by an Orioles rookie in a regular season game since Boddicker notched 12 strikeouts in September, 1983, at Detroit.

September 19

1961— Steve Barber throws his eighth shutout, the most in the majors since Bob Porterfield registered nine for the 1953 Senators, as the Orioles blank New York. Leadoff doubles in the first inning off Whitey Ford by Brooks Robinson and Jerry Adair account for the game's only run.

1974— The O's complete a three-game sweep of New York at Shea Stadium as Dave McNally wins, 7-0. The Birds move into first place for the first time since July 13.

1982— A crowd of 41,127 helps honor Earl Weaver on Thanks Earl Day in a moving one-hour, 15-minute ceremony. Rich Dauer capped the emotional afternoon with a dramatic two-out home run in the bottom of the 10th that gave the Orioles a 4-2 win over Cleveland.

1983— John Stefero, a Baltimore native and graduate of Mt. St. Joseph's High School, caps a dramatic 11th-inning comeback with a single to right, giving the Orioles an 8-7 win. The loss eliminated the defending-champion Brewers, who lost their 10th straight.

1989— Bob Milacki evens his record at 12-12 by beating Jack Morris and the Tigers, 6-2, at Memorial Stadium. The bottom third of the order (Craig Worthington, Tim Hulett and Jamie Quirk), collectively 3-for-40 going into the game, went 4-for-7 with five RBI. Worthington and Hulett homered while Quirk drove in the game winner.

1996— Cal Ripken smacks his 483rd career double in the second game of a doubleheader, passing Brooks Robinson for the most in Oriole history.

September 20

1930— First baseman Joe Hauser hits his 62nd and 63rd home runs of the season to lead the Orioles to a 5-1 victory at Newark.

1956— Catcher Tom Gastall, a young "bonus baby" who signed a big contract with the Orioles right out of Boston University in 1955, is killed at the age of 23 when the small plane he is piloting crashes into the Chesapeake Bay. Gastall, who played in 32 games in '56, was the second former player from Boston University to die in two years. Harry Agganis of the Red Sox died the year before of natural causes.

1958— Hoyt Wilhelm, the veteran reliever who had joined the club in August, pitches the first no-hit, no-run game in modern Orioles history, 1-0 over the Yankees. The only run is provided by Gus Triandos, who hit his 30th home run to tie Yogi Berra for most by an American League catcher in one season.

1961— Roger Maris hits his 59th home run as New York clinches the pennant by beating the Orioles, 4-2.

Jerry Adair

1970— Jim Palmer joins Mike Cuellar and Dave McNally as 20-game winners by pitching a four-hit shutout over Cleveland, 7-0. The Orioles became the first club to sport three 20-game winners since 1956 when Early Wynn, Bob Lemon and Herb Score did it in Cleveland.

1973— The Orioles turn an around-the-horn triple play at Tiger Stadium. With runners on first and second, Frank Howard hit a grounder to Brooks at third, who stepped on third for one out, fired to Bobby Grich at second, and on to Terry Crowley at first. Palmer won his 22nd and the Birds stole five bases, three by Don Baylor, and one each by Merv Rettenmund and Brooks Robinson.

1974— Boog Powell's homer over the Green Monster in left gives the Orioles a 2-1 win over Boston, their 19th win in the past 24 games.

1980— Steve Stone matches the Orioles' team record for most victories in a season, defeating the Blue Jays, 6-1, for his 24th win. Both Mike Cuellar and Dave McNally collected 24 wins in 1970.

1984— Ken Singleton's 246th and last major league home run is a grand slam off Boston's Al Nipper in a 15-1 trouncing of the Red Sox at Memorial Stadium. Singleton's last two home runs were grand slams as he connected in Seattle on September 1.

1989— Jeff Ballard wins his 18th game against just seven losses, 9-2, over the Tigers. The Orioles have supplied Ballard with an average of over six runs a game in each of his starts. With nine games remaining in the season the Orioles are in second place in the division, one game behind Toronto.

Brooks Robinson, Mark Belanger, Davey Johnson and Boog Powell

1996— Brady Anderson doubles in the 5-1 loss to Toronto, giving him his 86th extra base hit of the year, a new Orioles club record. The previous mark of 85 was shared by Frank Robinson ('66) and Cal Ripken ('91) who each won the MVP in those years. Brady finished the year with 92 extra base hits.

1998— Without fanfare or notice, Cal Ripken approaches manager Ray Miller 30 minutes before the Orioles' final home game and asks to be replaced in the lineup, thus ending the most remarkable consecutive games playing streak in sports history—2,632 consecutive games played. It began over 16 years before on May 30, 1982 and stretched a full 502 games more than Lou Gehrig's impossible-to-top total of 2,130 straight games that Cal eclipsed on September 6, 1995. Cal wasn't injured, nor was his performance suffering. He simply thought it was time and rather than end the streak on the road, he decided to do it before the home crowd and those who meant the most to him. Once the fans realized that Ryan Minor was stationed at third base and not Cal, they gave Cal a long ovation. The Yankee players joined the Orioles and the fans in the tribute. Said Ripken afterwards, "This shouldn't be a sad moment. I look at it as a happy moment. It's not going to change who I am or change the way I approach the game of baseball. I still consider myself an everyday player. I'm not going anywhere." The Streak began with Earl Weaver and outlasted six other managers. It included a run of 8,243 consecutive innings and only 130 games in which he left early, 27 this year. The Orioles lose, 5-4, to the Yankees and are officially eliminated from playoff contention.

September 21

1971— Dave McNally becomes a 20-game winner for the fourth straight year as he tosses a five-hit, 5-0, shutout over the Yankees.

1974— In a game that starts at 2:21 and ends at 8:48, the Orioles lose a heartbreaker to Boston, 6-5, as Deron Johnson drives in the game winner in the 10th. The game is stopped by three rain delays, the first lasting 2½ hours. Dwight Evans' three-run homer in the ninth helped tie it at 5-5 and set the stage for Johnson's heroics in the 10th.

1975— Mike Torrez pitches the Orioles to their fourth straight win and becomes a 20-game winner for the first timc in his career, 3-0, over Milwaukee.

1983— After losing to the Tigers, 14-1, the night before, the Orioles come back to sweep Detroit in a doubleheader, reducing the magic number to three. Rookie Mike Boddicker won his 15th in the opener, 6-0, on his league-leading fifth shutout. In the nightcap, trailing, 3-1, in the ninth, John Lowenstein hit his second grand slam in 10 days to help shock the Tigers, 7-3. The grand slam was the Orioles' eighth of the year, tying a club record, and was their sixth since August 29.

1996— Eddie Murray hits his 19th career grand slam in a 6-3 win over Toronto. The grand slam moves Eddie past Willie McCovey into second place on the all-time list behind Lou Gehrig's 23.

September 22

1953— In the deciding game of a playoff series between Rochester and the Orioles at Rochester, the Red Wings beat the Orioles, 8-1, to win the series, four games to three, in Baltimore's last minor league game.

1961— Jim Gentile sets an American League mark and ties Ernie Banks' major league standard by hitting his fifth grand slam of the year to lead the Orioles over Chicago, 8-6. The victim was old Oriole Don Larsen.

1966— The Orioles clinch their first pennant in the modern era as Jim Palmer goes the route to beat the A's in Kansas City, 6-1. The Birds were 10 games in front at the time.

1971— The Orioles bury New York, 10-1, as Bobby Grich hits his first major league homer, a three-run shot. Boog Powell homered twice.

1973— Rookie Al Bumbry sets a club record with three triples in one game in Milwaukee as the Orioles clinch the division title, 7-1. Bumbry is the first American Leaguer to hit three triples since Ben Chapman in 1939, and the first in the majors since Ernie Banks in 1966.

1979— The Orioles clinch the American League East title just moments before taking the field for a twi-night doubleheader against Cleveland at Baltimore, as Minnesota eliminates Milwaukee in an afternoon game. The Birds dropped both ends of the twin bill.

1992— A rainy night in Baltimore sees the Orioles' chances of overtaking the Blue Jays pretty much dashed as they fall six games back with 12 to play. Following a 3:18 rain delay at the start of the game, the first pitch was thrown at 10:17 pm and it ends at 1:20 am, a scant two minutes shy of the latest finish in club history. In between the Blue Jays took a 4-1 lead, but the O's battled back with a run in the seventh and another in the eighth, but the possible game-tying run was stranded at third base in the ninth inning. The Blue Jays win, 4-3.

1995— Harold Baines hits his 300th career home run at Milwaukee in a 10-3 Oriole victory. The blast comes off Mark Kiefer.

September 23

1923— In closing day of the International League season at Oriole Park, eccentric Rube Parnham pitches the Orioles to two wins over Jersey City—five to one on five hits in the first game, and 13-0 on three hits in the seven-inning nightcap. For Parnham, who rejoined the club that day after being AWOL for a week, it was his 19th and 20th consecutive wins, culminating a great 33-7 campaign.

1954— Bonus baby Billy O'Dell wins his first major league game, 2-1, over Chicago.

1970— An East Coast power shortage forces postponement of the O's-Tigers game in Baltimore. The game was played the next afternoon and Paul Blair slugged two home runs to power the Birds to a 7-4 win.

1978— In the nightcap of a doubleheader in Baltimore, Jim Palmer beats the Tigers, 6-1, to become the first American League pitcher in 43 years to win 20 games for the eighth season. Lefty Grove, who did it in 1935, also won 20 eight times, while Walter Johnson holds the league record with twelve 20-win seasons.

Al Bumbry

1979— Mike Flanagan beats the Indians, 3-1, for his 23rd victory and the club's 100th. It is the fourth time in Earl Weaver's 11-year tenure that the Orioles had reached the century mark (100-50).

1983— Back-to-back doubles by Rich Dauer and Rick Dempsey, and a single by Al Bumbry, produce three-runs in the second inning. The O's went on to beat Milwaukee, 4-2, behind Scott McGregor's 18th win. It was the Orioles' 10th win against Milwaukee in 11 games.

1985— Lefthanded pitcher Eric Bell becomes the first Oriole since Wally Bunker in 1963 to be promoted directly from Class A ball to the big leagues. He makes his debut the following night at Milwaukee and retires all three batters he faces, two on strikeouts.

1989— Bob Milacki beats the Yankees, 10-2, at Memorial Stadium before over 48,000 fans as Tim Hulett drives in three runs, two on a bases-loaded single. Hulett is now 5-for-5 with the bases loaded since joining the Orioles.

1990— Jeff Ballard, in relief of Ben McDonald, wins his first game ever in relief, 2-1, in 10 innings over Milwaukee. McDonald had held the Brewers to one run over nine innings. It was just Ballard's second win of the season against 10 losses.

September 24

1971— In a memorable doubleheader sweep of the Indians, the Orioles clinch their third straight eastern crown in the opener, 9-2, as Mike Cuellar wins his 20th. Pat Dobson joined Cuellar in the 20-win circle with a 7-0 shutout in the nightcap.

1972— Jim Palmer notches his 100th career win by defeating Milwaukee, 4-2, at County Stadium.

1974— Al Kaline, a Baltimore native, becomes the 12th player in big league history to reach the 3,000-hit plateau, doubling into the right-field corner off Dave McNally in Memorial Stadium.

1975— Jim Palmer wins his 22nd as the Birds top Detroit, 8-1, after a long rain delay. A crowd of only 4,000 pushed the O's over the million mark in attendance for the first time since 1971.

1980— Boston's Tony Perez and Baltimore's Terry Crowley knock two homers each in a home-run battle that ended, 12-9. Orioles' Doug DeCinces snapped a 9-9 tie with a three-run homer in the bottom of the seventh.

1989— In the final home game of the year the Orioles are blanked by the Yankees, 2-0, before a Memorial Stadium crowd of 51,173. The Birds set a new home attendance record of 2,535,208 for 78 dates, over 400,000 more fans than they had ever drawn before.

1996— Eddie Murray doubles in the 13-8 loss to Boston, giving him 20 or more doubles in 20 straight seasons. Only Eddie and Tris Speaker, who did it from 1908-1928, ever accomplished the feat. Eddie finishes the year with 79 RBI, his 20th consecutive season with 75 or more RBI, a new major league record, breaking Aaron's mark of 19 straight seasons with 75+ RBI.

1997— Despite going 10-13 over the final three weeks of the season, the Orioles clinch their first American League East title in 13 years with a 9-3 win at Toronto.

September 25

1954— Don Larsen loses his 21st game of the year against just three wins. The loss total led the league and set a dubious Oriole record that still stands.

1955— The Orioles close the season with their 15th win in the last 20 games to show a three-game improvement over the year before, when they won 54 and lost 100.

1970— Squandering a 5-0 lead, the Orioles beat Cleveland, 9-7, on Terry Crowley's two-run homer in the 13th. The win gives the Orioles a two-year victory total of 217, matching the 1927-28 Yankees with the best two-year record in league history.

1983— The Orioles clinch their seventh American League eastern championship since divisional play began in 1969 by beating Milwaukee, 5-1, at County Stadium. Home runs by Jim Dwyer and Joe Nolan helped eliminate Detroit with a week left in the regular season.

1988— The Orioles drop a doubleheader to Detroit and reach 100 losses for just the second time in club history. Jack Morris throws a one-hitter, allowing only a single to Mickey Tettleton in the seventh inning of the first game. It was the 34th anniversary of the Orioles only previous 100th loss in 1954.

1989— Starting the final week of the season just one game out of first place, the Orioles beat Milwaukee, 5-3, as Pete Harnisch pitches the best game of his career and Gregg Olson finishes up with his 20th consecutive scoreless appearance. Olson is named American League "Rookie of the Year" with his 27 saves. He is also the toughest pitcher in the league to homer off of, facing 365 batters (85 innings) and allowing only one homer, by Dwight Evans.

1990— The first eight Yankee batters hit safely off Anthony Telford and Mickey Weston to tie an American League record. The previous occurrences were in 1954 and 1960 and the Orioles were the victims both times. The Yankees score eight runs in the first inning en route to a 15-3 win.

1998— First baseman Rafael Palmeiro is overwhelmingly selected as the Orioles' Most Valuable Player by vote of media members who cover the club on a regular basis. Palmeiro also won in 1995 and 1996. Eddie Murray won the award a record seven times. For the season, Raffy played in all 162 games, batting .296 with 43 home runs and 121 RBI. Eric Davis, who hit .327 with 28 homers and 89 RBI and had a 30 game hitting streak, was runner-up to Palmeiro in the voting.

September 26

1961— The Yankees edge the O's, 3-2, as Roger Maris ties Babe Ruth's single-season record with his 60th home run of the year off Jack Fisher in Yankee Stadium.

1962— In the shortest game ever played in Memorial Stadium, Dave McNally, in his major league starting debut, shuts out Kansas City, 3-0, in just 1 hour and 32 minutes.

1968— Dave McNally wins his 22nd game, 7-1, over Cleveland, and in the process sets club records for wins, consecutive wins in one year (12), innings pitched (273), complete games (18), strikeouts (202) and ERA (1.95).

1971— Jim Palmer fires a three-hitter to shut out Cleveland, 5-0, and join the 20-win club, thereby making the Orioles the first team in 51 years to have four 20-game winners.

1978— Mike Flanagan loses his bid for a no-hitter with two outs in the ninth inning. Cleveland's Gary Alexander homers as the Orioles beat the Indians, 3-1, in Baltimore.

1956— Charlie Beamon becomes the first Oriole to pitch a shutout in his major league debut, blanking the Yankees, 8-0.

1984— Storm Davis surrenders the only home run he allows at home all season, in his last inning of work for the season as New York's Don Baylor connects with two-outs in the ninth. The homer breaks a string of 147-homerless innings by Davis at Memorial Stadium.

1992— Craig Lefferts wins his first game as an Oriole and first in the American League, a 2-0 decision over the Red Sox. No runner reached second base. Lefferts pitched 7.1 innings and Gregg Olson saved it.

1993— Detroit's Eric Davis, a future Oriole, hits the longest home run in Camden Yards' brief history, blasting an Arthur Rhodes offering 452 feet to center field. Detroit wins, 9-4, in the first game of a doubleheader. The Tigers win the second game, 6-5, to eliminate the Orioles from the A.L. East race.

1995— Mike Mussina begins a string of five consecutive shutouts to end the season, blanking the Blue Jays, 5-0. Orioles pitchers match a league and club record with the shutouts, four of which were complete games, by Mussina to start and end it, Scott Erickson and Kevin Brown. A shutout on the next to last day, a 12-0 win over Detroit, was a combined effort by Ben McDonald, Jimmy Haynes and Jesse Orosco. The Orioles concluded the '95 campaign with 45.0 consecutive shutout innings pitched. The American League and team record is 54 set by the '74 Orioles at the start of their amazing stretch run that began with two 1-0 shutouts over the Red Sox on Labor Day.

September 27

1959— The Orioles beat the Yankees to finish with a 12-10 record against New York, winning a season series against them for the first time. It was the first time since 1925 that the Yanks did not win 85 or more games, finishing 79-75. The O's finished 74-80.

1960— In the most one-sided victory in club history, the Orioles clobber Boston, 17-3, on 18 hits and five RBIs by Jim Gentile. The Birds amassed 35 total bases in the game.

1961— Steve Barber becomes the first Oriole pitcher to beat New York four times in one year, tying Chuck Estrada's club record for most wins in a season (18). The Birds win, 3-2, behind Boog Powell's first major league RBI on his first major league hit, a third-inning single.

Charlie Beamon

1963— Most Valuable Oriole Stu Miller sets an American League record for most appearances (71) and games finished (59), chalking up his 26th save as the Birds down Detroit. Miller also led the league with 31 relief points on five wins and 26 saves.

1970— Dick Hall celebrates his 40th birthday by working three perfect innings against Cleveland to gain credit for a 4-3 victory, his 10th of the season.

1974— Baltimore beats Milwaukee, 1-0, on Bob Oliver's slow roller in the bottom of the 17th and moves a full game in front of New York, the biggest lead of the year.

1977— Mike Flanagan strikes out a career-high 13 batters, pitching the Orioles to a 6-1 triumph over Detroit in Baltimore.

1978— Doug DeCinces extends his hitting streak to 17 games, and the Orioles defeat Cleveland, 3-1.

1986— Scott McGregor gives up a bunt single to Paul Molitor to lead off the game, then retires 24 straight Brewers, finishing with a two-hit, 7-0 win at County Stadium.

1989— Bob Milacki, Kevin Hickey and Mark Williamson combine on a six-hit shutout of the Brewers, 4-0. Mickey Tettleton, mired in a 1-for-17 slump and dropped to sixth in the batting order, hits a decisive three-run homer after failing to execute a sacrifice bunt. It's Milacki's fifth straight win as he becomes the first rookie in 71 years to lead the league in starts. The win sets up a dramatic three-game finale of the season in Toronto with the Orioles having to win at least two to set up a one-game playoff in Baltimore on Monday.

1991— Cal Ripken drives in five runs in a 9-7 win at Tiger Stadium. It's the first of a three-game stretch in which Cal drives in 11 runs while going 8-for-14 with two doubles, a triple and two home runs.

1992— Thinking they caught a break, the Orioles run into Joe Hesketh, subbing for the scratched Roger Clemens. Hesketh instead hurls a four-hit complete game win as Boston wins, 6-1, to eliminate the Birds from the division title race. On September 5, the O's were 19 games over .500 and only ½ game

Dick Hall uniform—1971

behind Toronto, but what followed was a 7-13 tailspin as they tumbled to a season-high seven games out. In the 21 games leading up to their elimination, the Birds failed to score more than four runs in any game. It matched the longest stretch in team history, August 3-25, 1954.

1996— In a nasty altercation with plate umpire John Hirschbeck, Roberto Alomar has to be restrained after spitting in Hirschbeck's face during an argument over ball-strike calls at Toronto's Skydome. Alomar later apologizes but is fined and suspended for the first five games of the 1997 season.

1997— One day after receiving a chemotherapy treatment in Milwaukee, Eric Davis goes 4-for-5 against the Brewers, smacking his first home run since May 6 in a 5-4 Orioles win.

September 28

1960— Ted Williams closes out his great career with the Red Sox at the age of 42. In his third plate appearance, he blasts a ball toward the bullpen in right center field but Al Pilarcik makes a leaping catch to rob Williams of a homer. However, on his final time up, Ted connects off Jack Fisher for his 521st lifetime homer, sending Fenway Park into a frenzy.

1973— The Birds set a Memorial Stadium record with 18 runs against Cleveland. Utility infielder Frank Baker's first major league homer is a grand slam off Dick Bosman. The final is 18-4.

1976— At Memorial Stadium, Wayne Garland becomes the American League's third 20-game winner as the Orioles defeat Milwaukee, 7-5, in the first game of a doubleheader. Jim Palmer had already reached the 20-victory plateau.

1977— Jim Palmer becomes a 20-game winner for the seventh time in the last eight years when the Orioles defeat Detroit, 3-2, in 11 innings, at Memorial Stadium.

1979— Billy Smith drives in six runs in Cleveland and hits a grand slam in the O's 14-6 win. It is the eighth bases-loaded smash of the year by the O's, a club record.

1987— Righthander John Habyan pitches 8.1 innings and combines with reliever Tom Niedenfuer on a 3-0 shutout win over Jack Morris and the Tigers, one of only four times the A.L. East champs are shut out.

1988— Rookie Bob Milacki tosses a three-hit, 132 pitch shutout and beats the Yankees, 2-0, at Memorial Stadium.

1992— In the final home game of the first season at Camden Yards, the Orioles beat Boston, 7-3, behind Brady Anderson's two home runs. His first was his 20th, making him the first player in American League history ever to hit 20 homers, steal 50 bases and drive in 75 runs (his totals were 21, 53, 80). He's also just the 17th leadoff hitter in Major League history to reach the 20-homer plateau. Brady's 53 steals is better than the entire team total in 1991. The final attendance of 3,567,819 is more than 1,000,000 better than the previous club record set just one year before at Memorial Stadium.

1993— Ben McDonald tosses the third two-hitter of his career in a 9-1 win over the Yankees before over 46,000 fans at Camden Yards.

1996— The Orioles beat Toronto, 3-2, at the Skydome and, coupled with a Seattle defeat in Oakland, clinch the American League Wild Card and notch their first postseason berth in 13 years.

Brady Anderson

1997— The Orioles close the season with a 7-6 win in Milwaukee as Jerome Walton homers twice. Cal Ripken runs his consecutive games streak to 2,478. Jimmy Key surrenders the first grand-slam homer of his career to Jeromy Burnitz, encompassing 2511 innings.

September 29

1953— The city of Baltimore is awarded the St. Louis Browns franchise, putting Baltimore back in the majors after 51 years.

1956— Brooks Robinson hits his first major league home run off Evilio Hernandez of the Washington Senators at Griffith Stadium.

1971— The Orioles cap the regular season with their 11th consecutive win, 1-0, over Boston. By winning 101 games, the Orioles tied the major league record for most consecutive 100-win seasons (109-108-101) and gave Earl Weaver 318 wins in his first three seasons as manager, an American League record.

1973— The playoff-bound Orioles finish the season with 97 wins, beating Cleveland, 7-3. Old pro Curt Motton hits a three-run homer as Mike Cuellar wins his 18th.

1976— Henry Aaron scores the 2,147th run of his career, tying Babe Ruth for second on the all-time list (behind Ty Cobb's 2,244) in the Brewers' 6-3 win over the Orioles in Baltimore.

1978— In a losing cause, Rich Dauer plays in his 86th-straight errorless game, to set a major league record for fielding by a second baseman in one season. His total of 426 chances accepted during the errorless streak also broke an American League record for his position. Detroit beat the Orioles, 3-2, at Tiger Stadium.

1980— Steve Stone sets an Oriole high by winning his 25th game, 4-3, over Boston, breaking the record of 24 set by Dave McNally and Mike Cuellar in 1970.

1984— Mike Boddicker becomes the first Oriole pitcher in four years, since Steve Stone and Scott McGregor in 1980, to win 20 games. Boddicker beats Boston, 6-3, at Fenway Park for his fifth straight complete game. It gives the Orioles 23 20-game winners in the last 17 seasons, beginning in 1968. Despite leading the league in wins (20) and ERA (2.79), Boddicker could finish no higher than fourth in the Cy Young balloting. Once again in 1998, no Oriole pitcher won 20 so Boddicker remains the last to do it.

1989— The first game of the dramatic final showdown for the Eastern Division pennant goes to Toronto, 2-1, as Lloyd Moseby lines a two-out RBI single off the left field wall in the bottom of the 11th against loser Mark Williamson. The record Skydome crowd of 49,636 had barely settled in their seats when Phil Bradley hit the very first pitch of the game from Todd Stottlemyre 420 feet into the left-field seats. Jeff Ballard left with a shutout in the eighth but Toronto tied the game on a Gregg Olson wild pitch. The Blue Jays lead the Orioles by two games with two to go.

1992— Ben McDonald's only win during his last 10 starts is a 7-2 decision over Frank Tanana and the Tigers in Detroit. McDonald had a no-hitter for 5.1 innings before Dave Bergman singled. The win snapped a six-game losing streak for Ben.

1996— Brady Anderson hits his 50th home run on the last day of the season, connecting off Toronto's Pat Hentgen for the Orioles only run in a 4-1 loss as Hentgen wins his 20th. Brady becomes the 14th player in history to hit 50 or more homers in a season. The 50 homers trailed Mark McGwire by two. Brady finishes with 110 RBI and a .247 average.

Jeff Ballard

September 30

1978— Rich Dauer's record string of fielding by a second baseman in one season comes to an end as the Orioles lose to Detroit, 5-4. Dauer handled 426 chances before a wild throw in the sixth inning. The former major league mark for one season was by Ken Hubbs (418 changes without an error), while with the Cubs in 1962.

1979— Dave Skaggs hits his second career homer in 439 at bats, off Rick Wise of the Indians, in a 6-5 loss to Cleveland on the last day of the season. Two years earlier, also on the last day of the season, Skaggs hit his first and only other home run, also off Rick Wise, who was then with the Red Sox.

1980— Al Bumbry's two hits enable him to become the first player in Oriole history to collect 200 hits in one season, as the Birds beat the Red Sox, 11-6, in Fenway Park.

1982— Earl Weaver is ejected for the 89th and last time in a dispute in Detroit. Umpire Rocky Roe did the honors as Earl was thrown out for the sixth time in 1982. Marty Springstead and Ron Luciano tied for the honors of ejecting Earl the most, with seven.

September 30

1988— For the second start in a row, Toronto's Dave Steib loses a no-hit bid in the ninth inning. Jim Traber's pinch bloop single to right with two outs in the ninth is the only hit in a 4-0 Blue Jay win. Traber had been in a 1-26 slump. Cleveland's Julio Franco spoiled Steib's no-hit bid in his previous start with a bad hop single.

1989— The pennant race ends in Toronto despite a gallant effort from righthander Dave Johnson who replaced Pete Harnisch as the Oriole starter after Harnisch had stepped on a nail, cutting his foot, while walking back to the hotel the night before. Johnson gave up a first inning run and then retired 18 of 19 batters before departing in the eighth with a 3-1 lead and having given up just two hits and walking three, including Nelson Liriano to open the eighth. Kevin Hickey walks the only man he faces, then Mark Williamson comes on and the next four batters bring the pennant to Toronto. Lloyd Moseby sacrifices, Mookie Wilson singles, scoring Liriano and Fred McGriff drives in the tie run with another single. George Bell's sacrifice fly wins it, 4-3, as the Orioles go down 1-2-3 in the ninth.

1995— Brady Anderson matches his career high with five RBI against the Tigers, in a 12-0 Oriole win at Camden Yards. Four of the five RBI come on his first career grand slam which he clubs off Sean Bergman. The five RBI matches the club high in '95. Ripken, Baines and Bret Barberie also had five RBI efforts.

Orioles Radio

OCTOBER

October 1

1969— The Orioles close the regular season with a 2-1 win over Detroit as Jim Palmer wins his 16th against just four losses. The win gives the Birds 109 wins, most since the 1961 Yankees.

1970— The Orioles close out the 1970 season with a 108-54 record beating Washington, 3-2, to win the division by 15 games.

1974— The Birds cap an amazing stretch run by winning 27 of their last 33 games, edging Detroit, 7-6, for their eighth straight win. Brooks Robinson scores the winning run from first on Andy Etchebarren's double. Milwaukee beat the Yankees that night on George Scott's bases-loaded single, and the pennant race is over.

1977— The Orioles, who were eliminated from the East Division race by the Red Sox the night before, eliminate Boston in turn, 8-7, at Fenway Park, and enable the Yankees to win the division title.

1982— Faced with sweeping the Milwaukee Brewers to win the east, the Orioles stay alive by taking both games of a Friday doubleheader. Behind the pitching of Dennis Martinez and Tippy Martinez, the Birds beat Cy Young-bound Pete Vuckovich, 8-3, in the opener. Twenty-year-old Storm Davis won the nightcap, 7-1, as the Birds pulled to within one game of Milwaukee and the crowd of over 51,000 chanted "sweep, sweep, sweep."

Storm Davis

1988— After winning his first two starts and at one point sporting a 4-5 record, Jay Tibbs loses his last 10 decisions, number 10 a 7-3 loss at Toronto to finish with a 4-15 record. It establishes an Oriole record for most consecutive losses in a season. The previous record was eight.

1989— In the final game of the season, the Orioles beat Toronto, 7-5, as Ben McDonald wins his first major league game. The final record of 87-75 marks a 32½ game improvement over 1988, the third greatest one-season improvement in modern major league history. The O's 87 wins tie the '67 Cubs for the most wins ever for a team following a 100-loss season. The Orioles spent 116 days in first place after spending a combined 23 days in first from 1984 through 1988. Not bad for a team that had 22 players with less than two years of big league experience.

1992 — Mike Devereaux hits a two-out, two-strike, two-run home run in the ninth inning to tie the game and Glenn Davis' solo homer in the 10th wins it for the Orioles, 3-2, in Cleveland. Mike Mussina finishes the season with 18 wins, the youngest Oriole at 23 to win that many games since 19-year-old Wally Bunker won 19 games in 1964.

1993 — The Orioles finally post a win against Todd Stottlemyre, beating the Blue Jays, 7-2. Stottlemyre had an 8-0 career record against the Birds going into the game.

1996 — In the first of the best-of-five Division Series with the Indians, the Orioles bomb the Tribe, 10-4, at Camden yards. David Wells, with help from Jesse Orosco, Terry Mathews, Arthur Rhodes and Randy Myers, gets the win over Charles Nagy. B.J. Surhoff homers twice, while Brady Anderson and Bobby Bonilla also homer, Brady's leading off the game.

1997 — Mike Mussina squares off against Randy Johnson at the Kingdome in the first game of the best-of-five Division Series. The Orioles break a 1-1 tie with four runs in the fifth and four in the sixth en route to a 9-3 win. Mussina limits the Mariners to two runs through seven innings to get the win.

October 2

1960 — After two sevenths, three sixths and one fifth-place finish, the Orioles break through to clinch second place on Milt Pappas' six-hitter over Washington, 2-1. Jackie Brandt wins it with an eighth-inning homer off Pedro Ramos at Griffith Stadium.

1982 — Beating Milwaukee for the fifth straight time and third in the crucial series, the Orioles tie for the division lead by crushing the Brewers, 11-3, and forcing a final showdown on Sunday. The heroes are pitchers Scott McGregor and Sammy Stewart, plus Rich Dauer and Jim Dwyer, who had reached 13 straight times by hit or walk, a club record.

1988 — The Orioles drop their 107th game of the season, 9-3, in Toronto as Cal Ripken's consecutive game streak reaches six seasons and 1,088 straight games, just 15 games behind Joe Sewell for fifth place on the all-time list. Larry Sheets homers off Jimmy Key, giving him his first RBI of the season against lefthanded pitching after 113 at bats.

1993 — In his last start of the season, Rick Sutcliffe beats Toronto, 8-4, to even his record to 10-10. It's Sutcliffe's first win in nearly two months and denies Blue Jays rookie Pat Hentgen his 20th victory.

1996 — The Orioles make it two straight over the Indians in the Division Series, beating the Tribe, 7-4, before 48,970 fans at Camden Yards. Armando Benitez gets the win in relief. Brady Anderson homers as the Birds take a 2-0 lead in the best-of-five series.

Jimmy Key

1997— The Orioles complete a two-game sweep of Seattle in the Kingdome in the Division Series, beating Jamie Moyer and the Mariners, 9-3. Moyer was forced out of the game with a 2-1 lead in the fifth inning with a strained left forearm and the Orioles took advantage by scoring eight runs off the Seattle bullpen, six against Bobby Ayala.

October 3

1970— Baltimore 10, Minnesota 6 in the American League Championship Series opener. Although Mike Cuellar was knocked from the mound in the fifth, he hit a wind-blown, grand-slam homer in the fourth inning off Jim Perry to give the Birds a 9-2 lead. Cuellar's grand slam is a record in ALCS play.

1972— Roric Harrison homers off Cleveland's Ray Lamb in a 4-3 win over the Indians, thus becoming the last American League pitcher to homer in regulation play (the designated hitter rule begins in 1973).

1979— A 10th-inning homer by John Lowenstein wins the opener of the ALCS, 6-3, over the California Angels. Jim Palmer pitched nine innings of seven-hit ball, with reliever Don Stanhouse pitching a perfect 10th inning. Nolan Ryan started for the Angels. Earl Weaver was so excited at Lowenstein's pinch three-run homer that he ran to second base to help escort the "hero" home.

1982— With everything on the line, Don Sutton out-pitches Jim Palmer and the Brewers beat the Orioles, 10-2, to win the Eastern Division title. Robin Yount hits two home runs for the Brewers, who score five runs in the ninth to break it open.

1988— Don Aase is released after going 41 appearances since his last win on opening day, 1987. Bothered by arm problems, Aase earned his last save on May 23, 1987 and had only one save opportunity after that, on September 26, 1988. Aase leaves the Orioles with 50 saves, sixth on the club's all-time list.

1993— The Orioles end the season on a losing note, 11-6, to Toronto as Joe Carter becomes the 25th player in baseball history to hit two home runs in one inning, hitting a pair off Ben McDonald in the second inning. The Orioles set another season attendance record in the process, drawing 3,644,965 fans to Camden Yards. It's the seventh highest figure in major league history. The Birds sold out their last 52 home games and 71 out of 80 in 1993. Chris Hoiles hit his 29th homer to go with a .310 average, just missing an opportunity to become the first American League catcher ever to hit .300 or better with 30 homers. Cal Ripken completes his 11th straight season without missing a game as his consecutive games streak reaches 1897, second to Lou Gehrig's 2,130. During the streak the Orioles have played 17,271 innings and Cal has played in 17,135 of them.

Chris Hoiles

October 4

1969— In the first ALCS game ever played, Paul Blair drops a perfect two-strike bunt down the third base line to score Mark Belanger from third and enable the Orioles to beat the Twins in 12 innings. Boog Powell had tied the score at 3-3 with a ninth-inning homer off Jim Perry. Frank Robinson and Mark Belanger had homered earlier. Tony Oliva hit a two-run homer off Mike Cuellar. Dick Hall, the fifth Oriole pitcher, was the winner.

1970— The Orioles score seven runs in the ninth to beat Minnesota, 11-3, and take a two-nothing lead in the best of five. Ron Perranoski, who had 34 saves in the regular season, was the ninth-inning victim, giving up a two-run double to Boog Powell and a three-run homer to Dave Johnson.

1971— The Orioles win their eighth straight ALCS game over three seasons, beating Oakland, 5-1, as Mike Cuellar bests Jim Hunter behind Boog Powell's two home runs and solo shots from Brooks Robinson and Elrod Hendricks.

1979— What begins as a Baltimore "laugher," ends as a nail-biting cliffhanger in the second game of the playoffs. Mike Flanagan was handed a 9-1 lead by the end of three innings, only to see it dwindle to one run before reliever Don Stanhouse rode to the rescue and saved the game, 9-8, before a crowd of 52,108 at Memorial Stadium.

1980— Reggie Jackson's home run helps the Yankees beat the Tigers and clinch the American League eastern title. It was the latest the Orioles, who played Cleveland two games that night, had ever been eliminated from a pennant race (just one day left in the season). That night, Gary Roenicke's solo homer in the 13th gave the O's a 3-2 first game win, while Mike Boddicker lost his major league debut, 6-4, in the nightcap.

1991— In the last night game at Memorial Stadium, former Oriole Mickey Tettleton homers in the 14th inning to give the Tigers a 4-2 win. The game ends at 12:13 a.m. and is followed by a fireworks show. The two teams both scored in the second and one each in the 13th before Tettleton's tie-breaker.

1992— The Orioles win the season finale in Cleveland, 4-3, in 13 innings to finish the season with an 89-73 record. It's the Orioles' best record since the 1983 World Series championship season and a major league high 22-game improvement over their 1991 record. Brady Anderson hits his 10th triple to become one of only three players in the majors in '92 to reach double figures in doubles, triples and homers. Teammate Mike Devereaux and Pittsburgh's Andy Van Slyke are the others. Devereaux likewise has a remarkable season, driving in 107 runs and hitting 24 homers as he leads the club in 10 offensive categories. "Devo" was 13-for-25 with the bases loaded for a .520 average with 38 RBI. Catcher Jeff Tackett had an unusual line in the game: AB-0, R-0, H-0, RBI-2. He entered the game in the eighth inning, driving in a run with a sacrifice bunt. He was walked intentionally his next time up and delivered the winning run in the 13th with a sac fly.

1993— American League owners unanimously approve the sale of the Orioles ownership from financially strapped Eli Jacobs to a group headed by Baltimore native Peter Angelos. The price tag, $173 million. Angelos made a fortune representing plaintiffs in the nation's massive amount of asbestos cases. Popular action novelist Tom Clancy, another Baltimorean, becomes a minority investor along with comic book king Steve Geppi, broadcaster Jim McKay and tennis star Pam Shriver.

1996— After a travel date to Cleveland, the Indians beat the Orioles, 9-4, to trail the best-of-five Division Series two games to one. Manny Ramirez and Albert Belle homer for Cleveland while B. J. Surhoff goes deep for the Orioles. Albert Belle's seventh-inning grand slam off Armando Benitez after Jesse Orosco walks the bases loaded decides the outcome.

1997— Seattle avoids a sweep of the Division Series thanks to the strong pitching effort by Jeff Fassero, who tosses eight shutout innings, retiring 18 straight Oriole hitters at one point en route to a 4-2 win at Camden Yards. Fassero escapes runners on second and third and a no-out situation in the third by striking out Geronimo Berroa, getting Rafael Palmeiro to tap back to the mound and striking out Cal Ripken. Fassero went on to retire the next 15 hitters.

October 5

1966— The underdog Orioles, playing their first World Series game ever, beat the Dodgers, 5-2, at Dodger Stadium. Frank and Brooks Robinson hit first-inning home runs off Don Drysdale. Moe Drabowsky, working the last 6⅔ innings in relief of Dave McNally, yielded just one hit and struck out 11 to set a series record. He struck out six straight in the fifth and sixth to tie another mark.

1969— Curt Motton's pinch single to right in the 11th scores Boog Powell with the only run of the game. Dave McNally outduels Dave Boswell, 1-0, to win the second game of the ALCS with the Twins.

1970— The Orioles complete their second straight playoff sweep of the Minnesota Twins, 6-1, as Jim Palmer goes all the way for the win at Memorial Stadium.

The October 10, 1966 Baltimore Sun *sports page.*

1971— Jim Palmer, who had pitched three previous complete-game victories to clinch titles in '66, '69 and '70, does it again, beating Oakland, 5-3, to complete a three-game sweep.

1974— Jim "Catfish" Hunter gives up homers to Paul Blair, Brooks Robinson and Bobby Grich as the Orioles take the first game of the ALCS, 6-3, at the Oakland Coliseum.

1979— California stays alive by taking the third game of the 1979 ALCS, 4-3, in Anaheim. Dennis Martinez led, 3-2, with one out in the ninth before the roof caved in. Bobby Grich's fly ball to short center, dropped by Al Bumbry, brought in the tie run. Former Oriole Larry Harlow's double off Don Stanhouse won it.

1980— Scott McGregor becomes a 20-game winner for the first time as the Orioles close the season with a 7-1 win over Cleveland. It was also the 100th win for the Orioles, the fifth time Earl Weaver won 100 or more games, tying him with Connie Mack for second place on the all-time list behind Joe McCarthy with six.

1983— The White Sox edge the Orioles, 2-1, behind the five-hit pitching of Lamarr Hoyt to take a 1-0 lead in the best of five ALCS. Tom Paciorek's single off Scott McGregor in the third scored the first run. Paciorek scored the game winner in the sixth when Ron Kittle grounded into a double play. Cal Ripken singled home Dan Ford, who had doubled, for the only Oriole run in the ninth.

1986— The Orioles lose, 6-3, to Detroit to finish the season with a 73-89 record, the fourth worst season in club history. The only seasons in which the Orioles fared worse were their first three seasons in the league in 1954, '55 and '56. It is the Orioles' first losing season since 1967, breaking a string of 18 consecutive winning campaigns, the second longest streak in major league history. It is the Orioles first ever last-place finish.

1991— The Orioles win for the last time at Memorial Stadium, 7-3, over Detroit, thanks in large measure to the final home run in the stadium's history, a two-run shot by Chito Martinez in the sixth. Brady Anderson's three-run triple puts the game out of reach. Martinez' homer off Mark Leiter puts the Orioles into the lead for good and gives Chito the game-winning RBI in their last victory in the park they called home for 38 years.

1996— In one of the most memorable games in club history, the Orioles edge the Indians, 4-3, in 12 innings in Cleveland to capture the Division Series, three games to one. Roberto Alomar is the hero. First he singles in the tying run in the top of the ninth, with two outs and two strikes, against Jose Mesa and then homers in the 12th off Mesa to win it and dethrone the defending American League champs. Indians starter Charles Nagy strikes out 12 of 15 batters at one point as the Birds fan 23 times on the day and still win. The Tribe is held hitless over the final five innings.

1997— The Orioles advance to the American League Championship Series as Mike Mussina outpitches Randy Johnson and the Mariners, winning, 3-1. Johnson allows solo homers to Geronimo Berroa and Jeff Reboulet. Mussina gives up just two hits through seven innings, including a solo homer to Edgar Martinez. Armando Benitiz pitches the eighth and Randy Myers saves it with a scoreless ninth.

October 6
1966— Jim Palmer, nine days short of his 21st birthday, becomes the youngest pitcher in World Series history as the Orioles blank the Dodgers, 6-0, to take a two-nothing lead in the series. The Dodgers

committed six errors, three in one inning by center fielder Willie Davis. Sandy Koufax, pitching his final major league game, is the loser.

1969— The Orioles crush the Twins, 11-2, in Minnesota to complete a three-game sweep of the playoffs. Lead-off man Don Buford had four hits, while Paul Blair went 5-for-6 with two doubles, a home run and five RBI's. While Jim Palmer went the route, Billy Martin used seven pitchers, to no avail.

1973— In game one of the 1973 ALCS, Jim Palmer struck out 12 A's and pitched a five-hit shutout to win, 6-0, before over 41,000 at Memorial Stadium. Vida Blue yielded four hits and two walks and was removed after retiring just two batters.

1974— Oakland evens the ALCS at one apiece behind Ken Holtzman's five-hit pitching at Oakland. Ray Fosse's three-run homer off Grant Jackson in the eighth was the big hit. Dave McNally makes his final appearance as an Oriole in a losing cause.

1979— Scott McGregor pitches a six-hit shutout as the Orioles blank California, 6-0, in Anaheim to win the American League pennant. Doug DeCinces helped bring the Birds their first pennant since 1971 with a sensational fielding play that killed the Angels' only serious threat in the fifth inning. Jim Anderson's smash could have been a three-run double. Instead, DeCinces dived, made the stop, hooked the bag with his leg to force Bobby Grich and threw out Anderson to end the inning. Pat Kelly's three-run homer in the seventh helped put it out of reach.

1983— Rookie Mike Boddicker strikes out 14 White Sox and pitches a five-hit shutout as the O's beat Chicago, 4-0, to knot the best of five ALCS at one game each. The Orioles scored single runs in the second and fourth off loser Floyd Bannister and scored two in the sixth when Cal Ripken, who had doubled, came home on Gary Roenicke's home run. Boddicker was voted MVP of the ALCS.

1991— In one of the most emotional and historic days in Baltimore baseball history, the Orioles ring down the curtain on Memorial Stadium, losing to the Tigers, 7-1, before 50,700 fans. The last pitch was thrown by winner Frank Tanana who gets Cal Ripken to ground into a double play to end it. The last Oriole to throw a pitch was Mike Flanagan who struck out Travis Fryman. The last Oriole hit was

Memorial Stadium

a single by Glenn Davis. It was the 25,431 Oriole hit at the stadium. Mike Devereaux tripled in the game to become only the second Oriole to reach double figures in doubles, triples, homers and stolen bases. Phil Bradley was the first in 1989. The total team attendance for the season, 2,552,753, sets a new club record, surpassing the 1989 high by 17,545. Since 1954 over 51 million fans paid their way into Memorial Stadium in 2,746 playing dates.

After the game, a Field of Dreams sequence unfolded in which over 100 former Orioles came out one-by-one to stand at their respective positions with the fans cheering and shedding tears at the same time. Fan favorite Rick Dempsey, who obtained permission from the Brewers to miss their final game in order to attend the O's Memorial Stadium finale, spelled out O-R-I-O-L-E-S one last time and rounded the bases in a home run trot ending in a belly slide at home plate. Home plate was then dug up and whisked away to Camden Yards where a new era of Oriole baseball would begin the following spring.

Mark Belanger

1998— Shortstop Mark Belanger, who teamed with Brooks Robinson to give the Orioles one of the greatest third-short fielding combinations in baseball history, dies of cancer at the age of 54. Nicknamed the "Blade" because of his reed-thin build, Belanger won eight Gold Gloves including six in a row from 1973 through 1978. Belanger retired after 17 seasons in Baltimore and one with the Dodgers in 1982, joining the players association as an assistant to player chief Donald Fehr.

October 7

1973— The Orioles' 10-game ALCS win streak ends as Catfish Hunter beats Dave McNally, 6-3. Sal Bando homered twice off McNally while Bert Campaneris and Joe Rudi hit solo shots for the A's, who evened the series at one apiece.

1983— In a wild and woolly affair at Comiskey Park, the Orioles blast Chicago, 11-1, to take a 2-1 lead in the ALCS. Eddie Murray's three-run first inning homer off loser Richard Dotson got the Orioles off and running. Mike Flanagan hit Ron Kittle on the knee leading off the White Sox fourth, and after Dotson hit Cal Ripken in the fifth, Eddie Murray took exception to an inside offering and both benches cleared. When play resumed, Murray walked and John Lowenstein doubled to score both Ripken and Murray. The Chicago strategy of hitting Ripken when two were out backfired. The Orioles scored a single run in the eighth and four more in the ninth to make it a rout.

October 8

1966— Wally Bunker and Paul Blair team up to give the Orioles a commanding 3-0 lead over the Dodgers in the World Series. Blair belted a 430-foot home run to left-center in the fifth inning to account for the game's only run while Bunker, bothered much of the year by a sore right elbow, fanned six and walked only one. Claude Osteen was the hard luck loser.

1974— Vida Blue pitches a two-hitter and strikes out seven, out-dueling Jim Palmer, 1-0, to take the third game of the ALCS. Palmer allowed only four hits, but one was a solo homer to Sal Bando in the fourth to account for the game's only run.

1983— In a play-off classic, Britt Burns of Chicago shuts the Orioles down for nine innings, while Storm Davis and Tippy Martinez hold the White Sox scoreless. With one out and nobody on in the top of the 10th, Burns made his only mistake as Tito Landrum homers into the left-field seats. The Orioles score two more off SaLome Barojas and Juan Agosto to win, 3-0, and clinch their sixth American League pennant.

1997— Brady Anderson and Roberto Alomar homer early off Chad Ogea and Scott Erickson and Randy Myers combine on a four-hitter as the Orioles blank the Indians, 3-0, in the first game of the American League Championship Series at Camden Yards. Brady leads off the first inning with a homer for the 29th time in his career, including two in the postseason.

October 9

1944— The baseball world takes Baltimore seriously as a future major league city when the fourth game of the Little World Series with Louisville draws a crowd of 52,833 at Baltimore Stadium. The crowd outdrew the major league World Series in St. Louis between the Cardinals and Browns. Louisville won the game, 5-4, to tie the series at two-all, but manager Tommy Thomas' Birds swept the next two games to win the series, four games to two.

1966— The Orioles complete a four-game sweep of the Dodgers to win their first World Championship. Dave McNally retired the side in order in seven of the nine innings, while Frank Robinson's fourth-inning homer off Don Drysdale accounted for the only run of the game. Paul Blair robbed Jim Lefebvre of a home run in the eighth with a leaping catch as the Dodgers went 33 consecutive innings without scoring. Frank Robinson was named series MVP

1971— The Orioles come back to beat Pittsburgh, 5-3, in the first game of the World Series in Baltimore. Frank Robinson's homer in the second, off Dock Ellis, coupled with Merv Rettenmund's three-run homer in the third, put the Orioles ahead to stay. Dave McNally retired 21 of the last 22 batters he faced to get the win.

1973— Despite 11 strikeouts in 10 innings and surrendering only four hits, Mike Cuellar finds himself a 2-1 loser in game three of the ALCS in Oakland. Campy Campaneris, who hit only four home runs in 151 regular season games, hit his second of the playoffs, leading off the 11th. Ken Holtzman pitched a three-hitter to win and Earl Williams hit a solo homer.

1974— The A's manage only one hit off the Orioles, but capitalize on nine Mike Cuellar walks in 4⅔ innings to win the fourth and deciding game of the 1974 ALCS, 2-1, in Baltimore. Cuellar walked in the first Oakland run in the fifth, and Reggie Jackson's seventh-inning double accounted for the second run. Boog Powell drove in the lone Oriole run in the ninth.

1996— In the first game of the best-of-seven American League Championship Series at Yankee Stadium, New York edges the Orioles, 5-4, in 10 innings. The Yankees tie the game on shortstop Derek Jeter's controversial home run in which 12-year-old Jeffey Maier reaches over the fence and catches the ball in his glove preventing Tony Tarasco from making a play on it. Bernie Williams homers off Randy Myers in the 10th to win it. Brady Anderson and Rafael Palmeiro homer for the Orioles.

1997— The Indians score three runs in the eighth inning to come back and stun the Orioles and the crowd, 5-4, to square the best-of-seven ALCS and head to Cleveland with a split. Marquis Grissom's three-run homer in the top of the eighth off Armando Benitez decides the game. Cal Ripken homers for the Orioles.

October 10

1961— Billy Hitchcock signs to manage the Orioles in 1962.

1970— In the first game of the World Series, the Orioles edge the Reds, 4-3, in Cincinnati's Riverfront Stadium. Boog Powell, Elrod Hendricks and Brooks Robinson homered for Baltimore. Brooks began one of the great one-man defensive shows in series history by throwing out Lee May at first after it appeared May's hard shot over the bag would get by for a double. Also in the sixth, a vehement argument ensued after plate umpire Ken Burkhart called Bernie Carbo out at the plate on Ty Cline's high chop in front of the plate. Catcher Elrod Hendricks grabbed the ball and dived at Carbo, knocking down Burkhart. Hendricks tagged Carbo with the glove hand, but the ball was in his throwing hand. Instant replays showed that Carbo failed to touch home plate.

Billy Hitchcock

1979— The opener is delayed a day because of rain, and snow fell in the morning, but the Orioles are hot despite the 41-degree game-time temperature, scoring five times in the first inning and holding on to beat Pittsburgh, 5-4, in the first game of the World Series. Before a chilled but packed house of 53,735 in Baltimore, Phil Garner threw away John Lowenstein's grounder to allow two runs to score, Bruce Kison uncorked a wild pitch to score Eddie Murray and Doug DeCinces capped the scoring with a two-run homer in his first series at bat. Mike Flanagan wiggled out of several jams as the Pirates stranded 10. Willie Stargell homered in the eighth to cut it to 5-4.

1996— The Orioles square the ALCS with a 5-3 win at Yankee Stadium as David Wells outpitches David Cone. Armando Benitiez gets the save in relief of Randy Myers. Todd Zeile and Rafael Palmeiro homer for Baltimore.

October 11

1969— Mike Cuellar beats the Mets and Tom Seaver, 4-1, in the first game of the World Series in Baltimore. Don Buford's lead-off homer off Seaver gave the Birds the lead to stay.

1970— The Reds lead, 4-0, after the first three innings, but the Orioles storm back with one in the fourth and five in the fifth to beat Cincinnati, 6-5, and take a two-games-to-none lead in the World Series. Brooks Robinson ended a Cincy threat in the third, robbing Lee May and starting an inning-ending double play. Boog Powell's second series homer and Ellie Hendricks' two-run double were the key offensive blows. Dick Hall retired the side in order in the eighth and ninth to preserve the win.

1971— The Orioles parlay 14 singles and seven walks into an 11-3 pasting of the Pirates to take a 2-0 edge in the World Series. Brooks Robinson had three hits and drove in three runs, while Merv Rettenmund tied a World Series record with two hits in one inning. Richie Hebner's three-run homer in the eighth cost Jim Palmer a shutout.

1973— Jim "Catfish" Hunter pitches the Oakland A's to their second straight American League Championship, shutting out the Orioles, 3-0, in game five of the ALCS in Oakland.

1979— Thirty-five-year-old Manny Sanguillen lines a two-out pinch single to right in the top of the ninth to give Pittsburgh a 3-2 win and even the World Series at one game apiece. Eddie Murray homered and doubled in the other run. The Orioles had two on and nobody out in the eighth before John Lowenstein grounded into a double play to end the threat. Don Stanhouse gave up the hit to Sanguillen, Manny had only four RBI all season.

1983— President Reagan watches from Oriole-owner Edward Bennett Williams' private box, as game one of the World Series is played in a steady rain. Garry Maddox hits Scott McGregor's first pitch of the eighth inning for a home run, and the Phillies win, 2-1. All the runs are home runs. Winner John Denny gave up a first-inning homer to Jim Dwyer, and 40-year-old Joe Morgan tied it in the sixth inning with a home run to right. Al Holland pitched the final 1⅓ innings after Denny gave up a two-out double to Al Bumbry in the eighth. Holland Strode to the rescue as the Phillies took a 1-0 lead in the best of seven.

October 11
1966— All-time Oriole saves leader Gregg Olson is born in Omaha, Nebraska.

1996— Veteran lefthander Jimmy Key outduels Mike Mussina at Camden Yards as the Yankees win, 5-2, to take a two-games-to-one lead in the best-of-seven American League Championship Series. John Wetteland notches the save as the Yankees win their seventh straight game at Oriole Park. Todd Zeile homers for the Orioles in a losing cause.

1997— The Indians beat the Orioles in bizarre fashion, 2-1, in 12 innings at Jacobs Field to take a two-games-to-one lead in the best-of-seven ALCS. A missed squeeze bunt by Omar Vizquel scores Marquis Grissom from third base as catcher Lenny Webster misses the tag. The game features 33 strikeouts to set a new championship series record. Mike Mussina strikes out 15 including the side three times to set an ALCS record. He strikes out five in a row at one stage. After Cleveland scores in the eighth, the Orioles tie it in the ninth when Brady Anderson's routine fly to center is lost in the twilight by Grissom, falling for an RBI double.

October 12
1969— In game two of the 1969 World Series, the Mets edge the Orioles, 2-1, to square the series at one game each. Left-hander Jerry Koosman held the O's hitless thru the first six innings, as Donn Clendenon's fourth-inning homer off Dave McNally had staked Koosman to a 1-0 lead. The Birds tied it on a Brooks Robinson single in the seventh, but three straight hits in the ninth by Ed Charles, Jerry Grote and Al Weis gave the Mets the lead and the game winner.

1971— After two defeats, Pittsburgh beats the Orioles, 5-1, at Three Rivers Stadium in the third game of the World Series. Steve Blass pitched a three-hitter. Bob Robertson's three-run homer in the seventh off Mike Cuellar broke it open after Frank Robinson had homered in the top of the seventh to bring the Birds to within one run, 2-1.

1979— Trailing, 3-2, to the Pirates after a 67-minute rain delay at Three Rivers Stadium, the Orioles spring to life and roll over Pittsburgh, 8-4, in the third game of the World Series. The Birds' first two runs in the third inning came on Benny Ayala's two-run homer. In the fourth inning, after the rain delay, the O's exploded for five runs, the big blow a bases-loaded triple by Kiko Garcia. Garcia had four hits and four RBI in the game as Scott McGregor went the distance.

1983— Mike Boddicker, the pride of tiny Norway, Iowa, pitches a three-hitter against the Phillies (the lone run was unearned), winning, 4-1, and squaring the series at one game apiece. Boddicker dazzled the Phillies with his remarkable array of breaking pitches, while Phillie rookie Charles Hudson ran out of gas in the fifth. John Lowenstein got the Orioles on the board with a home run and then the "three stooges," Ken Singleton's nickname for the lower third of the batting order, came through. Rich Dauer drilled a single to left, Todd Cruz beat out a bunt and Rick Dempsey doubled home Dauer with the go-ahead run. Boddicker then added a sacrifice fly to left. Cal Ripken singled home John Shelby in the seventh with the fourth run.

1993— Orioles manager Johnny Oates is named American League Manager of the Year by *The Sporting News*, guiding the Birds to an 85-77 record, tied for third in the American League East, 10 games behind Toronto. Oates beat out New York's Buck Showalter for the award. Oates joins Hank Bauer (1966), Earl Weaver (1977, 1979) and Frank Robinson (1989) as the fourth Oriole manager to win the award.

Johnny Oates

1996— A crowd of 48,974, the largest ever to see a game at Camden Yards, watch the Yankees win, 8-4, to take a commanding 3-1 lead in the best-of-seven ALCS. The two teams combine for five more homers and now have hit 13 in the first four games. The Yankees hit four tonight and lead wire-to-wire, marking the first time in the postseason they didn't have to come from behind to win. Darryl Strawberry homers twice for the Yankees.

1997— Once again the Indians win by a run on their last-at bat as they beat the Orioles for the third straight game, 8-7. Cleveland rallies from a 5-2 deficit in the fifth inning with four runs. The Orioles tie it in the ninth off Jose Mesa on Rafael Palmeiro's single off Mesa's foot. The Indians win it in the bottom of the ninth on Sandy Alomar's two-out RBI single off Armando Benitez to take a 3-1 lead in games.

October 13

1970— Dave McNally becomes the only pitcher to hit a grand slam in World Series competition, connecting in the sixth inning off Wayne Granger to pace the Orioles to a 9-3 win and a commanding three games-to-none lead over the Reds. Don Buford and Frank Robinson hit solo homers off loser Tony Cloninger. Brooks Robinson made a sparkling grab of Johnny Bench's liner in the sixth.

1971— The first World Series night game ever played (after 397 day games) draws a record attendance for Pittsburgh and the largest TV audience ever for a baseball game. Twenty-year-old Bruce Kison relieved Luke Walker in the first inning with the Orioles leading, 3-0, and pitched 6⅓ scoreless innings. Premier reliefer Dave Giusti retired six straight Orioles over the final two innings, and the Bucs went ahead in the seventh, winning, 4-3, to knot the series at two games apiece.

1979— Earl Weaver's "Deep Depth" proves vital as the Orioles send 11 men to the plate and score six runs in a 9-6 win over Pittsburgh in game four of the World Series. Leading, 6-3, in the eighth, Kent Tekulve replaced Don Robinson with the bases loaded. John Lowenstein greeted Tekulve with a bases-loaded double to score two runs and, after an intentional walk to Billy Smith, Terry Crowley delivered a pinch double to score Doug DeCinces and Lowenstein with the go-ahead runs. Tim Stoddard hit for himself and singled to right, scoring Smith. It was Stoddard's first hit in professional baseball. Stoddard got the win by shutting the door on the Pirates over the last three innings. The final score was 9-6 Baltimore and a 3-1 edge in the series.

1996— The Yankees end the Orioles' season by taking the ALCS in five games with a 6-4 win at Camden Yards as Andy Pettitte outpitches Scott Erickson. Once again the long ball takes center stage as Jim Leyritz, Cecil Fielder and Darryl Strawberry homer for the eventual world champions while Todd Zeile, Eddie Murray and Bobby Bonilla go deep for the Orioles.

1997— The Orioles stay alive in the ALCS by beating the Indians, 4-2, in Cleveland and sending the series back to Baltimore with the Tribe leading three games to two. The O's took a 2-0 lead in the third on Geronimo Berroa's two-run bases loaded single. Eric Davis homered in the ninth for the Orioles.

October 14

1914— Harry Brecheen, pitching coach for the Orioles in their first 14 seasons, is born in Broken Bow, Oklahoma.

1969— Tommy Agee is the hero for the Mets, homering in the first inning and making two great catches to save at least five runs. The improbable Mets shut out the Orioles, 5-0, to take a 2-1 lead in World Series games.

1970— Cincinnati wins its only game of the 1970 World Series, 6-5, as Lee May's eighth inning homer off Eddie Watt gives the Reds the win. Brooks Robinson has four hits in a losing cause, including a home run.

1971— Nellie Briles shuts out the Orioles on two hits to pace the Pirates to their third straight series win. The final is 4-0, and Bob Robertson's second-inning homer off Dave McNally provides all the scoring Briles needed.

1979— Jim Rooker and Bert Blyleven combine on a six-hitter as the Pirates stay alive by winning Game Five in Pittsburgh, 7-1. The Bucs had 13 hits on the day, including a perfect 4-for-4 for Bill Madlock.

1983— The Orioles climb into the driver's seat by beating Steve Carlton and the Phillies, 3-2, to take a 2-1 lead in the best-of-seven Series. With Pete Rose benched by manager Paul Owens, the Phillies jumped to a 2-0 lead off Mike Flanagan on homers by Gary Matthews and Joe Morgan. When Carlton escaped a bases loaded, no-out jam in the fourth by getting Eddie Murray to pop up and Gary Roenicke to bounce into a double play, it looked like Philadelphia would win. But Dan Ford's towering homer to left halved the deficit in the sixth, and the Orioles tied it in the seventh. Rick Dempsey's two-out double was followed by pinch hitter Benny Ayala's single to left that tied the score. Al Holland relieved Carlton and was greeted by a John

Shelby single. When Ford's hard smash to short was bobbled by Ivan DeJesus, Ayala sped home with the winning run. Jim Palmer pitched two innings of relief to get the win.

October 15

1969— Ron Swoboda's miraculous headlong, back-handed diving catch, inches off the grass in the ninth, helps the Mets stifle a potentially big inning as Tom Seaver beats the Orioles, 2-1, in game four of the World Series at Shea Stadium. The Mets scored the winning run in the 10th when J.C. Martin dropped a bunt down the first base line. Pete Richert fielded it, but his throw hit Martin in the back and rolled into right field, allowing Rod Gaspar to score the winning run from second. Replays showed Martin was running inside the baseline, but umpire Shag Crawford didn't see it that way. Earl Weaver was ejected by Crawford earlier in the game, only the third series ejection for a manager.

1970— Mike Cuellar pitches the Orioles to their second World Series championship, beating the Reds, 9-3, in Baltimore behind home runs by Frank Robinson and Merv Rettenmund. The top of the ninth provided a fitting climax to Brooks Robinson's storybook World Series. He lunged to grab Johnny Bench's foul liner and threw out Pat Corrales to end the game. Brooks was voted MVP of the series, hitting .429 and starring in the field.

1983— The Orioles beat the Phillies, 5-4, to take a commanding 3-1 lead in the World Series. Rich Dauer is the hitting star, breaking out of a 1-26 postseason slump with three hits and three runs batted in. Joe Altobelli used a record four pinch hitters in one inning (the sixth) when the O's scored two runs and took the lead for good. Storm Davis, with help from Sammy Stewart and Tippy Martinez, is the winner. John Denny, coming back with three days rest, is the loser.

1997— In the fourth one-run game of the series, Cleveland second baseman Tony Fernandez hits a solo homer to right off Armando Benitez in the top of the 11th inning for the only run of the game as the Indians eliminate the Orioles, 1-0, in six games. Fernandez was playing in place of Bip Roberts, who injured his thumb in pre-game warmups and was scratched from the line-up. A brilliant pitching effort from Mike Mussina was wasted. Mussina gave up only one hit while striking out 10 in eight innings. The Indians thus avenge their ouster by the Orioles the year before.

October 16

1969— The Miracle Mets upset the Orioles in five games, winning, 5-3, at Shea Stadium. An early Frank Robinson homer and a two-run shot by loser Dave McNally went for naught as Donn Clendenon hit a two-run homer and Al Weis tied it with his first homer ever in Shea Stadium in the seventh. Ron Swoboda doubled in the game winner in the eighth, and Jerry Koosman went the distance for the Mets.

1971— The Orioles rally in the 10th to beat the Pirates, 3-2, and force game seven of the World Series. Frank Robinson, his legs aching from a painful achilles-tendon injury, streaked from first to third on Merv Rettenmund's single to center and slid home safely when Brooks Robinson flied to center field. Roberto Clemente homered in the third and Don Buford put the Orioles on the board in the sixth with a home run.

1979— John Candelaria and Kent Tekulve combine to pitch the first World Series shutout since 1975, 4-0, and force a seventh game. Jim Palmer threw shutout baseball until the seventh, when the Pirates broke through for two runs. The Bucs got two more in the eighth as Tekulve faced only 10 men over the final three innings to pick up his second save.

Scott McGregor

1983— Eddie Murray, battling a 2-for-16 World Series slump, cracks two monstrous home runs and Scott McGregor pitches a five-hit shutout as the Birds win, 5-0, over the Phillies and clinch the third world championship in modern Oriole history. Rick Dempsey who hit only three regular-season homers, clouts a hanging curve from Charles Hudson over the left-field fence in the top of the third. Dempsey also doubled and scored two runs and was named Most Valuable Player. Mike Schmidt symbolized the Phillies' futility with an .050 Series average—one broken-bat single in 20 trips.

1994— Cleveland pitching coach Phil Regan, who spent 22 seasons as a scout, coach and minor league manager, signs a two-year contract to manage the Orioles. Regan was a darkhorse behind former major league managers Davey Johnson and Bill Virdon. At 58, Regan would become the oldest manager in Oriole history, older even than Jimmie Dykes, who managed the 1954 Orioles at the age of 57.

October 17

1971— World Series hero Steve Blass goes the distance, limiting the Orioles to four hits and one run, and out-dueling Mike Cuellar to win the seventh and deciding game of the series, 2-1. A Roberto Clemente homer and Jose Pagan double accounted for the Pittsburgh runs. The Orioles' only run scored on an eighth-inning groundout as Blass set down Boog Powell, Frank Robinson and Merv Rettenmund in the ninth.

1979— Eight years after the Pirates captured the '71 World Series in seven games, the Bucs culminate a brilliant three-game comeback to beat the Orioles, 4-1, in Baltimore and win in seven games. MVP Willie Stargell drove in two runs with a two-run homer off Scott McGregor as four Pirate pitchers limited the O's to just four hits. Rich Dauer's third-inning homer off Jim Bibby accounted for the only Oriole run as Pittsburgh became only the fourth team in league history to win the World Series after being down, three-games-to-one.

1983— A crowd estimated at over 200,000 lines the streets of downtown Baltimore to honor the '83 World Champions. Rick Dempsey led one final Oriole cheer from the steps of city hall as owner Edward Bennett Williams unveiled the World Series trophy.

October 18

1979— A crowd estimated at over a quarter of a million people turns out to honor the Orioles with a parade in downtown Baltimore. The massive outpouring was not deterred by the Orioles losing the World Series in seven games.

October 20

1971— Just three days after losing the World Series in seven games, the Orioles embark on a month-long trip to Japan to play 18 games against that country's best players and teams. The Orioles traveled to 14 cities via airplane, train, bus, ferry boat and hydrofoil, winning 12 games, losing two, and tying four before an estimated 450,000 fans.

1995— Phil Regan, the 11th manager in Orioles history, ends up with the shortest tenure of any one-season manager in club annals, fired after a disappointing 71-73 record in his first big league managerial opportunity.

October 22

1991— Cal Ripken becomes the first player to win *The Sporting News* Major League Player of the Year while playing on a losing club. The award was initiated in 1936. Cal finished third in the league with 34 homers, the most by a shortstop since Rico Petrocelli hit 40 in 1969. He also becomes the first righthanded batter to hit more than 30 homers and strike out less than 50 times (46) since Al Rosen in 1953. Cal, who led the Orioles in 14 offensive categories led the majors with a club record 368 total bases. He was the only player in the league to finish in the top 10 in hits, homers, average and RBI.

October 25

1984— The Orioles embark on a three-week, 15-game tour of Japan in which they win eight games, lose five with one tie. One game is rained out. They win four of five from the Hiroshima Carp and four of five from the Tokyo Giants, managed by home run legend Sadahara Oh. The Orioles blast 35 homers in the 14 games, nine by Eddie Murray.

October 30

1986— The Orioles trade right-hander Storm Davis to San Diego for catcher Terry Kennedy and pitcher Mark Williamson.

1995— Former Oriole second baseman and veteran manager Davey Johnson is named to manage the Orioles, replacing the ousted Phil Regan. Johnson has the highest winning percentage among active managers, leading the Mets to the best record in the majors over a six-year span, averaging nearly 96 wins per year and winning the 1986 World Series against Boston.

October 31

1942— All-time Oriole left-hander Dave McNally is born in Billings, Montana.

NOVEMBER

November 1

1979— Edward Bennett Williams officially takes over ownership of the Orioles from Jerry Hoffberger at a price of $12 million. Hoffberger remained as club president.

November 2

1971— Pat Dobson pitches a no-hitter against the Tokyo (Yomiuri) Giants in Toyama, Japan.

November 3

1968— Vern Stephens, an original Oriole back in 1954, dies in Long Beach, California, at the age of 48.

1975— Hank Peters, 51 years old, replaces Frank Cashen as executive vice president and general manager of the Orioles.

November 4

1933— Tito Francona, who spent two seasons with the Orioles (1955-56) before being traded to Cleveland, where he had his best seasons, is born in Aliquippa, Pennsylvania.

November 5

1958— Lee McPhail is appointed general manager of the Orioles, letting Paul Richards concentrate on managing duties.

1992— Cal Ripken wins his second consecutive Gold Glove Award as selected by the American League managers and coaches. It's the 50th won by the Orioles since the award was established in 1957, eight more than any other AL club (Yankees—42).

1997— In a startling development, Davey Johnson, who managed the Orioles to back-to-back postseason appearances, tenders his resignation through a letter to owner Peter Angelos. In a letter of reply, Angelos accepted the resignation. A misunderstanding over the fine issued to Roberto Alomar for spitting in umpire John Hirschbeck's face contributed to the rift between Johnson and Angelos.

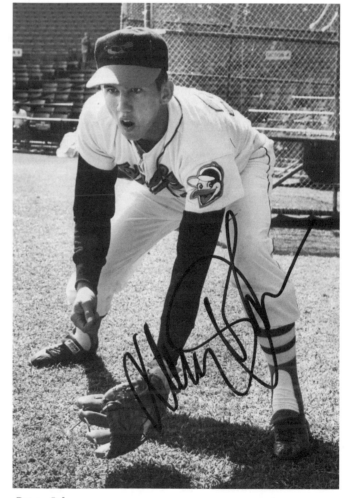

Davey Johnson

November 7

1989— Reliever Gregg Olson is named the American League Rookie of the Year. Olson saved 27 games in 33 opportunities, won five games against two losses and gave up only 14 earned runs in 85 innings pitched with 90 strikeouts. His earned run average was an impressive 1.69. Olson is the sixth Oriole to win rookie of the year honors.

November 9

1931— Whitey Herzog, who came to the O's from Kansas City in 1961 in a trade that sent Bob Boyd, Al Pilarcik, Wayne Causey, Jim Archer and Clint Courtney to the A's, is born in New Athens, Illinois.

1988— In one of the best deals in club history, the Orioles obtain popular Randy Milligan from Pittsburgh for a player to be named later. The Orioles sent pitcher Peter Blohm to Pittsburgh a month later to complete the deal.

November 10

1896— Jimmie Dykes, who hit .280 over 22 American League seasons and came down from Philadelphia to manage the Orioles in 1954, is born in Philadelphia, Pennsylvania.

1987— In a dramatic Memorial Stadium press conference, Oriole owner Edward Bennett Williams, calling it "the end of the beginning," announces that general manager Hank Peters has been fired after 12 seasons and replaced by former White Sox G.M. Roland Hemond.

November 11

1997— Pitching coach Ray Miller is named the 13th manager in Oriole history, signing a multi-year contract to replace Davey Johnson. Miller, who spent parts of two seasons as manager of the Twins in 1985 and '86, named Mike Flanagan as the club's new pitching coach and said hitting coach Rick Down, third base coach Sam Perlozzo and bullpen coach Elrod Hendricks will return. Flanagan had served as pitching coach in 1995 before a two-year stint in the broadcast booth.

November 12

1982— Joe Altobelli becomes the Orioles' seventh manager, signing a two-year contract as Earl Weaver's replacement.

November 16

1983— Cal Ripken becomes the first player in major league history to win the Rookie of the Year and Most Valuable Player awards in consecutive seasons, edging teammate Eddie Murray for American League MVP honors.

November 18

1954— Paul Richards negotiates a 17-player trade with the Yankees, one of the biggest in baseball history. Going to New York are pitchers Mike Blyzka, Don Larsen and Bob Turley, catcher Darrell Johnson, first baseman Dick Kryhoski, shortstop Billy Hunter and outfielders Ted del Guerico and Jim Fridley. The Birds in turn acquire pitchers Harry Byrd, Jim McDonald, and Bill Miller, catchers Hal Smith and Gus Triandos, second baseman Don Leppert, third baseman Kal Segrist, shortstop Willie Miranda, and outfielder Gene Woodling.

1976— The Orioles trade catcher Dave Duncan to the White Sox for outfielder Pat Kelly.

November 19

1942— Bonus boy Larry Haney, a catcher signed out of high school in 1961, is born in Charlottesville, Virginia. Larry joined the Orioles in July 1966, hitting a home run off Cleveland in his second at bat in the majors, and spent 1967 and 1968 in Baltimore before being selected by Seattle in the expansion draft.

1991— Cal Ripken becomes the first player in American League history to win Most Valuable Player honors on a sub-.500 team and the third in major league history, joining a pair of Chicago Cubs, Ernie Banks ('58 and '59) and Andre Dawson ('87). Cal becomes the first MVP in the 61 years of the award to play on a club with more than 85 losses. The Orioles were 67-95. Ripken collected 15 first place votes to nine for runnerup Cecil Fielder. Cal, who has now played in 1,573 consecutive games, hit a career high .323 with 210 hits, and career highs in home runs with 34 and RBI with 114.

November 21

1908— Paul Richards is born in Waxahachie, Texas.

1997— All-time Oriole great Eddie Murray retires as an active player and signs a two-year contract to be Ray Miller's bench coach with the Orioles. Eddie, who spent 12½ of his 21 big league seasons in Baltimore, retires with 3,255 hits and 504 home runs.

November 26

1962— The Orioles trade Gus Triandos and Whitey Herzog to the Tigers for catcher Dick Brown.

1991— Cal Ripken adds to his list of postseason honors by winning his first Gold Glove award and first by an Oriole since Eddie Murray in 1984. Cal led American League shortstops in fielding percentage (.986) for the second straight year; in putouts (267) for the fourth time; in assists (529) for the sixth time; total chances (807) for the fourth time; and double plays (114) for the fifth time. He committed only 11 errors, averaging one for every 73.4 chances. Cal's first Gold Glove

Paul Richards (left) and Dizzy Dean

comes a year after he should have won hands down, as in 1990 he established eight major league fielding records including fewest errors by a shortstop, just three in 680 chances for a .996 fielding percentage. He also set marks for consecutive errorless games (95) and consecutive errorless chances (431).

November 27

1978 — In one of the biggest bargains in their history, the Orioles purchase John Lowenstein's contract from Texas for the $20,000 waiver price.

November 28

1978 — For just the second time since the reentry draft began in 1976, the Orioles sign a player. Pitcher Steve Stone, who would win the 1980 Cy Young Award and set a club record of 25 wins, signed a four-year contract.

November 29

1967 — Don Buford, the best lead-off man the Orioles ever had, is acquired from the White Sox along with pitchers Bruce Howard and Roger Nelson in exchange for Luis Aparicio and Russ Snyder.

November 30

1959 — The Orioles trade pitchers Billy O'Dell and Billy Loes to the San Francisco Giants for Jackie Brandt.

Jackie Brandt

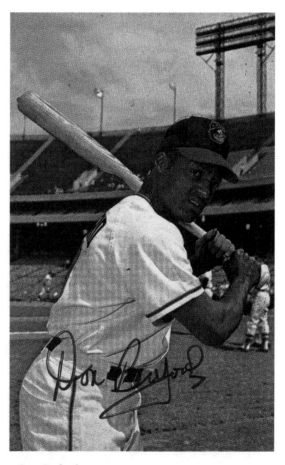

Don Buford

DECEMBER

December 1

1972— In not one of Baltimore's best trades, the Orioles send Dave Johnson, Pat Dobson, Johnny Oates and Roric Harrison to Atlanta for Earl Williams and Taylor Duncan. While Johnson went on to hit 43 homers as a Brave in 1973, Williams spent two turbulent seasons in Baltimore, hitting 36 homers and driving in 135 runs.

December 2

1971— To make room for Don Baylor in the outfield, the Orioles trade all-time great Frank Robinson and Pete Richert to the Dodgers for Doyle Alexander, Bob O'Brien, Sergio Robles and Royle Stillman.

December 3

1974— Lee May joins the Orioles from Houston in a deal for Rob Andrews and Enos Cabell. In six seasons in Baltimore, May hit 123 home runs and drove in 487 runs.

December 4

1974— In a great deal for Baltimore, the Orioles get Ken Singleton and Mike Torrez from Montreal for Dave McNally and Rich Coggins.

December 5

1962— Marv Breeding and Barry Shetrone head down the parkway to Washington for Bob "Rocky" Johnson and Pete Burnside.

December 6

1979— The Orioles acquire second baseman Lenn Sakata from Milwaukee for pitcher John Flinn.

1983— Cal Ripken is named *The Sporting News* Player of the Year, hitting .318 and leading the majors in hits with 211 and doubles, 47, both club records. Cal led the American League in runs with 121 and extra base hits (76), hitting 27 homers and driving in 102 runs.

1988— Agnes Neill Williams, who succeeded her late husband as chairman of the board of the Orioles, announces she has sold the club to a group of investors headed by computer tycoon Eli Jacobs. Jacobs is joined by fellow Yale Law School alums Larry Lucchino, the club president under Williams and Sargent Shriver as minority shareholders.

December 7

1977— The Orioles, who have had amazing success in dealing with Montreal, acquire Gary Roenicke, Don Stanhouse and Joe Kerrigan for pitchers Rudy May, Randy Miller, and Bryn Smith.

December 8

1968— Mike Mussina is born in Williamsport, Pennsylvania.

1996— Veteran lefthander Jimmy Key, who has won 164 games in 13 seasons with the Blue Jays and Yankees, signs a two-year free agent contract with the Orioles.

December 9

1965— On one of the most memorable dates in Oriole history, Frank Robinson officially becomes an Oriole. With the deal held up for two days because Lee McPhail joined the commissioner's office and Harry Dalton assumed command of the Orioles, Robinson, branded an "old 30" by Reds owner Bill DeWitt, joined the Orioles for veteran pitcher Milt Pappas, and young players Jack Baldschun and Dick Simpson. The Orioles promptly went from bridesmaid to the team to beat in the American League.

December 11

1924— Pitcher Hal "Skinny" Brown is born in Greensboro, North Carolina.

1984— The Orioles sign free-agent All-Star outfielder Fred Lynn to a five-year contract through the 1989 season.

1963 road cap

1993— Rafael Palmeiro, a .295 lifetime hitter in six seasons with the Cubs and Rangers, signs a five-year free agent contract with the Orioles.

December 12

1996— The Orioles sign free agent shortstop Mike Bordick to a three-year contract, thus paving the way for Cal Ripken's transition to third base. Bordick, one of the top glove men in the league, is also a pesky hitter, driving in a career-high 54 runs in 1996 with Oakland.

December 13

1954— Two of the Brooklyn Dodgers Boys of Summer, Preacher Roe and Billy Cox, come to Baltimore for two minor leaguers and cash. Roe retired without playing a game in Baltimore, while Cox played in 55 games, hitting .211 in 1955, after which he also retired.

1984— Despite only pitching in 23 games over a two-year span because of arm surgery, relief pitcher Don Aase signs a four-year contract with the Orioles through the 1988 season.

December 14

1963— The Orioles purchase the contract of pitcher Harvey Haddix from Pittsburgh. Nicknamed "Kitten" because of his resemblance to Oriole pitching coach Harry "The Cat" Brecheen, Haddix spent two seasons in Baltimore, appearing in 73 games, all in relief, and compiling an 8-7 record.

1995— Lefty reliever Randy Myers, who has amassed 30 or more saves with four different clubs, signs a two-year free agent contract with the Orioles.

December 15

1962— Stu Miller, Mike McCormick and John Orsino come over from the Giants for pitchers Jack Fisher and Billy Hoeft.

1985— The Orioles send popular reliever Sammy Stewart to Boston for infielder Jackie Gutierrez, the first trade between the two clubs in a quarter century.

December 16

1951— Oriole left-handed pitcher Mike Flanagan is born in Manchester, New Hampshire.

December 17

1953— In their very first deal, the Orioles trade pitcher Bob Cain to the Philadelphia A's for pitchers Joe Coleman and Frank Fanovich.

1935— Cal Ripken Sr., who became the first father ever to manage two sons simultaneously in the major leagues and who served as a player, manager, scout and coach for over 30 years in the Orioles system, is born in Aberdeen, Maryland.

December 19

1996— The Orioles sign former Red, Dodger and Tiger outfielder Eric Davis to a free-agent contract. After missing the 1995 season with a herniated disc in his neck, Davis came out of retirement in 1996 and hit .287 with 26 homers and 83 RBI in Cincinnati.

December 20

1995— Versatile Milwaukee Brewer B. J. Surhoff, coming off his finest year in which he hit .320 and led the Brewers in batting, runs scored and RBI, signs a three-year free-agent contract with the Orioles.

December 21

1995— Five-time All-Star second baseman Roberto Alomar signs a three-year free-agent contract with the Orioles. Alomar is a .298 lifetime hitter in over seven big league seasons.

December 22

1940— Elrod Hendricks, who celebrated his 30th season in an Oriole uniform as a player or coach in 1998, is born in St. Thomas, Virgin Islands.

December 26

1961— Storm Davis is born in Dallas, Texas.

1995— The Orioles obtain lefthanded pitcher David Wells from the Cincinnati Reds in exchange for outfielders Curtis Goodwin and Trovin Valdez.

December 27

1922— Connie Johnson, the Orioles' biggest winner in 1957 with a 14-11 record, is born in Stone Mountain, Georgia.

Elrod Hendricks

Statistics

ORIOLES IN AMERICAN LEAGUE STANDINGS, 1954-1998

YEAR	WON	LOST	PCT	GB/GA	PLACE	MANAGER(S)
1998	79	83	.488	35	4th	Ray Miller
1997	**98**	**64**	**.605**	**(2)**	**1st**	**Davey Johnson**
1996	88	74	.543	4	2nd	Davey Johnson
1995	71	73	.493	15	3rd	Phil Regan
1994	63	49	.563	6½	**2nd	Johnny Oates
1993	85	77	.525	10	&-3rd	Johnny Oates
1992	89	73	.549	7	3rd	Johnny Oates
1991	67	95	.414	24	6th	Frank Robinson/Johnny Oates (5)
1990	76	85	.472	11½	5th	Frank Robinson
1989	87	75	.537	2	2nd	Frank Robinson
1988	54	107	.335	34½	7th	Ripken Sr./Frank Robinson
1987	67	95	.414	31	6th	Cal Ripken Sr.
1986	73	89	.451	22½	7th	Earl Weaver
1985	83	78	.516	16	4th	Attobelli/Ripken/Weaver(3)
1984	84	77	.525	19	5th	Joe Altobelli
1983	**98**	**64**	**.605**	**(6)**	**1st**	**Joe Altobelli**
1982	94	68	.580	1	2nd	Earl Weaver
1981	59	46	.562	1	*2nd	Earl Weaver
1980	100	62	.617	3	2nd	Earl Weaver
1979	**102**	**57**	**.642**	**(8)**	**1st**	**Earl Weaver**
1978	90	71	.559	9	4th	Earl Weaver
1977	97	64	.602	2	2nd	Earl Weaver
1976	88	74	.543	10½	2nd	Earl Weaver
1975	90	69	.566	4½	2nd	Earl Weaver
1974	**91**	**71**	**.652**	**(2)**	**1st**	**Earl Weaver**
1973	**97**	**65**	**.599**	**(8)**	**1st**	**Earl Weaver**
1972	80	74	.519	8	3rd	Earl Weaver
1971	**101**	**57**	**.639**	**(12)**	**1st**	**Earl Weaver**
1970	**108**	**54**	**.667**	**(15)**	**1st**	**Earl Weaver**
1969	**109**	**53**	**.673**	**(19)**	**1st**	**Earl Weaver**
1968	91	71	.562	12	2nd	Hank Bauer/Earl Weaver (2)
1967	76	85	.472	15½	T-6th	Hank Bauer
1966	**97**	**63**	**.606**	**(9)**	**1st**	**Hank Bauer**
1965	94	68	.580	8	3rd	Hank Bauer
1964	97	65	.599	2	3rd	Hank Bauer
1963	86	76	.531	18½	4th	Billy Hitchcock
1962	77	85	.475	19	7th	Billy Hitchcock
1961	95	67	.586	14	3rd	Paul Richards/Luman Harris (1)
1960	89	65	.578	8	2nd	Paul Richards
1959	74	80	.481	20	6th	Paul Richards

YEAR	WON	LOST	PCT	GB/GA	PLACE	MANAGER(S)
1958	74	79	.484	17½	6th	Paul Richards
1957	76	76	.500	21	5th	Paul Richards
1956	69	85	.448	28	6th	Paul Richards
1955	57	97	.370	39	7th	Paul Richards
1954	54	100	.351	57	7th	Jimmie Dykes
TOTALS	3,775	3,305	.533			

*First Half: 31-23, .57, 2 GB. . .Second Half: 28-23, .549, 2GB
**—Strike on August 12, 1994 caused suspension of the rest of the season (no post-season play)
***—Qualified for post-season as American League Wild Card
T—Tie in standings ('93 with Detroit; '76 with Washington)
5—Oates (54-71) replaced Robinson (12-24) on May 23
4—Robinson (54-101) replaced Ripken (0-6) on April 12
3—Altobelli (29-26) was relieved after June 12 game; Ripken (1-0) managed June 13; Weaver (53-52) took over June 14
2—Weaver (48-34) replaced Bauer (43-37) on July 11
1—Harris (17-10) replaced Richards (78-57) on September 1

Hank Bauer

ORIOLES YEAR-BY-YEAR BATTING LEADERS

YEAR	AVG.		HOMERS		RBI		STEALS		YEAR
1954	Abrams	.293	Stephens	8	Stephens	46	Coan	9	1954
1955	Triandos	.277	Triandos	12	Triandos	65	Diering	5	1955
							Pope	5	
1956	Nieman	.322	Triandos	21	Triandos	88	Francona	11	1956
1957	Boyd	.318	Triandos	19	Triandos	72	Pilarcik	14	1957
1958	Woodling	.276	Triandos	30	Triandos	79	Pilarcik	7	1958
1959	Woodling	.300	Triandos	25	Woodling	77	Pilarcik	9	1959
1960	B. Robinson	.294	Hansen	22	Gentile	98	Breeding	10	1960
1961	Gentile	.302	Gentile	46	Gentile	141	Brandt	10	1961
1962	B. Robinson	.303	Gentile	33	Gentile	87	Brandt	9	1962
1963	A. Smith	.272	Powell	25	Powell	82	Aparicio*	40	1963
1964	B. Robinson	.317	Powell	39	B. Robinson	118	Aparicio*	57	1964
1965	B. Robinson	.297	Blefary	22	B. Robinson	80	Aparicio	26	1965
1966	F. Robinson	.316	F. Robinson*	49	F. Robinson	122	Aparicio	25	1966
1967	F. Robinson	.311	F. Robinson	30	F. Robinson	94	Aparicio	18	1967
1968	B. Robinson	.253	Powell	22	Powell	85	Buford	27	1968
1969	F. Robinson	.308	Powell	37	Powell	121	Blair	20	1969
1970	F. Robinson	.306	Powell	35	Powell	114	Blair	24	1970
1971	Rettenmund	.318	F. Robinson	28	F. Robinson	99	Buford	15	1971
							Rettenmund	15	
1972	Grich	.278	Powell	21	Powell	81	Baylor	24	1972
1973	T. Davis	.306	Williams	22	T. Davis	89	Baylor	32	1973
1974	T. Davis	.289	Grich	19	T. Davis	84	Baylor	29	1974
1975	Singleton	.300	Baylor	25	L. May	99	Baylor	32	1975
1976	Singleton	.278	R. Jackson	27	L. May*	109	Bumbry	42	1976
1977	Singleton	.328	L. May	27	L. May	99	Kelly	25	1977
			Murray	27	Singleton	99			
1978	Singleton	.293	DeCinces	28	Murray	95	Harlow	14	1978
1979	Murray	.295	Singleton	35	Singleton	111	Bumbry	37	1979
	Singleton	.295							
1980	Bumbry	.318	Murray	32	Murray	116	Bumbry	44	1980
1981	Murray	.294	Murray+	22	Murray*	78	Bumbry	22	1981
1982	Murray	.316	Murray	32	Murray	100	Bumbry	10	1982
1983	C. Ripken	.318	Murray	33	Murray	111	Shelby	15	1983
1984	Murray	.306	Murray	29	Murray	110	Shelby	12	1984
1985	Murray	.297	Murray	31	Murray	124	Wiggins	30	1985
1986	Murray	.305	C. Ripken	25	Murray	84	Wiggins	21	1986
1987	Sheets	.316	Sheets	31	C. Ripken	98	Wiggins	20	1987
1988	Murray	.284	Murray	28	Murray	84	Stanicek	12	1988
1989	Bradley	.277	Tettleton	26	C. Ripken	93	Devereaux	22	1989
1990	Finley	.256	C. Ripken	21	C. Ripken	84	Finley	22	1990
1991	C. Ripken	.323	C. Ripken	34	C. Ripken	114	Devereaux	16	1991
1992	Devereaux	.276	Devereaux	24	Devereaux	107	Anderson	53	1992
1993	Hoiles	.310	Hoiles	29	C. Ripken	90	Anderson	24	1993
1994	Palmeiro	.319	Palmeiro	23	Palmeiro	76	Anderson	31	1994
1995	Palmeiro	.310	Palmeiro	39	Palmeiro	104	Anderson	26	1995
1996	Alomar	.328	Anderson	50	Palmeiro	142	Anderson	21	1996
1997	Anderson	.288	Palmeiro	38	Palmeiro	110	Anderson	18	1997
1998	Davis	.327	Palmeiro	43	Palmeiro	121	Anderson	21	1998

*Led League   +Tied League

ORIOLES YEAR-BY-YEAR PITCHING LEADERS

YEAR	WON		LOST		INNINGS		ERA		YEAR
1954	Turley	14	Larsen	21	Coleman	221.1	Pilette	3.12	1954
1955	Wilson	12	Wilson	18	Wilson	235.1	Wilson	3.45	1955
1956	Moore	12	Wright	12	Moore	185.0	C. Johnson	3.42	1956
1957	C. Johnson	14	Moore	13	C. Johnson	242.0	C. Johnson	3.20	1957
1958	Portocarrero	15	Harshman	15	Harshman	236.1	Harshman	2.90	1958
1959	Wilhelm	15	O'Dell	12	Wilhelm	226.0	Wilhelm	2.19	1959
	Pappas	15							
1960	Estrada+	18	Estrada	11	Estrada	208.2	Brown	3.06	1960
			J. Fisher	11					
			Pappas	11					
1961	Barber	18	Fisher	13	Barber	248.1	Pappas	3.03	1961
1962	Pappas	12	Estrada+	17	Estrada	223.1	Roberts	2.78	1962
1963	Barber	20	Barber	13	Barber	258.2	Barber	2.75	1963
1964	Bunker	19	Barber	13	Pappas	251.2	Bunker*	2.69	1964
1965	Barber	15	Barber	10	Pappas	221.1	Pappas	2.61	1965
					Barber	220.2			
1966	Palmer	15	Palmer	10	McNally	213.0	McNally	3.17	1966
1967	Phoebus	14	S. Miller	10	Phoebus	208.0	Phoebus	3.33	1967
			Richert	10					
1968	McNally	22	Phoebus	15	McNally	273.0	McNally	1.95	1968
1969	Cuellar	23	Cuellar	11	Cuellar	290.2	Palmer	2.34	1969
1970	Cuellar+	24	Palmer	10	Palmer+	305.0	Palmer	2.71	1970
	McNally+	24							
1971	McNally+	21	Cuellar	9	Cuellar	292.0	Palmer	2.68	1971
			Palmer	9					
1972	Palmer	21	Dobson+	18	Palmer	274.1	Palmer	2.07	1972
1973	Palmer	21	McNally	17	Palmer	296.0	Palmer*	2.40	1973
1974	Cuellar	22	Grimsley	13	Grimsley	296.0	Grimsley	3.07	1974
1975	Palmer+	23	Grimsley	13	Palmer	323.0	Palmer+	2.09	1975
1976	Palmer*	22	Cuellar	13	Palmer*	315.0	Palmer	2.51	1976
			Palmer	13					
1977	Palmer+	20	R. May	14	Palmer*	319.0	Palmer	2.91	1977
1978	Palmer	21	Flanagan	15	Palmer*	296.0	Palmer	2.46	1978
1979	Flanagan*	23	D. Martinez+	16	D. Martinez+	292.0	Flanagan	3.08	1979
1980	Stone*	25	Flanagan	13	McGregor	252.0	Stone	3.23	1980
1981	D. Martinez+	14	Palmer	8	D. Martinez	179.0	Stewart	2.33	1981
			Stewart	8					
1982	D. Martinez	16	D. Martinez	12	D. Martinez	252.0	Palmer	3.13	1982
			McGregor	12					
1983	McGregor	18	D. Martinez	16	McGregor	260.0	Boddicker	2.77	1983
1984	Boddicker*	20	Flanagan	13	Boddicker	261.1	Boddicker	2.79	1984
1985	McGregor	14	Boddicker	15	Boddicker	204.0	Dixon	3.67	1985
1986	Boddicker	14	McGregor	15	Boddicker	218.1	Flanagan	4.24	1986
1987	Bell	10	Bell	13	Boddicker	226.0	Boddicker	4.18	1987
	Boddicker	10							
	Schmidt	10							
1988	Ballard	8	Bautista	15	Bautista	171.2	Bautista	4.30	1988
	Schmidt	8							
1989	Ballard	18	Schmidt	13	Milacki	243.0	Ballard	3.43	1989
1990	D. Johnson	13	Harnisch	11	Harnisch	188.2	D. Johnson	4.10	1990
			Ballard	11					
1991	Milacki	10	Ballard	12	Milacki	184.0	Milacki	4.01	1991
1992	Mussina	18	Sutcliffe	15	Mussina	241.0	Mussina	2.54	1992
1993	Mussina	18	McDonald	14	McDonald	220.1	McDonald	3.39	1993
1994	Mussina	16	McDonald	7	Mussina	176.1	Mussina	3.06	1994
			Moyer	7					
1995	Mussina*	19	Brown	9	Mussina	221.2	Mussina	3.29	1995
			Mussina	9					
1996	Mussina	19	Wells	14	Mussina	243.1	Mussina	4.84	1996
1997	Erickson	16	Key	10	Mussina	224.2	Mussina	3.20	1997
	Key	16							
1998	Erickson	16	Erickson	13	Erickson	251.1	Mussina	3.49	1998

*Led League   +Tied League

THE ORIOLES HALL OF FAME

The Orioles Hall of Fame was conceived in 1977 by the Oriole Advocates at the suggestion of two former presidents, Allen Barrett and Jack Buckley, both of whom have since passed away. The Advocates continue to administer the annual elections under the direction of their Hall of Fame Committee.

Candidates may be elected to the Orioles Hall of Fame through two channels: the regular vote by a panel of some 80 people, comprising sportswriters, broadcasters, Oriole Advocates and Oriole personnel; or by a vote of the veterans committee, a group of 25 senior representatives from the sports media, Oriole Advocates and the Orioles front office.

Procedures for election to the Orioles Hall of Fame are based on those used by the National Baseball Hall of Fame, requiring mention on 75% of ballots cast. All candidates must have served a minimum of three full seasons with the Orioles and must have been active in that capacity within the last 15 years. To be eligible for regular election, a player, manager or coach must have ceased serving in the position for which he was nominated for at least one year. For consideration by the veterans committee, formed in 1989, a candidate must have ceased serving in the capacity of consideration for at least 15 years.

Herbert E. Armstrong Award: The Orioles Hall of Fame Veterans Committee also selects winners of the Herbert E. Armstrong Award, presented annually to non-uniformed personnel who have distinguished themselves in their service to the Orioles. The Armstrong Award was established in 1995 in honor of the beloved former educator, professional baseball player and manager and longtime official for both the Orioles' International League and American League clubs, who dedicated nearly 70 years of his life to the people of Baltimore, his adopted hometown.

MURRAY, CASHEN ARE 1999 ELECTEES TO O'S HALL

Eddie Murray, a six-time Most Valuable Oriole and one of three major leaguers to amass more than 3,000 hits and 500 home runs, and former general manager Frank Cashen, whose 10 years with the club included the team's first six trips to the post-season, are the newest elected members of the Orioles Hall of Fame. Murray was elected through a vote of the Hall of Fame Committee and its 80 electors, while Cashen received the Herbert E. Armstrong Award for nonuniformed personnel in a vote of the Hall's veterans committee.

Murray, currently an Orioles coach, batted .294 and hit 343 homers during 12½ seasons with the Orioles in a 21-year career. Cashen, a native Baltimorean who began his career as a sportswriter, joined the Orioles front office following the 1965 season and oversaw the business and baseball sides as executive vice president and general manager before moving on to the Commissioner's Office and then the New York Mets.

The election of Murray and Cashen bring Oriole Hall of Fame membership to 38 people:

ORIOLES HALL OF FAME MEMBERS (38)

Brooks Robinson, 3b (1977)	Al Bumbry, of (1987)	Jerold Hoffberger, owner (1996)—A
Frank Robinson, of (1977)	Steve Barber, lhp (1988)	Bill Hunter, coach (1996)—V
Dave McNally, lhp (1978)	Jim Gentile, 1b (1989)	Luis Aparicio, ss (1982)
Boog Powell, 1b (1979)	Stu Miller, rhp (1989)—V	Cal Ripken, Sr., coach (1996)
Gus Triandos, c (1981)	Dick Hall, rhp (1989)	Harry Dalton, executive (1997)—A
Mike Cuellar, lhp (1982)	Hank Bauer, mgr (1990)—V	Rick Dempsey, c (1997)
Mark Belanger, ss (1983)	Scott McGregor, lhp (1990)	Davey Johnson, 2b (1997)—V
Earl Weaver, mgr (1983)	Hal Brown, rhp (1991)—V	Bobby Grich, 2b (1998)—V
Paul Blair, of (1984)	Gene Woodling, of (1992)—V	Lee May, 1b (1998)—V
Milt Pappas, rhp (1985)	Don Buford, of (1993)—V	Lee McPhail, executive (1998)—V
Jim Palmer, rhp (1986)	Mike Flanagan, lhp (1994)	Frank Cashen, executive (1999)—A
Ken Singleton, of (1986)	George Bamberger, coach (1995)	Eddie Murray, 1b (1999)
	Chuck Thompson, broadcaster (1995)—A	
V—Veteran's Committee selection		A—Herbert Armstrong Award winner

MOST VALUABLE ORIOLES 1954-1998

The Louis M. Hatter Most Valuable Oriole Award is presented annually by the Sports Boosters of Maryland, Inc. In 1998, first baseman Rafael Palmeiro was voted winner for the third time in four years, joining Eddie Murray (7) Brooks Robinson (4), Cal Ripken (4) and Frank Robinson (3) as the only players to win the award more than twice. A total of 27 different Orioles have been honored in the club's 45 seasons (no award was given in 1994). Palmeiro also won the award in 1995 and 1996.

The Sports Boosters initiated the MVO award when the Orioles returned to the majors in 1954. Several years ago, they renamed the award in memory of Hatter, the distinguished and lovable "dean" of Baltimore baseball writers who covered the Orioles for *The Sun* for 27 years.

The award winner is selected through a vote of writers and broadcasters who cover the O's on a regular basis. There have been four ties, and no award was given in 1994.

Winners by position: outfielders—14; first basemen—14; pitchers—9; third basemen—4; shortstops—4; catchers—2; and second basemen—1

MOST VALUABLE ORIOLES, '54-'98

1954-Chuck Diering (OF)	1976-Lee May (1B)
1955-Dave Philley (OF)	1977-Ken Singleton (OF) Murray (1B)
1956-Bob Nieman (OF)	1979-Ken Singleton (OF)
1957-Billy Gardner (2B)	1980-Al Bumbry (OF)
1958-Gus Triandos (C)	1981-Eddie Murray (1B)
1959-Gene Woodling (OF)	1982-Eddie Murray (1B)
1960-Brooks Robinson (3B)	1983-Eddie Murray (1B)/C Ripken (SS)
1961-Jim Gentile (1B)	1984-Eddie Murray (1B)
1962-Brooks Robinson (3B)	1985-Eddie Murray (1B)
1963-Stu Miller (RHP)	1986-Don Aase (RHP)
1964-Brooks Robinson (3B)	1987-Larry Sheets (OF)
1965-Stu Miller (RHP)	1988-E. Murray (1B)/C. Ripken (SS)
1966-Frank Robinson (OF)	1989-Gregg Olson (RHP)
1967-Frank Robinson (OF)	1990-Cal Ripken (SS)
1968-Dave McNally (LHP)	1991-Cal Ripken (SS)
1969-Boog Powell (I 1B)	1992-Mike Devereaux (OF)
1970-Boog Powell (1B)	1993-Chris Hoiles (C)
1971-B. Robby (3B)/F. Robby (OF)	1994-No award given
1972-Jim Palmer (RHP)	1995-Rafael Palmeiro (1B)
1973-Jim Palmer (RHP)	1996-Rafael Palmeiro, (1B)
1974-Paul Blair (OF)/Mike Cuellar (LHP)	1997-Randy Myers (LHP)
1975-Ken Singleton (OF)	1998-Rafael Palmeiro (1B)

ORIOLES ALL-STAR GAME SELECTEES

1954
Bob Turley (DNP)

1955
Jim Wilson (DNP)

1956
George Kell (ST)

1957
George Kell (ST)
Billy Loes
Gus Triandos (DNP)

1958
Billy O'Dell
Gus Triandos (ST)

1959
Billy O'Dell2
Gus Triandos (ST)1
Jerry Walker (ST)+2
Hoyt Wilhelm (DNP 1st)
Gene Woodling2

1960
Chuck Estrada (DNP 2nd)
Jim Gentile (DNP 2nd)
Ron Hansen (ST both)
Brooks Robinson

1961
Jack Brandt (DNP 2nd)
Jim Gentile (DNP 2nd)
Brooks Robinson (ST both)
Hoyt Wilhelm*

1962
Jim Gentile (ST both)
Milt Pappas (both)
Brooks Robinson (both)
Steve Barber*

1963
Luis Aparicio
Brooks Robinson
Steve Barber*

1964
Luis Aparicio*
Brooks Robinson (ST)
Norm Siebern

1965
Milt Pappas (ST)+
Brooks Robinson (ST)

1966
Steve Barber (DNP)

Andy Etchebarren (DNP)
Brooks Robinson (ST)
Frank Robinson (ST)

1967
Andy Etchebarren (DNP)
Brooks Robinson (ST)
Frank Robinson (DNP)

1968
Dave Johnson
Boog Powell
Brooks Robinson (ST)

1969
Paul Blair
Dave Johnson
Dave McNally
Boog Powell (ST)
Brooks Robinson
Frank Robinson (ST)

1970
Mike Cuellar (DNP)
Dave Johnson (ST)+
Dave McNally (DNP)
Jim Palmer (ST)+
Boog Powell (ST)
Brooks Robinson
Frank Robinson (ST)

1971
Don Buford
Mike Cuellar
Jim Palmer
Boog Powell
Brooks Robinson (ST)
Frank Robinson (ST)

1972
Pat Dobson (DNP)
Bobby Grich (ST)+
Dave McNally
Jim Palmer (ST)+
Brooks Robinson (ST)

1973
Paul Blair
Brooks Robinson (ST)

1974
Mike Cuellar (DNP)
Bobby Grich
Brooks Robinson (ST)

1975
Jim Palmer (DNP)

1976
Mark Belanger
Bobby Grich (ST)

1977
Jim Palmer (ST)+
Ken Singleton

1978
Jim Palmer (ST)+
Mike Flanagan (DNP)
Eddie Murray (DNP)

1979
Ken Singleton
Don Stanhouse (DNP)

1980
Al Bumbry
Steve Stone (ST)+

1981
Scott McGregor (DNP)
Eddie Murray
Ken Singleton (ST)

1982
Ken Singleton (ST)

1983
Tippy Martinez (DNP)
Eddie Murray
Cal Ripken

1984
Mike Boddicker (DNP)
Eddie Murray
Cal Ripken (ST)

1985
Eddie Murray (ST)
Cal Ripken (ST)

1986
Don Aase
Eddie Murray (ST)
Cal Ripken (ST)

1987
Terry Kennedy (ST)
Cal Ripken (ST)

1988
Cal Ripken (ST)+

1989
Mickey Tettleton
Cal Ripken (ST)

1990
Greg Olsen (DNP)
Cal Ripken (ST)

1991
Cal Ripken (ST)

1992
Brady Anderson
Mike Mussina
Cal Ripken (ST)

1993
Mike Mussina
Cal Ripken (ST)

1994
Mike Mussina
Cal Ripken (ST)
Lee Smith

1995
Cal Ripken (ST)

1996
Roberto Alomar (ST)
Brady Anderson (ST)+
Cal Ripken (ST)

1997
Roberto Alomar (ST)
Brady Anderson (ST)
Jimmy Key ***
Mike Mussina (DNP)
Randy Myers
Cal Ripken (ST)

1998
Roberto Alomar (ST)
Rafael Palmeiro
Cal Ripken (ST)

Managers: Paul Richards, 1961**, Hank Bauer, 1967; Earl Weaver, 1970, 1971, 1972, 1974++, 1980; Joe Altobelli, 1984.

*Selected but did not attend due to injury
+Started but not elected
++Honorary Manager
**Replaced Casey Stengel who left Yankees after they won pennant in 1960
***Selected but did not attend—getting married
1-Selected for 1st game only
2-Selected for 2nd game only

NICKNAMES

The nickname "Orioles" is, traced all the way back to 1883, when a new ballpark on the southwest corner of York Road and Huntingdon Avenue (now Greenmount Avenue) was named Oriole Park. The reason is uncertain except a big mardi-gras type affair called The Order of the Oriole was staged. Soon the team too was being called Orioles, although the name really did not take hold until the 1890s. From the champion Orioles of the Gay Nineties, featuring such legends as John McGraw, Wee Willie Keeler, Wilbert Robinson and Hughie Jennings, right on up to the champions of 1983 and beyond, the nickname "Orioles" has been synonymous with Baltimore baseball.

THE MODERN-DAY ORIOLES HAVE FEATURED A HOST OF PLAYER NICKNAMES. HERE ARE A FEW:

Bamby	George Bamberger		Junior	Vern Stephens
Bee	Al Bumbry		Kitten	Harvey Haddix
Big Foot	Tim Stoddard		Mo, Big Bopper	Lee May
Blade	Mark Belanger		Moose	Mike Mussina and Randy Milligan
Boog	John Powell		Old Blue	Ray Moore
Buck	Grant Jackson		Otter	Gregg Olson
Bullet	Bob Turley		Rabbit	Ray Miller
	Bob Reynolds		Raffy	Rafael Palmeiro
Cakes	Jim Palmer		Rev	Pat Kelly
The Cat	Harry Brecheen		Rhino	Gary Roenicke
Clank	Curt Blefary		Rocky	Bob Johnson
The Crow	Terry Crowley		Rooster	Rick Burleson
Cuz	Curt Motton		Rope	Bob Boyd
Deacon	Ray Murray		Roy Hobbs	Jack Voight
Devo	Mike Devereaux		Scrap Iron	Clint Courtney
Diamond	Jim Gentile		Skinny	Hal Brown
Digger	Billy O'Dell		Snake	Pat Dobson
The Dipper	Rick Dempsey		Stan the Man	Don Stanhouse
E-Z	Billy Smith		Storm	George Davis
Fearless	Jim Fridley		T-bone	John Shelby
Flakey	Jackie Brandt		Tito	John Francona
Fuzzy	Al Smith			Terry Landrum
Groove	Don Baylor		Tippy	Felix Martinez
Hawk	Larry Harlow		Turkey	Dick Hall
Honey Bear	Floyd Rayford		War Eagle	Billy Hitchcock
Hoot	Walter Evers		Wizard of Waxahachie	Paul Richards

NATIONAL BASEBALL HALL OF FAME

Lee MacPhail's election to the Baseball Hall of Fame by the Veteran's Committee in 1998 brought to 10 the number of modern Orioles who have been enshrined at Cooperstown. During his long and meritorious career in baseball, MacPhail served as general manager and later president and GM of the Orioles from 1958 through 1965. He later served as president of the American League.

There are four modern Orioles enshrined in the Hall of Fame wearing Oriole hats for their official busts/portraits: Earl Weaver, Jim Palmer, and Brooks and Frank Robinson.

Palmer, the Robinsons and Reggie Jackson all were selected in their first year of eligibility for the Hall. They are four of only 29 first-ballot electees among the 240 Hall of Fame members (not including this year's Veteran's committee vote). Palmer polled 92.6% of the total vote (411 of 444 ballots cast) in 1990, the highest percentage ever by an Oriole.

Another beloved Oriole was honored by the Hall of Fame in 1993 when veteran O's broadcaster Chuck Thompson was the recipient of the Ford C. Frick Award, presented by the Hall of Fame to a broadcaster for major contributions to the game of baseball.

And in 1998, Sam Lacy, longtime sports editor of the *Baltimore Afro-American* newspaper, became the first local writer selected for the J.G. Taylor Spink Award, honoring sportswriters "for meritorious contributions to baseball writing."

In addition, there are six members of the 1890s Orioles juggernaut immortalized in the Hall of Fame.

MODERN ORIOLES IN BASEBALL HALL OF FAME

Robin Roberts (1976, 87%)	Luis Aparicio (1984, 85%)	Reggie Jackson (1993, 94%)
Frank Robinson (1982, 89%)	Hoyt Wilhelm (1985, 84%)	Earl Weaver (1996, VCS+)
Brooks Robinson (1983, 92%)	Jim Palmer (1990, 93%)	Lee MacPhail (1998, VCS+)
George Kell (1983, VCS+)		

+ Veterans' Committee Selection

Sixteen others who played and/or managed for the Orioles during the early days of Baltimore's rich baseball heritage also are enshrined at Cooperstown:

OLD ORIOLES IN BASEBALL HALL OF FAME

Frank (Home Run) Baker (3b)	Edward (Ned) Hanlon (mgr)	Joe (Iron Man) McGinnity (rhp)
Charles (Chief) Bender (rhp)	Rogers Hornsby (2b)	John McGraw (mgr, 3b)
Roger Bresnahan (c)	Hughie Jennings (ss)	Wilbert Robinson (mgr, c)
Dan Brouthers (1b)	Wee Willie Keeler (of)	George Herman (Babe) Ruth (of)
William (Candy) Cummings (rhp)	Joe Kelley (of-if)	
Robert M. (Lefty) Grove (lhp)	Rube Marquard (lhp)	

There are three additional Hall of Famers to have represented the Orioles, though not as players: George Weiss, who immortalized himself as a general manager of the Yankees, served part of his apprenticeship as an International League Orioles general manager; the late Luke Appling, a legendary hitter/shortstop for the White Sox coached one year under Birds' Manager Billy Hitchcock; and the late Burleigh Grimes, the famed spitball pitcher who won 270 games in the majors, scouted for the Orioles from '60 thru '71.

Notes: John McGraw had a 334 lifetime batting average in 16 big league seasons but was elected to the Hall of Fame primarily because of his achievements as a manager. The same is true of his buddy, Wilbert Robinson. Rube Marquard pitched only 30 innings for the Orioles, all in '27.

Baltimore-born Babe Ruth signed his first pro contract with Jack Dunn Sr. in '14, and made his professional debut with the I.L. Orioles that year as a pitcher. Chief Bender was based in Baltimore twice. He pitched both for the '27 Orioles (G-18, W-6 L-3) and the '15 Baltimore Terrapins (W-4, L-16) in the ill-fated Federal League.

Other native Marylanders in the Hall of Fame include "Home Run Baker" (Trappe), Lefty Grove (Lonaconing) and four others who never played for the Orioles: Jimmie Foxx (Sudlersville), Judy Johnson (Snow Hill), Al Kaline (Baltimore) and Vic Willis (Elkton), who was elected in 1995.

ABOUT THE AUTHOR

Ted Patterson, generally recognized as the foremost expert on Orioles history, arrived in Baltimore in 1973. He first served as sports director for WBAL before moving to WMAR-TV to assume the nighttime sports anchor position. From 1982 through 1998, Patterson was sports director at WPOC radio. Today, he serves as a host on the Liberty Works Radio Network. Through the years, Patterson has been behind the microphone for the Baltimore Orioles, Blast and Spirit, Washington Senators, and Cleveland Cavaliers and Crusaders. At collegiate level, he has been the voice for Navy football and basketball and Towson State basketball. Patterson is a three-time winner of Maryland's Sportscaster of the Year Award and a six-time winner of the Chesapeake Associated Press Sportscaster of the Year Award. This is his third book on the Orioles.

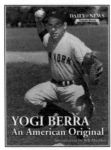
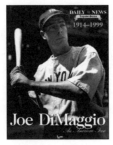
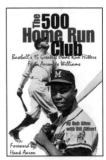